"In this masterful analysis, Schumacher shows the gender theory framework to be a complete inversion of the longstanding tradition of metaphysical realism. She traces the philosophical roots of this inversion to Sartre's atheistic existentialism, which reverses the realist claim that essence precedes existence. This reversal prompts a cascade of reversals that leaves nothing unaltered: ethics, language, art, medicine—even the very contours of what it means to be human. In this upside-down world, culture supplants nature; gender dethrones sex; creature becomes Creator; and human freedom is uprooted from any enduring good. Our culture needs a substantive, scholarly account of what's at stake in this great undoing and how to regain our footing. This is precisely what Schumacher provides."

ABIGAIL FAVALE
University of Notre Dame

"Michele Schumacher provides a tour de force, reading carefully both the *philosophia perennis* and its foes and calling out the substitution of nature by human artifice in the latter. But not content with critique, she also paints a portrait of the goodness of created nature, a goodness that extends down to our sex. She brings into view the divine Artist who lovingly fashions us in his image and calls us to the perfection of that image through our wise knowing and acting."

ANGELA FRANKS
St. John's Seminary

"In a culture that has lost its bearings on sex and gender identity, Schumacher attempts to restore some sorely needed sanity by drawing us back to the ground of sexual difference and of gender identity that tracks this difference: that of the order of being, of reality, of metaphysics. With this as the foundation, Schumacher deftly points out how nature, biology, teleology, and human knowledge of a created world order emerge as the normative frame for any proper understanding of sex and gender, as well as art and ethics. Schumacher has provided a great service in writing this work; the insights she offers are profound and philosophically rich. Here Schumacher sets the record straight on the notion of gender. I highly recommend this work."

PAUL GONDREAU
Providence College

"Everyone is talking about sex these days, but you can't do it intelligibly without talking about the nature of fundamental reality—metaphysics. *Metaphysics and Gender* is a penetrating analysis of the atheistic existentialism of self-creation at the heart of gender ideology with roots in John Paul Sartre, Simone de Beauvoir, and Judith Butler. In response, Michele Schumacher proposes a traditional Aristotelian-Thomistic understanding of nature as God's creation, and of our natures, our bodies, our identities, and our fulfillments as grounded in the fullness of our being."

Ryan T. Anderson,
President of the Ethics and Public Policy Center

"This book is the fruit of over twenty years of reflection as a wife, mother, and theologian by one of the most creative and independent thinkers in theology today."

Michael Sherwin, O.P.
University of Fribourg, Switzerland

METAPHYSICS *AND* GENDER

METAPHYSICS *AND* GENDER

The Normative Art of Nature and Its Human Imitations

MICHELE M. SCHUMACHER

EMMAUS
ACADEMIC
Steubenville, Ohio

Steubenville, Ohio
A Division of The St. Paul Center for Biblical Theology
Editor-in-Chief: Scott Hahn
1468 Parkview Circle
Steubenville, Ohio 43952

Printed in the United States of America

Library of Congress Cataloging-in-Publication Data applied for
ISBN: 978-1-64585-290-2 hc / 978-1-64585-291-9 pb / 978-1-64585-292-6 eb

Cover design and layout by Emma Nagle and Emily Morelli.

Cover credit: *Creation of Eve* by Lorenzo Maitani. Photograph by Georges Jansoone.

My appreciation to *The Thomist* for according me the right to republish material with substantial revision that first appeared in volume 80, no. 3 (2016): 363–423: "Gender Ideology and the 'Artistic' Fabrication of Human Sex: Nature as Norm or the Remaking of the Human?"

For the beloved men in my life:

my grandfather Alfred†

my father Daniel†

my husband Bernard

and

my son Nicolas

Thou dost not make God
But God thee.
If, then, thou art God's workmanship,
await the hand of thy Maker
which creates everything in due time;
in due time as far as thou art concerned,
whose creation is being carried out.
Offer to Him thy heart
in a soft and tractable state,
and preserve the form
in which the Creator has fashioned thee,
having moisture in thyself,
lest, by becoming hardened,
thou lose the impressions of His fingers.

Saint Irenaeus of Lyons
Adversus Haereses IV, 39:2

CONTENTS

ACKNOWLEDGEMENTS

I wish to express my sincere gratitude to Paul Gondreau of Providence College for bringing to my attention important references and developments that I touch upon in my first chapter and for sharing with me a still-unpublished manuscript that he has authored on that subject. My thanks also for his unwavering encouragement and fraternal support of my work.

So too am I grateful to Matthew Levering for his constant encouragement and in a particular way for his intercession with Emmaus Academic, whose staff has been especially helpful and kind.

I am particularly indebted to Father Michael Sherwin, O.P., whose solicitude toward me has been unwavering throughout the twenty years he served in Fribourg.

Special thanks to the wonderful women at the Catholic Women's Forum, who have generously shared their insights and research with me. In particular, I am grateful to Angela Franks, Janet Smith, Margaret Harper McCarthy, and Mary Rice Hasson.

And, as always, my deepest gratitude goes to my husband, Bernard, who encourages and accompanies me at every turn.

ABBREVIATIONS

CCC	*Catechism of the Catholic Church*
De An.	*De Anima* (Aristotle)
De Pot.	*Quaestiones Disputatae de Potentia Dei* (St. Thomas Aquinas)
De Ver.	*Quaestiones Disputatae de Veritate* (St. Thomas Aquinas)
Eth. Nic.	*Ethica Nicomachea* (Aristotle)
GA	*De Generatione Animalium* (Aristotle)
Met.	*Metaphysics* (Aristotle)
SCG	*Summa contra Gentiles* (St. Thomas Aquinas)
ST	*Summa Theologiae* (St. Thomas Aquinas)
Phys.	*Physica* (Aristotle)
Super Ioan.	*Super Evangelium S. Ioannis Lectura* (St. Thomas Aquinas)
Super Rom.	*Super Epistolam B. Pauli ad Romanus Lectura* (St. Thomas Aquinas)

INTRODUCTION

Metaphysics and Gender

"Until quite recently," the famous English novelist C. S. Lewis remarked in 1959, "it was taken for granted that the business of the artist was to delight and instruct his public"—that is to say, to address simultaneously their passions and their intellects. "There were, of course, different publics. . . . And an artist might lead his public on to appreciate finer things than they had wanted at first; but he could do this only by being; from the first, if not merely entertaining, yet entertaining, and if not completely intelligible, yet very largely intelligible." This constraint—let us call it *intelligent* (or purposeful) *design*, in keeping with a basic analogy that we will draw upon in these pages—had however been lost, Lewis observed. Hence, even "in the highest aesthetic circles one now hears nothing about the artist's duty to us. It is all about our duty to him. He owes us nothing; we owe him 'recognition,' even though he has never paid the slightest attention to our tastes, interests, or habits."[1] In short, the artist of modernity need not pay the slightest attention to an intention, not even his own. After all, modern art need not be an expression of *intelligence* or understanding; it is *expression* as such (tout court): personal and autonomous.[2]

UNDERLYING ANALOGIES: NATURE AND ART, NATURE AND ETHICS

Lewis's remarks do not point merely to the increasingly relativist tendencies of art in the Western world: to the lack of objective criteria or norms governing

[1] C. S. Lewis, "Good Work and Good Works," in *The World's Last Night and Other Essays* (San Diego: Harcourt and Brace, 1987), 78–79.

[2] As Melissa Ho, assistant curator at the Hirshhorn Museum (Washington, DC), puts it, modern art is characterized by "its own existential reason for being," whence the popular maxim, "art for art's sake." The emphasis lies on "being original and doing something innovative." As if to echo Lewis, Ho thus points to the underlying idea: "I am the artistic genius and you need me" (Megan Gambino, "Ask an Expert: What Is the Difference between Modern and Postmodern Art?," *Smithsonian Magazine*, September 22, 2011, http://www.smithsonianmag.com/arts-culture/ask-an-expert-what-is-the-difference-between-modern-and-postmodern-art-87883230/).

the artistic disciplines. They also point to the growing disregard among artists for the sociocultural expectations of their *publicum*. Mediating between the two is, without a doubt, the basis upon which both artistic and social norms were traditionally founded: nature, which served as a classic analogy for both art (understood in the broad sense, so as to include not only the fine arts but also technology and the practical sciences) and ethics in virtue of nature's intrinsic inclination toward its defining end and perfection.

With regard to the first of these analogies (that of art and nature), Harvard University professor of classics Mark Schiefsky explains: although art does bring about "results that nature itself cannot," it does so in the classic understanding "by acting in a natural way—the way nature *would* act if it could generate the products of art."[3] As for the difference between the two, nature is moved to its specifying end by way of intrinsic inclinations that are implicit to it, whereas a work of art is moved to its end extrinsically, and thus with more or less violence.[4] A sculptor, for example, who introduces a form into a piece of marble does so by chiseling and hammering away at the fine stone.[5] "Art is," Aristotle explains, "the principle and form of the thing that comes to be [let us say, a sculpture]; but it is located elsewhere [in, for example, the artist's mind or in a sketch that he has made] than in that thing, whereas the movement of nature is located in the thing itself that comes to be [a tree, for example, or a baby], and is derived from another natural organism [a tree or human parents] which possessed the form in actuality."[6]

This classic distinction between art and nature parallels the distinction between art and ethics. Ethics "does not affect human action in the same way as do art and technique," the Belgium theologian Servais Pinckaers explains. Unlike art and technique, which are concerned with the concrete produced by human action—this particular painting or that specific machine, for example—ethics is concerned with immanent principles, qualifying the actor as such: the stable dispositions (*habitus*: virtues or vices) at the origin of "the

---

3 Mark J. Schiefsky, "Art and Nature in Ancient Mechanics," in *The Artificial and the Natural: An Evolving Polarity*, ed. Bernadette Bensaude-Vincent and William R. Newman (Cambridge, MA: Massachusetts Institute of Technology Press, 2007), 72.

4 Such, more specifically, is the distinction between immanent and transitive actions. Whereas the latter have the effect of transforming matter outside of the agent, such as works of production or fabrication, the former take place within the agent and transform the actor himself. Examples of immanent actions are those of knowing, willing, intending, and loving.

5 See the example of Michelangelo by Pierre-Marie Emonet in *The Dearest Freshness Deep Down Things: An Introduction to the Philosophy of Being*, trans. Robert R. Barr (New York: Crossroad, 1999), 55.

6 Aristotle, *De generatione animalium* (On the Generation of Animals), in *The Complete Works of Aristotle: The Revised Oxford Translation*, vol. 1, ed. Jonathan Barnes (Princeton, NJ: Princeton University Press, 1984), 2.1.735a 2–4 (p. 1140) (hereafter, *GA*).

active willing that is the principle source of the action."[7] These immanent principles at the source of ethical action are—to complete our analogy—creative in only a limited sense. The human person is indeed free to choose, but he or she is not free to decide what is good or evil as such nor what is good or bad for him or her. In other words, the human being exercises the power to will within the context of what is perfective of the person as such: "to the good life as befits a human being who has developed to the fullest his human potential," as the French philosopher Yves Simon puts it.[8] It follows that "the human mind has no more power of inventing a new value, than of imagining a new primary colour, or, indeed, of creating a new sun and a new sky for it to move in."[9] In fact, the difference between the ethicist, who recognizes natural inclinations as prescriptive for human behavior, and the one who would invent a whole new moral code is like the difference between the man who says, "'You like your vegetables moderately fresh; why not grow your own . . . ?' and a man who says, 'Throw away that loaf and try eating bricks . . . instead.'"[10]

In short, the analogy between art and ethics invites us to consider what Simon identifies as the "problem of values": a "problem" that merits utmost "caution" today because "more often than not [the] consideration of 'values' . . . takes place within the framework of an idealistic, mechanistic philosophy whose vision of the world excludes finality."

> In this [modern and now postmodern] vision, things including man, have no ends and have, therefore, to be assigned "values" from outside. Without a nature of his own that would determine what is good and bad for him, man has no other choice but to let his imagination create his own "values." . . . In a world devoid of finality, all values must of necessity be both subjective and artificial; and when these "values" collapse, despair is all that is left. By contrast, in a world of natures, values reside in the nature of things. Thus if man has a nature, he also has a destiny, and we can relate what is right and wrong for him to do to his nature and to his end objectively.[11]

7 Servais Pinckaers, *The Sources of Christian Ethics*, trans. Sr. Mary Thomas Noble (Washington, DC: The Catholic University of America Press, 1995), 85.

8 Yves R. Simon, *The Definition of Moral Virtue* (New York: Fordham University Press, 1986), 118–19. Simon continues: "Understanding human nature, we can train ourselves in virtues according to objective standards" (119).

9 C. S. Lewis, *The Abolition of Man: Reflections on Education with Special Reference to the Teaching of English in the Upper Forms of Schools* (Oxford: Oxford University Press, 1943), 56–57.

10 Lewis, *The Abolition of Man*, 58–59.

11 Simon, *Definition of Moral Virtue*, 107.

THE INVERSION OF THESE ANALOGIES BY SARTRIAN PHILOSOPHY AND GENDER THEORISTS

Perhaps nowhere is the weight of Simon's words more apparent, as I will argue in these pages, than in the inversion of the analogy of art and ethics by gender theorists based upon the Sartrian presumption that there is no human nature. Hence, ethics becomes an "art" akin to the "art" of transforming the human body according to one's particular self-image, subjective desire, or so-called sexual "orientation," a highly ironic term insofar as it denies the psychological and biological structure proper to human sexuality, a structure aiming (whence the corresponding notion of *orientation*) simultaneously at communion between man and woman and at the birth of new persons. In the absence of nature-based inclinations toward nature-specified ends, on the other hand, sexual "orientation" signifies little more than an attempt to reify concupiscent desires—to "essentialize" *dis*oriented tendencies or to "enflesh" radically *non*-oriented tendencies—as typifies the euphuism of gender fluidity.[12] In both cases—that of "essentializing" concupiscent desires and that of "enfleshing" them—we are confronted with an attempt to reverse the traditional metaphysical order between nature and its appetites, inclinations, or desires. Whereas these have traditionally been understood as rooted in nature and as serving nature's movement toward its perfecting end—so as also to be judged as fitting to this movement and thus to be fostered, or as opposed and thus to be checked—the rhetoric of sexual orientation seeks to dethrone nature and set concupiscent inclinations in its place. This is the attitude that has birthed a whole androgynous anthropology.[13]

As Lewis predicted in his book appropriately entitled *The Abolition of Man*, "If man chooses to treat himself as raw material, raw material he will be: not raw material to be manipulated, as he fondly imagined, by himself [as a rational being], but by mere appetite, that is, mere Nature."[14] Indeed, as he foresaw it already in 1943, the "rebellion" of certain "new ideologies" against natural law

[12] See Michael W. Hannon, "Against Heterosexuality," *First Things* (March 2014), http://www.firstthings.com/article/2014/03/against-heterosexuality; and Michael W. Hannon, "Against Obsessive Sexuality: A Reply to My Critics," *First Things* (web exclusive), August 13, 2014, http://www.firstthings.com/web-exclusives/2014/08/against-obsessive-sexuality.

[13] See David S. Crawford, "Liberal Androgyny: 'Gay Marriage' and the Meaning of Sexuality in our Time," *Communio* 33, no. 2 (2006): 237–65.

[14] Lewis, *Abolition of Man*, 84. Similarly, "If you will not obey the *Tao* [that is, natural law], or else commit suicide, obedience to impulse (and therefore, in the long run, to mere 'nature') is the only course left open" (79).

is "a rebellion of the branches against the tree: if the rebels could succeed they would find that they had destroyed themselves."[15]

In this way, the tables are being turned on sexual realists—namely, those of us who believe that sex is more than skin deep—by so-called "theorists," who would disembody human sexuality and propose a new (presumably) better (because custom-made) way of being "gendered."[16] Hence Judith Butler, who is commonly regarded as the mastermind behind this trend, confronts us with a much too subtle shift in meaning. Throughout much of the history of the English language, "gender" was simply synonymous with sex: pointing, by way of its common root (*gyn*), to the reproductive potentialities and thus also to the sociohistorical dimensions of sex in virtue of which it necessarily transcends the individual/subjective domain.[17] It is thus only recently—after the sexual revolution had widely exercised its influence throughout the Western world—that the word *gender* has been used to refer to the social dimension of our sexual identity: to the sociocultural *expression* of the masculine or the feminine sex, whence the *distinction* between nature (in this case *sex*) and nurture (here *gender*).[18] Still more recently, however, it has come to denote—due largely to Butler, whose highly influential book *Gender Trouble* was first published in 1990—an actual *separation* between the two in view of reducing the former (sex) to the latter (gender).[19] Rather than referring—even culturally—to the concretely embodied and culturally rooted person, "gender" has thus become a sort of catchword for an uninhibited "freedom" to sexual self-determination: a license to freely determine not only one's own sexual inclination but also one's own sex in the absence of both natural and sociocultural factors.[20]

15 Lewis, *Abolition of Man*, 56–57.

16 In using the term "theory," its proponents would have us believe that the so-called theory of gender is an already validated scientific hypothesis, explains former European parliament deputy Élizabeth Montfort: "But, this so-called theory is apparently an opinion at best, an ideology at worst" (*Le genre démasqué: Homme ou femme? Le choix impossible*... [Valence, France: Peuple Libre, 2011], 15 [my translation]).

17 See Sr. Mary Prudence Allen, "Gender Reality vs. Gender Ideology: Ransoming the Concept of Gender," *Solidarity: The Journal of Catholic Social Thought and Secular Ethics* 4, no. 1 (2014): article 1, esp. 14–19, http://researchopruennline.nd.edu.au/solidarity/vol4/iss1/1/.

18 As of 1976, *The Concise Oxford Dictionary of Current English* still presents the word "gender" in purely grammatical terms and only secondarily as *synonymous* with sex. The social connotation is entirely absent. See *The Concise Oxford Dictionary of Current English: Based on The Oxford English Dictionary and Its Supplements*, ed. J. B. Sykes, 6th ed. (Oxford: Clarendon, 1976).

19 See Judith Butler, *Gender Trouble: Feminism and the Subversion of Identity* (New York: Routledge, 1990).

20 "*Gender* was the magic word" that made all of this possible, the German sociologist Gabriele Kuby explains. "The word sex had to be replaced; for prior to that, if someone was asked, 'What is your sex?,' they could answer only one of two things: man or woman" (Gabriele Kuby, *The Global Sexual Revolution: Destruction of Freedom in the Name of Freedom*, trans. James Patrick Kirchner [Kettering, OH: LifeSite, 2015], 44). See also Marguerite A. Peeters, *Le Gender, une norme mondiale? Pour un discernement* (Paris: Mame, 2013) (my translation); Michele M. Schumacher, "The Nature of Nature in Feminism, Old and New," in

Fighting against all forms of determinism—whether natural, biological, or cultural—recent gender "theorists" thus seek independence, or autonomy, with respect to faith and reason, nature and education, God and the human community. Because, it is reasoned more specifically, both the human body and the human community limit the exercise of freedom, we must be liberated from anything resembling a created world: a world composed of beings who are bound to one another by relations that are not of our making and in relationships that are simultaneously given and realized. In the words of Jean-Paul Sartre, whose philosophy is foundational for this ideology, not excepting the mediating role of Simone de Beauvoir,[21] "there is no human nature, since there is no God to conceive it. Not only is man what he conceives himself to be, but he is also only what he wills himself to be. . . . Man is nothing else but what he makes of himself."[22] "In him alone" lies, Beauvoir adds, "the power of laying the foundation of his own existence."[23] There is thus "no determinism": "no explaining things away by reference to a fixed and given human nature."[24] Because, furthermore, "there is no human nature," there is also "no 'feminine nature.' It's not something given," Beauvoir explains. Instead, the human person—whether male or female—is "defined by his presence to the world, his consciousness, and not [by] a nature that grants him *a priori* certain characteristics."[25] In short, in his attempt to draw "all the consequences of a coherent atheistic position," Sartre argues that to admit that man is free means that "man is freedom."[26]

Women in Christ: Toward a New Feminism, ed. Michele M. Schumacher (Grand Rapids, MI: Eerdmans, 2004), 17–51, esp. 17–28; and Beatriz Vollmer Coles, "New Feminism: A Sex-Gender Reunion," in *Women in Christ*, 52–66.

[21] On Beauvoir and Sartre's influence upon Judith Butler, see Deniz Durmus, "Existentialist Roots of Feminist Ethics: A Dissertation in Philosophy" (Ph.D. diss., The Pennsylvania State University, 2015), 117–46, https://etda.libraries.psu.edu/files/final_submissions/11104; as well as Butler's own works, *Subjects of Desire: Hegelian Reflections in Twentieth-Century France* (1987; repr., New York: Columbia University, 2012); and Judith Butler, "Sex and Gender in Simone de Beauvoir's *Second Sex*," *Yale French Studies* 72 (1986): 35–49. On the connection between Sartre's philosophy and that of Simone de Beauvoir, whom Sr. Prudence Allen qualifies as providing "the first articulation of existentialist feminism," see Allen's "Can Feminism Be a Humanism?," in *Women in Christ*, 270.

[22] Jean-Paul Sartre, *Existentialism and Human Emotions*, trans. Bernard Frechtman and Hazel E. Barnes (New York: Philosophical Library, 1957), 15.

[23] Simone de Beauvoir, *The Ethics of Ambiguity*, trans. Bernard Frechtman (New York: Open Road Integrated Media, 2018), 169.

[24] Sartre, *Existentialism and Human Emotions*, 22–23.

[25] Margaret A. Simons, Simone de Beauvoir, and Jane Maine Todd, "Two Interviews with Simone de Beauvoir (1982)," *Hypatia* 3, no. 3 (Winter 1989): 19. Or, as Sylvie le Bon perfectly summarizes Beauvoir's thought, "Far from being at the start point of history, the reality of woman is situated at its completion. It is always praxis, singular ideologies that have modeled this completely historical reality which is proposed as an Idea, a Being, a Fact" (Sylvie le Bon, "Le deuxième sexe, l'esprit et la lettre," *L'Arc* 61 [1975]: 56).

[26] Sartre, *Existentialism and Human Emotions*, 51, cf. 15, 23.

This is not to say that gender "theorists," who build upon this philosophy, recognize themselves as divorced from the world in which they live. Their final goal, after all—and this is what ultimately qualifies their work as an "ideology"[27] and simultaneously likens it to Sartrian doctrine[28]—is precisely *to transform this world* by establishing a new set of norms.[29] This goal of reorganizing society, if not the world itself, is sought by means of a reconceptualization of human sexuality so as also to transform the manner in which we conceive of marriage and family, as well as human rights.[30] Not surprisingly, then, the legal and juridical systems, which act as guarantors of these rights, are also targeted, as is the educational system, by which these new concepts and ideas are diffused.[31]

A PRESENTATION OF THE CHAPTERS

In an effort to argue against the inversion—by gender ideology and the existentialist philosophy of Jean-Paul Sartre upon which it is based—of the classic analogy between divine knowledge and art, on the one hand, and human

---

27 See Montfort, *Le genre démasqué*, 15; Jutta Burggraf, "Gender," in *Lexicon: Ambiguous and Debatable Terms Regarding Family Life and Ethical Questions*, ed. Pontifical Council for the Family (Front Royal, VA: Human Life International, 2006), 399–408; Joseph-Marie Verlinde, *L'idéologie du gender comme identité reçue ou choisie?* (Mesnil Saint-Loup, France: Le Livre Ouvert, 2012); and Kuby, *Global Sexual Revolution*. Marguerite Peeters, on the other hand, argues that gender is "not an ideology in the proper sense of the term," since the word "evokes systems of thought linked to Western modernity," and gender is, she insists, "a postmodern phenomenon" (Marguerite A. Peeters, "Gender: An Anthropological Deconstruction and a Challenge for Faith," in *Woman and Man: The* Humanum *in Its Entirety: International Congress on the 20th anniversary of John Paul II's Apostolic Letter* Mulieris Dignitatem, *1988–2008*, ed. Pontifical Council for the Laity [Vatican City: Libreria Editrice Vaticana, 2010], 289–90).

28 Sartre, *Existentialism and Human Emotions*, 41: "For us, . . . man is in an organized situation in which he himself is involved. Through his choice, he involves all mankind, and he can not avoid making a choice." Sartre, 45: "When I declare that freedom in every concrete circumstance can have no other aim than to want itself, if man has once become aware that in his forlornness [in the absence of God] he imposes values, he can no longer want but one thing, and that is freedom, as the basis of all values."

29 As a case in point, one might consider the connection between Dr. Jay Stewart's notion of a "gender revolution" and Judith Butler's *Notes Toward a Performative Theory of Assembly*, which he cites to strengthen his argument. See Stewart, "Trans Youth Are Real," *Gendered Intelligence* (blog), January 20, 2017, https://genderedintelligence.wordpress.com/2017/01/20/trans-youth-are-real/; and Judith Butler, *Notes Toward a Performative Theory of Assembly* (Cambridge, MA: Harvard University Press, 2015).

30 See Kuby, *Global Sexual Revolution*; Peeters, *Le Gender, une norme mondiale?*; Michele M. Schumacher, "A Plea for the Traditional Family: Situating Marriage within John Paul II's Realist, or Personalist, Perspective of Human Freedom," *Linacre Quarterly* 81, no. 4 (2014): 314–42; and Abigail Favale, "The Eclipse of Sex by the Rise of Gender," *Church Life Journal*, March 1, 2019, https://churchlifejournal.nd.edu/articles/the-eclipse-of-sex-by-the-rise-of-gender/.

31 In addition to the references cited in the note above, see Congregation for Catholic Education, "'Man and Woman He Created Them': Towards a Path of Dialogue on the Question of Gender Theory in Education" (Vatican City, February 2, 2019), https://www.vatican.va/roman_curia/congregations/ccatheduc/documents/rc_con_ccatheduc_doc_20190202_maschio-e-femmina_en.pdf; Heather Brunskell-Evans, *Transgender Body Politics* (North Geelong, Australia: Spinifex, 2020).

knowledge and art, on the other hand, this volume begins by sketching in *chapter 1* an important practical consequence of the philosophy of "gender": that of the rapidly growing trend of sexual "reassignment" surgery (or the more socially correct "gender confirmation" surgery), whose long-term effects are highly problematic, as testified by patients, doctors, and researchers.

This introduction to the practical stakes opens the way for my exposition in *chapter 2* of the theoretical aspect of this philosophy as it has been articulated by Judith Butler. The famous "gender" theorist maintains, more specifically, that the divine prerogative of creating nature has been replaced by social norms, which are said to grant even materiality, or corporeality, to human bodies. In this way, the foundation is laid for what is treated as an "artistic" reversal of norms, such that what was traditionally ascribed to nature is awarded instead to the human will. Hence, the gradual replacing of the notion of sexual *identity* with that of sexual *orientation* in our public vocabulary has allowed for "the introduction of the voluntary precisely in that domain where the subject experiences the involuntary," as the French philosopher Bérénice Levet observes.[32] Such, to be more specific, is the replacing of God's art (nature) with human "art" (manipulation): the "reduction of nature," as Joseph Ratzinger remarks, "to facts that can be completely grasped and therefore controlled" and the reduction of morality to that which is entirely "posited by man."[33]

In contrast to this characteristically modern trend of reducing nature to what is vulnerable to human manipulation and human sexuality to what is called "orientation," *chapter 3* points to their traditional meaning: one implying necessity and purposefulness, as befitting the doctrine of creation.[34] This, in

---

[32] Bérénice Levet, *La théorie du genre ou le monde rêvé des anges* (Paris: Bernard Grasset, 2014), 91 (my translation).

[33] Joseph Ratzinger, *A Turning Point for Europe? The Church in the Modern World: Assessment and Forecast*, 2nd ed., trans. Brain McNeil (San Francisco: Ignatius, 1994), 37. Hence, morality "does not precede vis-à -vis us: we precede it and fashion it" (37). Similarly, Lewis observes that "we reduce things to mere Nature *in order that* we can 'conquer' them. We are always conquering Nature, because 'Nature' is the name for what we have, to some extent, conquered." Hence, just as the stars are considered "nature" when "we can weigh and measure them," and the human soul is likewise when "we can psycho-analyse her" (*Abolition of Man*, 82–83).

[34] Josef Pieper points out that "there exists a current in Western thought, extending from St. Augustine to, let us say, Immanuel Kant, in which the meaning of the phrase 'by nature' is identical to that of 'by virtue of the created state.'" Josef Pieper, "Future without a Past and Hope with No Foundation?," in *Josef Pieper: An Anthology*, trans. Jan van Heurck (San Francisco: Ignatius, 1989), 211. Because, on the other hand, much of modern philosophy is "defined as rejections of both Christianity and antiquity, . . . nature is not seen as the pattern of necessities in man and the world; it is rather taken [in the opinions that are dominant in the Western world] as that which is to be mastered and transformed by man. Nature is defined in function of technology and the human projects technology serves" (Robert Sokolowski, *The God of Faith and Reason: Foundations of Christian Theology* [Notre Dame, IN: University of Notre Dame Press, 1982], 22).

turn, serves as the context wherein is treated the classic, Aristotelian-Thomistic notion of art as imitating nature in its internal directedness, or orientation, to precise ends, or goods. From this perspective, nature is regarded as the necessary presupposition for all that human beings are capable of creating or achieving. In this way, the plea is made for a return to the classic understanding of nature as norm: a norm that is invested with positive value prior to the influence of the human will and concupiscent appetites. That is why natural norms inspire the human person to willfully act in accord with nature's own intrinsic order and goodness in view of a normative plenitude of goodness, identical with being.

This normative plenitude is also of importance in understanding freedom from the perspective of excellence and thus in accord with the traditional metaphysical understanding of an end (*telos*) as a thing's perfected natural state of being: its complete goodness. In contrast, as pointed out in *chapter 4*, is the culturally prevalent understanding of freedom as an absence of constraint, so as to be essentially unaffected by natural inclinations. In opposition to the normative vision of nature and its inclinations is thus the Sartrian effort to uproot appetites, or desires, from both nature and natural ends, which are no longer given in the dual sense of the term as factual (*datum*) and as gratuitous (*donum*). In place of inclinations toward perfection, Sartre inserts desires that are a simple projection of consciousness in view of subjecting the freedom of others to one's own life project. Hence, Sartre's self-made man realizes himself with the help of the man-made woman, whose goal—as second-wave gender theorist Andrea Long Chu argues—is to become the perfect object of his desire. Such is the definition that Chu gives to both femaleness and to gender: the process of internalizing "misogynistic expectations" or "the self's gentle suicide in the name of someone *else's* desires, someone *else's* narcissism."[35]

Within the context of arguing for a return to the normative value of nature, *chapter 5* treats the distinction between biology and morphology and thus also between natural powers (in view of the specific good of procreation) and the manipulation of nature by surgical intervention. In the latter case, the body is "artistically" adapted to the ever-changing patterns of human fancy. Not surprisingly, gender ideology is now teaming up with artificial reproductive technologies, whence the coining of the term "*trans*biology" to signify the engineering of life itself and its potencies. Such is presumably the final frontier that gender ideology has yet to cross, but the project is well underway. The consequences of doing so—however incredible or frightful to our

[35] Andrea Long Chu, *Females* (New York: Verso, 2019), 35.

imaginations—nonetheless remain largely unknown to us. Due to the reversal of the traditional order between theoretical and practical knowledge, it can hardly be otherwise. Such is the option for Francis Bacon's dictum "knowledge is power" over the commonsensical "think before you leap." Henceforth the human will assumes primacy over knowledge of things in particular and of nature in general.

This reversal is just one consequence, among the many studied in *chapter* 6, of the failure to respect the difference at the basis of the classic metaphysical tradition between divine knowledge and human knowledge. Although the human intellect does indeed measure the things that it makes, it is nonetheless itself measured—as are all created things—by the divinely created things of this world. Each of these is said to reflect an eternal idea in the divine intellect just as a house, to borrow from St. Thomas, is measured by the image in the mind of its architect. Unlike the divine intellect, which is always in act, the human intellect is first of all passive and receptive before it is active and assertive, being potentially "all things." For it is like a "blank slate" upon which nothing is written. Because, moreover, human knowledge, like human art, is necessarily limited by the real—by the divine art that both precedes and measures it—our words are likewise measured by the real that they serve to convey. As differing from the divine Word in which the world and its inhabitants were created, human words are creative only as expressions of what is first of all understood. That is to say, they express what has first been received from this world by means of the senses, which serve to in-*form* our intellects. That is why they also differ from the culturally empowered word of Butler's philosophy, which is said to create bodies and their sex by its pronouncement.

Other conscious beings nonetheless present a constant limit to the Butlerian project of creating bodies by means of language. After all, the objective (as distinct from the subjective) value of my bodied being is thought to reside for today's "psychological" self in the consciousness of others—in what they think of me—and this remains inaccessible to me if not for the words they employ to communicate its content. That is why language must be policed to assure the success of the "gender" regime. And this in turn accounts for the systematic attempt throughout much of the Western world to change words that are charged with gendered meaning: "she," "he," "mother," "father," "uterus," "penis," "vagina," and so on. Because these words are a constant reminder of a natured past—of the long reign of natural law, under which nature was normative with respect to both being (ontology) and acting (ethics)—they must, "gender" activists argue, be erased from our lips. Only in this way might they eventually be erased from our minds, where they are said to receive their social meaning and even their metaphysical significance in the first place.

Finally, in the *conclusion*, it will be argued that the confrontation between the classic metaphysical tradition, beginning with Aristotle, and the new philosophy of "gender"—which is presented as an offspring of the existential but profoundly atheistic philosophy of Jean-Paul Sartre—entails the question of whether or not one is willing to respect the "ever-greater difference" between God and man. This primary question, in turn, implies the fundamental distinction between divine causality (or art) and human causality (or art). Ultimately, then, it is this distinction that determines the difference between the natural creature, with its sex, and man-made "gender."

CHAPTER 1

The Artistic Altering of Bodily Sex: An Ideological Revolution

True to the goal of changing cultural norms, recent developments in gender "theory" are not meant to remain in discussion among intellectuals in ivory towers. As a case in point, *The Boston Globe* reported in December 2011—nearly four years before gold-medal Olympian Bruce Jenner's famous transition to "Caitlyn"—the instance of twin boys who "were identical in every way but one. Wyatt [whose name has since been changed to Nicole] was," the reporter explains, "a girl to the core, and now lives as one with the help of a brave, loving family and a path-breaking doctor's care."[1]

It is well worth noting that against all (now "outdated") arguments of early gender theorists, who claimed that we choose sexual behaviors according to our education—that, in other words, we are programmed to behave in certain ways in accord with social expectations—Wyatt had to surmount his mother's insistence that he change out of his princess dress before presenting himself to guests in the family home and his father's tears when, at the age of four, he admitted that he hated his (later "her") penis and wanted to get rid of it. "Even when we did all the boy events to see if she would 'conform,'" writes Wyatt's (now "Nicole's") mother, who has since accepted that he is a girl, "she would just put her shirt on her head as hair, strap on some heels and join in. It wasn't really a matter of encouraging her to be a boy or a girl. That came about *naturally*."[2] Indeed, as if to stress the fact that there is no question of these parents socially programming Wyatt, *The Globe* entitles this story "Led by the Child Who Simply Knew."

"I have always known I was a girl," says Nicole, aged fourteen when the article was published. "I think what I'm aiming for is to undergo surgery to get a

[1] Bella English, "Led by the Child Who Simply Knew," *The Boston Globe*, December 11, 2011, http://articles.boston.com/2011-12-11/lifestyle/30512365_1_twin-boys-transgender-jonas.

[2] Emphasis added. The use of the word "naturally" in this context might serve to highlight the fact that it has become "natural" to separate the human body from the realm of affectivity.

physical female body that matches up to my image of myself."[3] At the time, that surgery was difficult to obtain for those under the age of legal consent in the US and Europe. However, at least 56 patients aged 13 to 17 years underwent genital surgeries between 2019 and 2021, and at least 776 underwent mastectomies in the United States alone.[4]

A GROWING BUSINESS

As for Boston Children's Hospital, it has come to boast of a "skilled team" that "includes specialists in plastic surgery, urology, endocrinology, nursing, gender management, and social work, who collaborate to provide a full suite of surgical options for transgender teens and young adults." More specifically, they are willing to "help young people with gender identity concerns transfer seamlessly to surgical care if and when they are ready."[5] Its website explains that one can, for example, receive chest reconstruction and breast augmentation at the age of fifteen,[6] vaginoplasty at the age of seventeen,[7] and either metoidioplasty (the construction of a penis from existing genital tissue) or phalloplasty (the construction of a penis from skin and other tissue harvested from another part of a patient's body) at the age of eighteen.[8] In Vermont, such surgeries may be funded for youth of at least sixteen years of age by taxpayers,[9] and in Oregon, eligibility begins already at fifteen, even in the absence of parental consent![10]

As for Nicole, although surgery was not yet an option at the time of *The*

---

3 English, "Led by the Child."

4 See Robin Respaut and Chad Terhune, "Putting Numbers on the Rise in Children Seeking Gender Care," Reuters, October 6, 2022, https://www.reuters.com/investigates/special-report/usa-transyouth-data/.

5 Center for Gender Surgery, Boston Children's Hospital (website), https://www.childrenshospital.org/centers-and-services/programs/a-_-e/center-for-gender-surgery-program#.

6 See "Breast Augmentation," Boston Children's Hospital (website), https://www.childrenshospital.org/treatments/breast-augmentation.

7 See "Vaginoplasty," Boston Children's Hospital (website), https://www.childrenshospital.org/conditions-and-treatments/treatments/vaginoplasty.

8 See "Metoidioplasty," Boston Children's Hospital (website), https://www.childrenshospital.org/conditions-and-treatments/treatments/metoidioplasty; and "Phalloplasty," Boston Children's Hospital (website), https://www.childrenshospital.org/conditions-and-treatments/treatments/phalloplasty.

9 See Susan Berry, "Vermont to Allow Taxpayer-Funded Transgender Sex Reassignment Surgeries for Children," Breitbart, June 13, 2019, https://www.breitbart.com/politics/2019/06/13/vermont-taxpayer-funded-transgender-sex-reassignment-surgeries-children/.

10 See Rina Marie Doctor, "Oregon Allows 15-Year-Olds to Have Sex Reassignment Surgery Even without Parental Consent?" Tech Times, July 13, 2015, https://www.techtimes.com/articles/68319/20150713/oregon-allows-15-year-olds-to-have-sex-reassignment-surgery-even-without-parental-consent.htm; and Basic Rights Oregon, "Oregon Health Plan Coverage for Gender Dysphoria," November 2015, https://www.basicrights.org/wp-content/uploads/2015/09/Gender_Dysphoria_Coverage_Within_OHP.pdf.

Globe's report, at the age of eleven, she joined thousands of American teens—not to mention those in Europe, where the trend was set[11]—in taking puberty blockers: drugs that suppress the release of sex hormones, namely, testosterone and estrogen.[12] The next step was to add female hormones so that "she" underwent puberty as a girl and developed as a woman, with breasts and curvy hips. These "benefits" come, however, at a price: the treatment not only threatens infertility and normal brain and bone development; it is also thought to cause cardiovascular problems, weight gain, diabetes, hypertension, gall bladder problems, and adrenal suppression.[13] None of these threats stopped Nicole, however. In 2015, at the age of eighteen and thanks to funds obtained from a lawsuit,[14] "her" masculine reproductive organs were removed and replaced by a simulation of female organs: breasts that cannot lactate and a vagina that does not open into a womb but that nonetheless requires, as the Boston Children's website reports, "a lifetime commitment to aftercare."[15]

---

[11] See Laura E. Kuper, "A Note on Research Methods and Gender Clinic Locations," in "Puberty Blocking Medication: Clinical Research Review IMPACT LGBT Health and Development Program," December 2014, p. 6, http://www.impactprogram.org/wp-content/uploads/2014/12/Kuper-2014-Puberty-Blockers-Clinical-Research-Review.pdf. It is worth noting that certain countries in Europe have since begun to introduce strict regulations on puberty blockers in light of "the significant risks and uncertainties of hormonal interventions" as well as questions concerning "the minor's maturity level and ability to provide true informed consent" (Society for Evidence Based Gender Medicine, "Sweden's Karolinska Ends All Use of Puberty Blockers and Cross-Sex Hormones for Minors Outside of Clinical Studies," May 5, 2021, updated May 8, 2021, and February 2022, https://segm.org/Sweden_ends_use_of_Dutch_protocol). See also the Society for Evidence Based Gender Medicine's "Policy Change Regarding Hormonal Treatment of Minors with Gender Dysphoria at Tema Barn—Astrid Lindgren Children's Hospital," https://segm.org /sites /default /files /Karolinska%20Policy%20Change%20K2021 -3343%20March%202021%20 %28English%2C%20unofficial%20translation%29.pdf; and Sanchez Manning, "'A Live Experiment on Children': Mail on Sunday Publishes the Shocking Physicians' Testimony That Led a High Court Judge to Ban NHS's Tavistock Clinic from Giving Puberty Blocking Drugs to Youngsters as Young as 10 Who Want to Change Sex," *Daily Mail*, January 9, 2021, https://www.dailymail.co.uk/news/article-9130157/The-physicians-testimony-led-High-Court-judge-ban-child-puberty-blocker-drugs.html.

[12] Talbot, "About a Boy," reports that Boston's Children's Hospital was the first to offer these in 2009, but Los Angeles, San Francisco, New York, and Seattle soon followed, and Chicago, Cleveland, and Philadelphia were lined up to do the same. She also reports the caution of Eli Coleman, the psychologist who drafted the latest guidelines for the World Professional Association for Transgender Health approving the use of puberty blockers: "We still don't know the subtle or potential long-term effects on brain function or bone development. Many people recognize it's not a benign treatment."

[13] See Walter J. Meyer III, "Gender Identity Disorder: An Emerging Problem for Pediatricians," *Pediatrics* 129, no. 3 (March 2012): 571–73; Manning, "'A Live Experiment on Children'"; and Faith Kuzma, "Are You Spiralling? Testosterone May Be the Reason," Psychreg, February 25, 2020, updated March 13, 2020, https://www.psychreg.org/testosterone-spiralling/.

[14] Nicole's family launched a discrimination suit against her school district (Maine Supreme Judicial Court, Doe v. Clenchy) for refusing to allow her to use the girls' restroom. See Jennifer Senior, "Review: 'Becoming Nicole': A Young Boy's Journey to Girlhood," *New York Times*, October 21, 2015, https://www.nytimes.com/2015/10/22/books/review-becoming-nicole-a-young-boys-journey-into-girlhood.html; and Amy Elles Nutt, Becom*ing Nicole: The Transformation of an American Family* (New York: Random House, 2015).

[15] "Vaginoplasty," Boston Children's Hospital (website).

COOPERATING WITH "MENTAL ILLNESS"?

Not surprisingly, Paul R. McHugh, former psychiatrist-in-chief at Johns Hopkins Hospital and Distinguished Service Professor of Psychiatry, refers to the practice of administering hormones in view of sexual reassignment as "close to child abuse." After all, 80 percent of children who make claims like that of Nicole will "abandon their confusion and grow naturally into adult life *if untreated*."[16] The "lack of data on gender dysphoria patients who have withdrawn from puberty-suppressing regimens and resumed normal development," on the other hand, poses the question of whether these treatments might actually "contribute to the persistence of gender dysphoria in patients who might otherwise have resolved their feelings of being the opposite sex," McHugh points out in union with Paul W. Hruz and Lawrence S. Mayer.[17]

McHugh, who helped put a stop to so-called sex-reassignment surgery (more commonly known today as "gender confirmation" surgery) at Johns

---

16 Michael W. Chapman, "Johns Hopkins Psychiatrist: Transgender is 'Mental Disorder'; Sex Change 'Biologically Impossible,'" CNS News, June 2, 2015, http://cnsnews.com/news/article/michael-w-chapman/johns-hopkins-psychiatrist-transgender-mental-disorder-sex-change (my emphasis). That statistic (that 80 to even 90 percent of gender-dysphoric children will align with their biology if allowed to pass through puberty naturally without transgender treatments) is consistent with figures cited by the World Professional Association for Transgender Health, *Standards of Care for the Health of Transsexual, Transgender, and Gender Nonconforming People*, 7th version (2012), 11, https://www.wpath.org/publications/soc. See also the recent (December 2019) North Carolina University study reporting that one in five teenagers reports some change in sexual orientation during adolescence: J. L. Stewart et al., "Developmental Patterns of Sexual Identity, Romantic Attraction, and Sexual Behavior among Adolescents over Three Years," *Journal of Adolescence* 77 (December 2019): 90–97; as well as Paul W. Hruz, Lawrence S. Mayer, and Paul R. McHugh, "Growing Pains: Problems with Puberty Suppression in Treating Gender Dysphoria," *The New Atlantis* (Spring 2017): 3–36; Kelley Drummond et al., "A Follow-Up Study of Girls with Gender Identity Disorder," *Developmental Psychology* 44 (2008): 34–45; Devia Singh, "A Follow-up Study of Boys with Gender Identity Disorder" (PhD diss., University of Toronto, 2012), http://images.nymag.com/images/2/daily/2016/01/SINGH-DISSERTATION.pdf; Kenneth J. Zucker, "The Myth of Persistence: Response to 'A Critical Commentary on Follow-Up Studies and "Desistance" Theories about Transgender and Gender Non-Conforming Children' by Temple Newhook et al. (2018)," *International Journal of Transgenderism* 19, no. 2 (May 2018): 1–15; Madeleine Wallien and Peggy Cohen Kettenis, "Psychosexual Outcome of Gender-Dysphoric Children," *Journal of the American Academy of Child and Adolescent Psychiatry* 47, no. 12 (December 2008): 1413–23; James Cantor, "Do Trans- Kids Stay Trans- When They Grow Up?," Sexology Today, January 11, 2016, http://www.sexologytoday.org/2016/01/do-trans-kids-stay-trans-when-they-grow_99.html; and Meyer, "Gender Identity Disorder." As for Amy Ellis Nutt, author of Becom*ing Nicole*, she admits that "only a quarter of the kids who identify as transgender continue to do so once they've hit adolescence." See Senior, "Review: 'Becoming Nicole.'"

17 Hruz, Mayer, and McHugh, "Growing Pains," 25. The authors argue, in fact, that "gender identity for children is elastic (that is, it can change over time) and plastic (that is, it can be shaped by forces like parental approval and social conditions)." We are thus alerted to the following problem: "If the increasing use of gender-affirming care does cause children to persist with their identification as the opposite sex, then many children who would otherwise not need ongoing medical treatment would be exposed to hormonal and surgical interventions" (6). See also Ryan T. Anderson, *When Harry Became Sally: Responding to the Transgender Moment* (New York: Encounter Books, 2018), 117–44.

Hopkins, has heard it all.[18] "Not uncommonly" people come to his clinic saying, "As long as I can remember, I've thought I was in the wrong body." When, however, "you discuss what the [male] patient means by 'feeling like a woman,' you often get," McHugh explains, "a sex stereotype in return—something woman physicians note immediately is a male caricature of women's attitudes and interests."[19] One can hardly help but think of Caitlyn Jenner's remark that "the hardest part of being a woman is figuring out what to wear": a remark that so infuriated the widower of Moira Smith, a female police officer killed in the 9/11 attacks, that he returned his late wife's 2001 "Woman of the Year" award when Jenner received the same in 2015.[20] At any rate, it is with good reason that Leonard Sax points to the irony of "the mainstream consensus" regarding gender. For the most part, it is considered as an entirely malleable social construction, "*unless* you happen to be *transgender*, in which case your gender identity is inviolate, hardwired, and impossible to change."[21]

As for Jenner, "she" also corresponds to McHugh's observation that post-surgical transgendered subjects tend to wear "high heels, copious makeup, and flamboyant clothing," to speak of themselves as freed to express "their natural inclinations"[22]—inclinations which do *not* include a desire for children (whom, after all, they cannot conceive within themselves, as do natal women) but *do* include typical stereotypes of women, such as that of being more "invested with being than with doing"—and to present themselves as "lesbians" because they remain attracted to women.[23] This last point, combined with the fact that only 4 to 13 percent of transgender "women" actually undergo lower body surgery, vindicates the natal women who, despite shameful accusations of "bigotry," are uncomfortable sharing private spaces, such as

---

[18] John Hopkins has since resumed performing this surgery.

[19] Paul R. McHugh, "Psychiatric Misadventures," *The American Scholar* 61, no. 4 (Autumn 1992): 502. See also McHugh, "Transgender Surgery Isn't the Solution: A Drastic Physical Change Doesn't Address Underlying Psycho-Social Troubles," *The Wall Street Journal*, June 12, 2014, http://www.wsj.com/articles/paul-mchugh-transgender-surgery-isnt-the-solution-1402615120.

[20] See Katia Heller, "Widower of 9/11 Cop Returns Glamour Award over Caitlyn Jenner," CNN, November 17, 2015, http://edition.cnn.com/2015/11/16/living/widower-911-officer-glamour-award-caitlyn-jenner-feat/index.html.

[21] Leonard Sax, *Why Gender Matters: What Parents and Teachers Need to Know about the Emerging Science of Sex Differences* (New York: Harmony Books, 2005), 288–89. Or, as Heather Brunskell-Evans puts it, "Far from rejecting biological essentialism, queer theory endorses it since it untethers gender from its social context, mirroring the traditional claim that masculinity and femininity are pre-social and interior" (Heather Brunskell-Evans, "The Medico-Legal 'Making' of 'The Transgender Child,'" *Medical Law Review* 27, no. 4 [June 25, 2019]: 649).

[22] Paul R. McHugh, "Surgical Sex: Why We Stopped Doing Sex Change Operations," *First Things* (November 2004), http://www.firstthings.com/article/2004/11/surgical-sex.

[23] McHugh, "Psychiatric Misadventures," 502.

battered women's emergency shelters, jails, bathrooms, and locker rooms, with transgender "women."[24]

Moreover, although most of the men who have undergone sexual-reassignment surgery as adults at Johns Hopkins did not express regret for having done so, they did continue to experience the same psychological problems that haunted them prior to their surgeries.[25] That is why McHugh concludes that the psychiatric department at John Hopkins has been "cooperating with a mental illness."[26]

> It is not obvious how this patient's feeling that he is a woman trapped in a man's body differs from the feeling of a patient with anorexia nervosa that she is obese despite her emaciated, cachectic state. We don't do liposuction on anorexics. Why amputate the genitals of these poor men? Surely, the fault is in the mind not the member.[27]

Like those who are "dangerously thin" and who nonetheless believe that they are overweight or those otherwise "consumed by the assumption 'I'm ugly,'" the transgendered suffer "a disorder of 'assumption' . . . that departs from physical reality," McHugh explains.[28] Because, however, sexual orientation is falsely equated with *the feeling* of "gender," which in turn is said to be subjectively determined,[29] its defenders argue that it cannot be called into question; whence the

[24] See Ian T. Nolan et al., "Demographic and Temporal Trends in Transgender Identities and Gender Confirming Surgery," *Translational Andrology and Urology* 8, no. 3 (2019): 187.

[25] See McHugh, "Surgical Sex." To be more specific, McHugh's colleague Jon Meyer, who conducted a follow-up study of adult men who had undergone sexual reassignment surgery, observed that these patients fell into two groups: (1) homosexual men "who saw sex-change as a way to resolve their conflicts over homosexuality by allowing them to behave sexually as females with men," and (2) heterosexual (and some bisexual) men "who found intense sexual arousal in cross-dressing as females," an illness known as "autogynephilia." See Jon Meyer and Donna J. Reter, "Sex Reassignment Follow-Up," *Archives of General Psychiatry* 36, no. 9 (1979): 1010–15. See also Richard P. Fitzgibbons, Philip M. Sutton, and Dale O'Leary, "The Psychopathology of 'Sex Reassignment' Surgery: Assessing Its Medical, Psychological and Ethical Appropriateness," The National Catholic Bioethics Center, 2009, http://ncbcenter.org/document.doc?id=581.

[26] McHugh, "Surgical Sex." See also Sax, *Why Gender Matters*, 269–73.

[27] McHugh, "Psychiatric Misadventures," 503.

[28] See McHugh, "Transgender Surgery Isn't the Solution."

[29] As Talbot, reports in "About a Boy," "In trans circles, it is a given that sexual orientation and gender identity are separate matters." A so-called "Genderbread Person" (resembling a gingerbread man), which is a pictorial designed by trans activists, points to the following distinctions: "sexual orientation" is depicted by the heart; "gender identity" is depicted by the brain; "biological sex" is depicted by the sexual organs; and "gender expression" (the manner in which one presents oneself to others in terms of behavior and dress) is depicted by a dotted line surrounding the figure. See also Sax, *Why Gender Matters*, 263–65. We should not be surprised, then, that Tinder now offers more than fifty gender options and nine sexual orientation options to its users. See Business Today Desk, "Tinder's 'Let's Talk Gender' Online Glossary is the Guide We All Needed," *Business Today*, June 22, 2022: https://www.businesstoday.in/technology/news/story/tinders-lets-talk-gender-online-glossary-is-the-guide-we-all-needed-338709-2022-06-22.

now common practice of publicly defending "the right" of each citizen to change not only his or her "gender"[30] but also his or her physical sex accordingly: even with the help of public funding.[31] In fact, thirty-four of the fifty US states (or 68 percent) finance so-called "gender-affirming" hormone therapy with public tax monies and twenty-five (50 percent) pay for genital "gender-affirming" surgery.[32] Even in the absence of public funding, "sexual-reassignment" surgeries have been realized on youth thanks to crowdfunding online, which has the added "advantage" of bypassing certain governmental health standards and measures of protection.[33]

QUESTIONABLE STUDIES

Those funds would be far better spent treating the illness, McHugh argues, rather than dismembering the body.[34] In fact, in another of his articles, he cites a 2011 study by the Karolinska Institute in Sweden that followed 324 sex-reassignment patients over a period of thirty years (1973–2003).[35] The study revealed that the patients began to experience mental disorders about ten years

[30] See, for example, Selim Algar, "Changing Gender Is Easier Than Ever in NYC Schools," *New York Post*, June 28, 2019, https://nypost.com/2019/06/28/changing-gender-is-easier-than-ever-in-nyc-schools/.

[31] McHugh notes that on May 30, 2014, a US Department of Health and Human Services review board ruled that Medicare can pay for the sexual reassignment surgery. See McHugh, "Transgender Surgery Isn't the Solution," and Stephanie Armour, "Medicare Ban on Sex-Reassignment Surgery Lifted," *The Wall Street Journal*, May 30, 2014, http://www.wsj.com/articles/medicare-ban-on-sex-reassignment-surgery-lifted-1401478303. See also the extensive and well-documented argument to this effect by Gabriele Kuby, *The Global Sexual Revolution: Destruction of Freedom in the Name of Freedom*, trans. James Patrick Kirchner (Kettering, OH: LifeSite, 2015), and the map of the United States highlighting the twenty states (plus the District of Columbia) that "prohibit licensed mental health practitioners from subjecting LGBT minors to [so-called] harmful 'conversion therapy' practices that attempt to change their sexual orientation or gender identity," that is to say, that seek to bring about a correspondence between a patient's sexual orientation or so-called gender identity and their biological sex: http://www.lgbtmap.org/equality-maps/conversion_therapy. See also supra notes 9 and 10.

[32] See Michael Zaliznyak et al., "Which U.S. States' Medicaid Programs Provide Coverage for Gender-Affirming Hormone Therapy and Gender-Affirming Genital Surgery for Transgender Patients?: A State-by-State Review, and a Study Detailing the Patient Experience to Confirm Coverage of Services," *Journal of Sexual Medicine* 18, no. 2 (February 2021): 410–22.

[33] See Sue Reid, "How Children as Young as 13 Are Asking Strangers Online to Crowdfund Their Sex Change Drugs . . . And Even More Disturbingly—They Are Bypassing NHS Safeguards to Get Them," *Daily Mail*, January 28, 2022, https://www.dailymail.co.uk/news/article-10453837/How-children-young-13-asking-strangers-online-crowdfund-sex-change-drugs.html.

[34] The "most astonishing" example cited by McHugh, "Surgical Sex," is that of a surgeon in England, "who is prepared to amputate the legs of patients who claim to find sexual excitement in gazing at and exhibiting stumps of amputated legs." As for the categorizing of transgenderism as an illness, McHugh, "Transgender Surgery Isn't the Solution," argues that it "constitutes a mental illness in two respects": (1) the idea of sex misalignment "does not correspond with physical reality" and (2) "it can lead to grim psychological outcomes."

[35] See C. Dhejne et al., "Long-Term Follow-Up of Transsexual Persons Undergoing Sex Reassignment

after their surgeries and that their suicide rate was twenty times above that of the general (non-transgendered) population.[36] This is not a minor fact to keep in mind when regarding the results of a more recent (2019) study drawing from a much-expanded database—the world's largest to date—of the same population, supplied by the Swedish Total Population Register of over 9.7 million Swedes, 2,679 of whom were diagnosed with gender incongruence and 1,018 of whom had "gender-affirming" surgery. Because only nineteen of the more than one thousand respondents reported their last surgery as completed more than ten years prior to the study—in contrast to the 574 whose surgery was reported as having occurred less than two years prior—Dr. Mark Regnerus of the University of Texas at Austin has good reason to question the study's "trumpeted conclusion"[37] in favor of so-called gender-affirming surgeries.[38]

In light of these figures, Regnerus argues that this highly influential conclusion hinges on as few as three persons. That is why the scholarly interpretations of the "otherwise excellent data and analyses" are "remarkably out of step," suggesting a "complicity with activist groups in favor of seeking to normalize infertility-inducing and permanently disfiguring surgeries." Regnerus himself concludes *from the same data* that the beneficial effect of such surgeries is "so small that a clinic may have to perform as many as 49 gender-affirming surgeries before they could expect to prevent one additional person from seeking subsequent mental health treatment." As for hormonal interventions, they were found to cause "no mental health benefits . . . in this population."[39]

Given these utter incoherencies, it is not surprising that the editors of *The American Journal of Psychiatry* and the authors of the study were forced to

---

Surgery: Cohort Study in Sweden," *PLoS ONE* (February 22, 2011), http://www.ncbi.nlm.nih.gov/pubmed/21364939.

[36] See McHugh, "Transgender Surgery Isn't the Solution." Likewise striking is the review by the University of Birmingham's Aggressive Research Intelligence Facility (ARIF) of over one hundred international medical studies of post-operative transsexuals, a review which found "no robust scientific evidence that gender reassignment surgery is clinically effective." See David Batty, "Sex Changes Are Not Effective, Say Researchers," *The Guardian*, July 30, 2004, http://www.theguardian.com/society/2004/jul/30/health.mentalhealth.

[37] Mark Regnerus, "New Data Show 'Gender-Affirming' Surgery Doesn't Really Improve Mental Health. So Why Are the Study's Authors Saying It Does?" Public Discourse, November 13, 2019, https://www.thepublicdiscourse.com/2019/11/58371/.

[38] "The longitudinal association between gender-affirming surgery and reduced likelihood of mental health treatment lends support to the decision to provide gender-affirming surgeries to transgender individuals who seek them" (Richard Bränström and John E. Pachankis, "Reduction in Mental Health Treatment Utilization among Transgender Individuals after Gender-Affirming Surgeries: A Total Population Study," *The American Journal of Psychiatry* 177, no. 8 [August 2020]: 727–34).

[39] Regnerus, "'Gender-Affirming' Surgery." See also Ryan T. Anderson, "'Transitioning' Procedures Don't Help Mental Health, Largest Dataset Shows," The Heritage Foundation, August 3, 2020, https://www.heritage.org/gender/commentary/transitioning-procedures-dont-help-mental-health-largest-dataset-shows.

publish a correction admitting that their original conclusion was "too strong." Indeed, "the results demonstrated no advantage of surgery in relation to subsequent mood or anxiety disorder-related health care visits or prescriptions or hospitalizations following suicide attempts in that comparison."[40] Moreover, similar studies conducted in Denmark and Switzerland reveal a lower quality of life among those who have undergone these surgeries and an increased level of disease and death.[41]

THE REIMER CASE: THE INVENTION OF "SEX CHANGE"

Not unlike these questionable—even regrettable—effects of "sexual-reassignment" surgery on adults are those of castrating male infants having sexually ambiguous genitalia and raising them as females: a practice that was almost universally conducted in the 1970s. Both illustrative and innovative was the famous John/Joan case: a pseudonym for Bruce/Brenda/David Reimer, "the boy who was raised to be a girl," in accord with the advice of the famous psychologist John Money.[42] This predecessor of Paul McHugh at Johns Hopkins found in Bruce Reimer the perfect subject to confirm his hypothesis that "like hermaphrodites, all the human race follow the same pattern, namely, of psychological undifferentiation at birth."[43]

[40] Editors, "Correction to Bränström and Pachankis," *The American Journal of Psychiatry*, August 1, 2020, https://ajp.psychiatryonline.org/doi/10.1176/appi.ajp.2020.1778correction. The correction also occurs on page 734 of the study.

[41] "Of 98% of all Danish transsexuals who officially underwent SRS [sexual reassignment surgery] from 1978 through 2010" (104 individuals), "one in three had somatic morbidity and approximately 1 in 10 had died" (Rikke Kildevaeld Simonsen et al., "Long-Term Follow-Up of Individuals Undergoing Sex -Reassigment Surgery: Somatic Morbidity and Cause of Death," *Sexual Medicine* 4 [2016]: 60). As for the Swiss study that followed fifty-five transsexuals fifteen years after their sexual reassignment surgery, it reports: "Quality of life as determined by the King's Health questionnaire," which is designed to assess the impact of lower urinary tract symptoms, including urinary incontinence, on health related quality of life, "was significantly lower in general health, personal, physical and role limitations. Patients' satisfaction was significantly lower compared with controls." See Annette Kuhn et al., "Quality of Life 15 Years after Sex Reassignment Surgery for Transsexualism," *Fertility and Sterility* 92, no. 5 (November 2009): 1685–89; results cited from the résumé at https://pubmed.ncbi.nlm.nih.gov/18990387/.

[42] See John Colapinto, *As Nature Made Him: The Boy Who Was Raised to Be a Girl* (New York: HarperCollins, 2000).

[43] John Money, "Cytogenetic and Psychosexual Incongruities with a Note on Space Form Blindness," *American Journal of Psychiatry* 119, no. 9 (1963): 820, https://www.researchgate.net/publication/9631137_Cytogenetic_and_Psychosexual_Incongruities_with_a_Note_on_Space_Form_Blindness. For a critique of Money's false reasoning "from the exception to the rule," see Sr. Mary Prudence Allen, "Gender Reality vs. Gender Ideology: Ransoming the Concept of Gender," *Solidarity: The Journal of Catholic Social Thought and Secular Ethics* 4, no. 1 (2014): 6–7. Similarly, Milton Diamond and H. Keith Sigmundson make reference to six articles critiquing the theory that hermaphrodites and pseudohermaphrodites offer a model for normal development, including a reply by Money. See reference notes 19–24 in Milton

Following a botched circumcision, Reimer underwent a so-called sex-change operation at the age of twenty-two months and was raised as a girl, in complete ignorance of his birth sex, while his twin brother acted as the control subject. Despite repeated—and non-retracted[44]—claims in print by Money of the success of his experiment,[45] Reimer did not adjust to "being" a girl. He rejected girl's toys, clothes, and activities. He imitated his father in shaving rather than his mother in applying makeup. He refused to use the girl's bathroom, and he urinated standing up. Finally, at the age of fourteen, he discovered the truth about his sex reassignment and asked to surgically and socially reappropriate his male identity.[46] He eventually married, but he remained greatly depressed and committed suicide in 2004.[47]

Given the notoriety of the Reimer case, combined with its false claims, it is not surprising that subsequent researchers had a wide body of case studies to draw upon in conducting sex reassignment follow-up studies.[48] In so doing, they concluded that "there is no known case where a 46 chromosome, XY male, unequivocally so at birth, has ever easily and fully accepted an imposed life as an androphilic female regardless of the physical and medical intervention." Indeed, "the sex reassignment did nothing to effect sexual orientation" because "sexual orientation is prenatally organized or at least predisposed."[49] If

Diamond and H. Keith Sigmundson, "Sex Reassignment at Birth: Long-Term Review and Clinical Implications," *Archives of Pediatrics and Adolescent Medicine* 151, no. 3 (1997): 298–304, http://hawaii.edu/PCSS/biblio/articles/1961to1999/1997-sex-reassignment.html.

44 See Milton Diamond, "Money's Sex Claims," Letter to the Editor, *The Listener*, September 5, 1998, http://hawaii.edu/PCSS/biblio/articles/1961to1999/1998-listener.html. See also Allen, "Gender Reality vs. Gender Ideology," 11–12.

45 See, for example, John Money and Anke A. Ehrhardt, *Man & Woman, Boy & Girl: The Differentiation and Dimorphism of Gender Identity from Conception to Maturity* (New York: New American Library, 1972).

46 As Diamond and Sigmundson, "Sex Reassignment at Birth," put it, "The contrast between the female gender-typical behaviors the child was being asked to accept and his inner directed behavior preferences presented a discordance that demanded resolution."

47 See John Colapinto, "Gender Gap: What Were the Real Reasons behind David Reimer's Suicide?," Slate, http://www.slate.com/articles/health_and_science/medical_examiner/2004/06/gender_gap.html.

48 See especially the study by William G. Reiner and John P. Gearhart, "Discordant Sexual Identity in Some Genetic Males with Cloacal Exstrophy Assigned to Female Sex at Birth," *New England Journal of Medicine* 350 (2004): 331–41. Also worth noting is the fact that Diamond and Sigmundson make reference to seven articles (see reference notes 19, 32, and 58–62 at the conclusion of their article, "Sex Reassignment at Birth"), reporting cases, including the Reimer one, in which males lacking a normal penis were reassigned as girls but eventually switched back to live "successfully" as males.

49 Diamond and Sigmundson, "Sex Reassignment at Birth." See especially notes 33–40 of the references listed at the completion of the article. Similarly, McHugh argues, based on studies by William G. Reiner (2004) and Jon Meyer (1979), that "human sexual identity is mostly built into our constitution by the genes we inherit and the embryogenesis we undergo" (McHugh, "Surgical Sex"). On the other hand, McHugh and Mayer insist that "the understanding of sexual orientation as an innate, biologically fixed property of human beings—the idea that people are 'born that way'—is not supported by scientific

not for the fact that it is easier to surgically construct a vagina than to correct a malformed or damaged penis, and significantly less expensive, one might even question why so-called sex reassignment was ever performed in the first place.[50] On the other hand, despite amazing gains in surgical practice in the interim—one need only consider the fact that Reimer eventually had penal reconstruction and was capable of "coital orgasm with ejaculation"[51]—these gains continue to serve the same "trendy idea" that provided the initial zeal for sexual-reassignment surgery in the seventies: "not [one] derive[d] from critical reasoning or thoughtful assessments," McHugh reports, but from the "if it feels good, do it" philosophy, which for surgeons meant: "if you can do it and he wants it, why not do it?"[52] This philosophy, in turn, was parasitic of the notion that "nature is totally malleable" and that sexual identity is primarily determined by "postnatal, cultural, nonhormonal influences,"[53] whence also the portrayal of the body as "a suit of clothes to be hemmed and stitched to style."[54]

CULTURAL PRESSURE TO TRANSITION

evidence." In fact, "as many as 80% of male adolescents who report same-sex attractions no longer do so as adults" (Paul McHugh and Lawrence S. Mayer, "Sexuality and Gender: Findings from the Biological, Psychological, and Social Sciences," *The New Atlantis* 50 Special Report [2016]: 7). McHugh and Mayer propose to show that "though sexual orientation is not a choice, neither is there scientific evidence for the view that sexual orientation is a fixed and innate biological property" (13). Hence, for example, "there is no reliable scientific evidence that sexual orientation is determined by a person's genes. But there is evidence that genes play a role in influencing sexual orientation" (31). More recently, a study by MIT and Harvard scientists of the genetic material of nearly a half million individuals reveals that the genetic influence on same-sex orientation is quite minimal: only 0.32 on a scale from zero to one. Results suggest "that same-sex sexual behavior, like most complex human traits, is influenced by the small, additive effects of very many genetic variants." In other words, "genetic influences on same-sex sexual behavior are highly polygenic," with "no single genetic determinant (sometimes referred to as the 'gay gene' in the media)" (Andrea Ganna et al, "Large-Scale GWAS Reveals Insights into the Genetic Architecture of Same-Sex Sexual Behavior," *Science* 356, no. 882 [2019]: 3–4, 6). "This means," Paul Sullins explains in his commentary, "that a person's developmental environment—which includes diet, family, friends, neighborhood, religion, and a host of other life conditions—is twice as influential on the probability of developing same-sex behavior or orientation as a person's genes are" (Paul Sullins, "'Born That Way' No More: The New Science of Sexual Orientation," Public Discourse, September 30, 2019, https://www.thepublicdiscourse.com/2019/09/57342/).

50 Talbot reported in 2013 that the construction of a vagina by inverting the penis costs approximately fifteen thousand dollars, whereas phalloplasty (the surgical construction of a penis) can cost more than a hundred thousand dollars. See Talbot, "About a Boy"; and Mayer and McHugh, "Sexuality and Gender," 91.

51 Diamond and Sigmundson, "Sex Reassignment at Birth."

52 McHugh, "Psychiatric Misadventures," 503.

53 McHugh, "Surgical Sex." On the challenges of determining sexual orientation, see Mayer and McHugh, "Sexuality and Gender," 13–58. The authors point out that "there are currently no agreed-upon definitions of 'sexual orientation,' 'homosexuality,' or 'heterosexuality' for purposes of empirical research" (21).

54 McHugh, "Psychiatric Misadventures," 503.

Meanwhile, this spirit of extreme subjectivism distracted the medical community, McHugh believes, from conducting "genuine investigations" into the cause of the distress and torment, as testified by the patients themselves,[55] prompting them to undergo such radical surgical interventions.[56] Indeed, the very fact

[55] One need only consider that one detransition chat group has over 19,000 members. See https://www.reddit.com/r/detrans/. See also Scott Newgent, "We Need Balance When It Comes to Gender Dysphoric Kids. I Would Know," *Newsweek*, February 9, 2021, https://www.newsweek.com/we-need-balance-when-it-comes-gender-dysphoric-kids-i-would-know-opinion-1567277; the important testimony of Walt Heyer, a reverted transsexual, and others at http://www.sexchangeregret.com/; Walt Heyer, *Trans Life Survivors* (self-pub., 2018); the testimony of Patrick Mitchell, aired on Australia's *60 Minutes* on September 10, 2017, https://www.youtube.com/watch?v=vqSdcvIz4VI; BBC News Night, "Detransitioning: Reversing a Gender Transition," November 26, 2019, https://www.youtube.com/watch?v=fDi-jFVBLA8; GuessImAfab, "GenderFlux: How One Young Woman Fell Down the Rapid Onset Rabbit Hole," 4thWaveNow, May 15, 2019, https://4thwavenow.com/2019/05/16/genderflux-how-one-young-woman-fell-down-the-rapid-onset-rabbit-hole/; Stella Morabito, "Trouble in Transtopia: Murmurs of Sex Change Regret," The Federalist, November 11, 2014, https://thefederalist.com/2014/11/11/trouble-in-transtopia-murmurs-of-sex-change-regret/; Nicole Russell, "What The First Nonbinary American Wants the Supreme Court to Know about Transgenderism," The Federalist, October 8, 2019, https://thefederalist.com/2019/10/08/what-the-first-nonbinary-american-wants-the-supreme-court-to-know-about-transgenderism/; Jill Stark, "I Will Never Be Able to Have Sex Again. Ever," *The Sydney Morning Herald*, May 31, 2009, https://www.smh.com.au/national/i-will-never-be-able-to-have-sex-again-ever-20090530-br41.html; Jill Stark, "Sex-Change Clinic 'Got it Wrong,'" *The Sydney Morning Herald*, May 31, 2009, https://www.smh.com.au/national/sexchange-clinic-got-it-wrong-20090530-br3u.html; Transgender Trend, "Parents Questioning the Transnarrative" (East Sussex, UK, 2019), https://www.transgendertrend.com/detransition/; the example of Kiera Bell in Heather Brunskell-Evans, *Transgender Body Politics* (North Geelong, Australia: Spinifex, 2020), 77–81, as well as Bell's own testimony at https://www.persuasion.community/p/keira-bell-my-story; and the numerous examples cited by Anderson in *When Harry Became Sally*, 49–76.

[56] On the extreme subjectivism of the medical community on this issue, see, for example, Mayer and McHugh, "Sexuality and Gender," who point to "a large gap between the certainty with which beliefs are held about these matters [those of gender identity] and what a sober assessment of the science reveals." After all, "the majority of children who identify as a gender that does not conform to their biological sex will no longer do so by the time they reach adulthood." That is why the authors are "disturbed and alarmed by the severity and irreversibility of some interventions being publicly discussed and employed for children" (12). See also Anderson, *When Harry Became Sally*, 93–116; Katherine Cave, "The Medical Scandal that the Mainstream Media Ignores," Public Discourse, April 8, 2019, https://www.thepublicdiscourse.com/2019/04/50959/; Madeleine Kearns, "A Thousand Parents of Trans-Identifying Children Beg Doctors to Listen," *National Review*, October 24, 2018, https://www.nationalreview.com/corner/american-academy-of-pediatrics-transgender-statement-parents-beg-doctors-to-listen/; Daniel Payne, "Casualties of a Social, Psychological, and Medical Fad: The Dangers of Transgender Ideology in Medicine," Public Discourse, January 31, 2018, https://www.thepublicdiscourse.com/2018/01/20810/; Leonard Sax, "Politicizing Pediatrics: How the AAP's Transgender Guidelines Undermine Trust in Medical Authority," Public Discourse, March 13, 2019, http://www.the publicdiscourse.com/2019/03/50118; Jane Robbins and Erin Tuttle, "What's Wrong with the New NIH Study on Transgender Kids?," Public Discourse, January 17, 2018, http://www.thepublicdiscourse.com/2018/01/20844/; Michael K. Laidlaw, "The Gender Identity Phantom," Mercatornet, November 12, 2018, https://mercatornet.com/the-gender-identity-phantom/23780/; Michelle Cretella, "I'm a Pediatrician. Here's What You Should Know about a New Study on Transgender Teen Suicide," The Daily Signal, September 18, 2017, https://www.dailysignal.com/2018/09/18/new-study-on-transgender-teen-suicide-doesnt-prove-kids-need-gender-transition-therapy/; Michelle Cretella, "I'm a Pediatrician. Here's What I Did When a Little Boy Patient Said He Was a Girl," The Daily Signal, December 11, 2017, http://dailysignal.com/2017/12/11/cretella-transcript/; Michelle Cretella, "Gender Dysphoria in Children," American College of Pediatricians (website),

that Boston Children's Hospital—to name just one of the increasing number of hospitals and clinics worldwide with similar protocols—is actively encouraging young patients like Wyatt to change their physical sex by way of hormone treatments in view of reassignment surgery despite ample research pointing to the devastating long-term effects thereof[57] stands as proof of the "power of cultural fashion to lead psychiatric thought and practice off in false, even disastrous, directions."[58] Such might well be viewed as "collaborat[ing] with madness."[59] As for the constantly growing number of children and adolescents flirting with transgenderism—thanks, no doubt, to "a flurry of mostly positive media [including popularized internet] attention"[60] and a powerful LGBTQ+ lobby attempting to silence those who speak against transition[61]—would it not be

---

November 2018, https://www.acpeds.org/the-college-speaks/position-statements/gender-dysphoria-in-children; Andre Van Mol, "Transing California Foster Children and Why Doctors Like Us Opposed It," Public Discourse, October 28, 2018, https://www.thepublicdiscourse.com/2018/10/42612/; Sydney Wright, "I Spent a Year as a Trans Man. Doctors Failed Me at Every Turn," The Daily Signal, October 7, 2019, https://www.dailysignal.com/2019/10/07/i-spent-a-year-as-a-trans-man-doctors-failed-me-at-every-turn/.

57 In addition to the studies already mentioned, e.g., Reiner and Gearhart, "Discordant Sexual Identity," Diamond and Sigmundson, "Sex Reassignment at Birth," Dhejne et al., "Long-Term Follow-Up," Kuhn et al., "Quality of Life," and Simonsen et al., "Long-Term Follow-Up," see also Mayer and McHugh, "Sexuality and Gender: Findings from the Biological, Psychological, and Social Sciences," who report "a disproportionate rate of mental health problems" in the LGBT community "compared to the population as a whole" (6). Members of this population are, for example, "estimated to have about 1.5 times higher risk of experiencing anxiety disorders," and "roughly double the risk of depression." They have "1.5 times the risk of substance abuse, and nearly 2.5 times the risk of suicide." Particularly alarming is the "rate of lifetime suicide attempts across all ages of transgender individuals," which is "estimated at 41%, compared to under 5% in the overall U.S. population" (8). As for those who undergo sex reassignment, they are "about 5 times more likely to attempt suicide and about 19 times more likely to die by suicide" (9, see also 66–70). Moreover, "compared to heterosexuals, non-heterosexuals are about two to three times as likely to have experienced childhood sexual abuse" (7, see also 42–50) and "as many as 80% of male adolescents who report same-sex attractions no longer do so as adults" (7, see also 50–57).

58 McHugh, "Psychiatric Misadventures," 498.

59 McHugh, "Surgical Sex."

60 Talbot, "About a Boy." See also Talbot, "Being Seen: Video Diaries of Transgender Youth," *The New Yorker*, March 11, 2013, http://www.newyorker.com/news/news-desk/being-seen-video-diaries-of-transgender-youth; Abigail Shrier, *Irreversible Damage: The Transgender Craze Seducing Our Daughters* (Washington, DC: Regnery, 2020); and Anderson, *When Harry Became Sally*, 117–44. A very poignant example is the BBC program, "Just a Girl," available on the BBC website (https://www.bbc.co.uk/programmes/b04v8czp), which, according to Sanchez Manning, depicts "an 11-year-old's struggle to get hormones that stunt puberty, making it easier to have sex-change surgery in the future"; Sanchez Manning, "Does your child really need to know how 'Ben' became 'Amy'? Furious parents slam 'damaging' BBC sex change show aimed at six-year-olds," Mail Online, October 29, 2016, http://www.dailymail.co.uk/news/article-3885922/Parents-slam-damaging-BBC-sex-change-aimed-six-year-olds.html. See also Telegraph Reports, "Row over BBC Transgender Programme Aimed at Children," October 30, 2016, http://www.telegraph.co.uk/news/2016/10/30/row-over-transgender-programme-as-children-as-young-as-six-expos/. Not surprisingly, Walter J. Meyer III notes an increase in pediatric referrals due to high media coverage (see "Gender Identity Disorder").

61 As a case in point, an already approved research project by psychotherapist James Caspian at the Bath

better, as the mother of a transitioning art student suggested, to encourage budding young artists to find an artistic medium other than that of their own bodies? "Many teen-agers," she remarks, seem "to regard their bodies as endlessly modifiable, through piercings, or tattoos, or even workout regimens." She therefore wonders "if sexual orientation was beginning to seem boring as a form of identity; gay people were getting married, and perhaps seemed too settled." Within this cultural climate it is indeed difficult to recognize, as journalist Margaret Talbot notes, "what a radical social experiment" transgenderism really is.[62]

Within this context we do well to consider the warning of Heather Brunskell-Evans, a philosopher and social theorist at Kings College in London. Those campaigning for the rights of the so-called transgender child too often "presume what they need to prove," she argues; "namely that gender identity exists *a priori*." In fact, Brunskell-Evens observes that transgenderism is quickly becoming a "self-fulfilling prophecy: children self-identify as transgender; the GIDS [Gender Identity Development Service, commissioned by England's National Health Service, also known as the Tavistock clinic] (and other gender identity services) confirm and intensify the child's self-diagnosis; parents, teachers, and educational professionals are induced to understand gender non-conformity as evidence of transgenderism, to accept transgender doctrine as 'truth' and to collude with social and medical intervention."[63] And this is no small matter when one considers the 3,363 percent increase in youth referrals at GIDS within a ten-year period or the 1,500 percent soar in gender dysphoria diagnoses among youth within the same period in Sweden.[64] In

Spa University in the United Kingdom on the subject of "detransitioning" was rejected by the university's ethics committee "because it could be 'politically incorrect'" ("Bath Spa University 'Blocks Transgender Research,'" *BBC News*, September 25, 2017, https://www.bbc.com/news/uk-41384473). Caspian, who had proposed studying the growing number of people who regret their "gender reassignment" procedures, said in February 2019 that since his project was vetoed in mid-2017, fifty people have contacted him to express their regret over their transitions to the opposite sex. See Sam Petherid, "Ex -Bath Spa Student James Caspian Fails in Court Fight Against University," SomersetLive, February 20, 2019, https://www.somersetlive.co.uk/news/somerset-news/bath-spa-university-james-caspian-2557060.

62 Talbot, "About a Boy."

63 Brunskell-Evans, "The Medico-Legal 'Making' of 'The Transgender Child,'" 657, 656. See also Shrier, *Irreversible Damage*, 25–57; and Lisa Littman, "Parent Reports of Adolescents and Young Adults Perceived to Show Signs of a Rapid Onset of Gender Dysphoria," *PLoS ONE* (August 16, 2018), https://journals.plos.org/plosone/article?id=10.1371/journal.pone.0202330.

64 See Robert Orange, "Teenage Transgender Row Splits Sweden as Dysphoria Diagnoses Soar By 1,500%," *The Guardian*, February 22, 2020, https://www.theguardian.com/society/2020/feb/22/ssweden-teenage-transgender-row-dysphoria-diagnoses-soar. Moreover, Hruz, Mayer, and McHugh report that GIDS experienced a whopping 2,000 percent relative increase in referrals between the year 2009/2010 (with 94 referrals) and the year 2016/2017 (with 1,986) and a 430 percent increase in the same time period for children under the age of six. Dramatic increases were likewise reported by a gender clinic in Toronto, by Boston Children's Hospital, and by the Indianapolis pediatric endocrinology clinic. See Hruz, Mayer, and McHugh, "Growing Pains," 5.

light, moreover, of frightening testimonies from victims scarred by so-called "sex-change" treatments[65] and from leading medical experts concerning the "irreversible, life-changing dangers" of puberty blockers and the "live experiment" that their prescribers are conducting on vulnerable children (especially those with "identity issues" such as Autism), a UK High Court judge banned the clinic in January 2020 from providing puberty-blocking drugs to children under sixteen without consent from the courts.[66] Nevertheless, this decision was reversed the following year by an appeal court, which argued that it is "for clinicians rather than the court to decide on competence [to consent]." In so doing, they granted reason to the Tavistock clinic's position that the original court ruling "interfered with the entitlement of children to make decisions for themselves"—in, that is to say, the absence of parental consent.[67]

As for Boston Children's Hospital and Massachusetts General Hospital, they actively encourage the use of puberty-suppressing drugs on their websites, with reference to an arguably self-serving study—a study conducted by their own researchers—linking puberty blockers to fewer suicidal thoughts.[68] Besides the vested interests of the hospitals—not to mention the many "competing interests" of the main author (including monies received from pharmaceuticals) announced amidst numerous critical commentaries of his study on the same journal page—we are warned by critics of weaknesses in the study's methodology (including a "biased sample" due to self-reporting), in its control group (including an "insufficient cross-sectional design"), and in its brief follow-up time, despite "lifetime" claims. Even more striking, as one critic points out, is the study's failure to acknowledge that in the absence of puberty

[65] See supra note 55.

[66] Manning, "'A live experiment on children.'" For the judgement itself, see Bell v. Tavistock, [2020] EWHC 3274 (Admin), available online at https://www.judiciary.uk/wp-content/uploads/2020/12/Bell-v-Tavistock-Judgment.pdf.

[67] Haroon Siddique, "Appeal Court Overturns UK Puberty Blockers Ruling for Under 16s," *The Guardian*, September 17, 2021, https://www.theguardian.com/society/2021/sep/17/appeal-court-overturns-uk-puberty-blockers-ruling-for-under-16s-tavistock-keira-bell. See Robin Respaut and Chad Terhune, "Putting Numbers on the Rise in Children Seeking Gender Care," Reuters, October 6, 2022, https://www.reuters.com/investigates/special-report/usa-transyouth-data/.

[68] See Jack L. Turban et al., "Pubertal Suppression for Transgender Youth and Risk of Suicidal Ideation," *Pediatrics* 145, no. 2 (February 2020), https://pediatrics.aappublications.org/content/145/2/e20191725; Jessica Cerretani, "First-of-Its-Kind Study Links Puberty Blockers to Lower Odds of Suicidal Thoughts," Discoveries: Stories and News from Children's Hospital, January 24, 2020, https://discoveries.childrenshospital.org/puberty-blockers-suicidal-thoughts/; and Massachusetts General Hospital Journal, "Access to Pubertal Suppression Linked to Lower Suicidal Ideation Risks in Transgender Young Adults," July 1, 2020, https://advances.massgeneral.org/neuro/journal.aspx?id=1591. Stanford Children's Health (Lucile Packard Children's Hospital) is more discrete, although it is obvious that they too are providing puberty blockers. See the page of their Pediatric and Adolescent Center Clinic, https://www.stanfordchildrens.org/en/service/gender.

blockers, "on average only about 15% [of patients with gender dysphoria] persist [in that state]." That figure changes to "virtually 100%" when they are in fact administered. "Thus, an indiscriminate prescription of puberty blockers will significantly increase the number of adolescents who continue to full transition, which may worsen long-term outcomes in attempted suicides." Not surprisingly, the critic—an emeritus professor of neurophysiology at the University of Oslo—concludes: "prescription of PB [Puberty Blockers] is not warranted."[69] The Karolinska Hospital in Sweden apparently agrees, having suspended prescription of puberty blockers to minors under sixteen in April of 2021.[70]

[69] Avi Ring, "Re: Pubertal Suppression for Transgender Youth and Risk of Suicidal Ideation," *Pediatrics*, February 12, 2020, https://pediatrics.aappublications.org/content/145/2/e20191725/tab-e-letters#re-pubertal-suppression-for-transgender-youth-and-risk-of-suicidal-ideation.

[70] Society for Evidence Based Gender Medicine, "Sweden's Karolinska."

CHAPTER 2

The Gendering of Sex as a Fabrication: Judith Butler's Philosophy of "Gender"

This increasingly prolific trend toward sexual "reassignment" is what Sr. Prudence Allen seems to have in mind when she addresses the practical consequences of the philosophy of "gender" as "going viral."[1] Such is the "artistic" attempt to revolutionize the world by changing the meaning of reality and ultimately by reinventing the human body-person. As Pope Benedict expressed it in his Christmas address to the clergy in 2012:

> It is now becoming clear that the very notion of being—of what being human really means—is being called into question. . . . According to this philosophy [of gender], sex is no longer a given element of nature, that man has to accept and personally make sense of: it is a social role that we choose for ourselves, while in the past it was chosen for us by society. . . . People dispute the idea that they have a nature, given by their bodily identity, that serves as a defining element of the human being. They deny their nature and decide that it is not something previously given to them, but that they make it for themselves.[2]

---

1 "An analogy with the way a virus spreads and the contemporary expression about an electronic photo or story 'going viral' seemed to apply. A virus has to find a willing host cell to attach itself to, and it usually destroys the host cell or ends its normal activities before moving on to infect another cell" (Sr. Mary Prudence Allen, "Gender Reality vs. Gender Ideology: Ransoming the Concept of Gender," *Solidarity: The Journal of Catholic Social Thought and Secular Ethics* 4, no. 1 [2014]: 14–15, http://researchopruennline.nd.edu.au/solidarity/vol4/iss1/1/). See also Abigail Shrier's treatment of "rapid-onset gender dysphoria," which she describes in similar terms: that of a "craze," which she defines as "a cultural enthusiasm that spreads like a virus." Shrier explains that this is a technical term in sociology, which she applies in the case at hand to describe a "crowd mental illness." See Abigail Shrier, *Irreversible Damage: The Transgender Craze Seducing Our Daughters* (Washington, DC: Regnery, 2020), 27; and Lisa Littman, "Parent Reports of Adolescents and Young Adults Perceived to Show Signs of a Rapid Onset of Gender Dysphoria," *PLoS ONE* (August 16, 2018), https://journals.plos.org/plosone/article?id=10.1371/journal.pone.0202330.

2 Pope Benedict XVI, "Address of His Holiness Benedict XVI on the Occasion of Christmas Greetings to the Roman Curia" (December 21, 2012), http://w2.vatican.va/content/benedict-xvi/en/speeches/2012/december/documents/hf_ben-xvi_spe_20121221_auguri-curia.html.

We are thus witnessing an evolution—or more appropriately, a "corruption"—of thought and language, such that the social construction of *gender* has given place to the social construction of *nature*, and thus of sex.[3] The recent trend, which was initiated by Judith Butler, is now to argue for a reversal of the so-called "patriarchal" or heterosexual ordering of the relationship between culture and nature, politics and physiology. Hence, as Elaine Graham explains, "the constructs of human *culture* may be seen as defining our concepts of '*nature*,' and not the other way around."[4] The God-made universe is being replaced by a man-made one: virtual reality is becoming chillingly real!

THE CULTURAL CONSTRUCTION OF SEX

Butler thus reasons far beyond the gender-sex distinction proposed by Simone de Beauvoir in her 1949 classic *Le deuxième sexe* (*The Second Sex*): "One is not born, but rather becomes a woman."[5] "For Beauvoir," Butler explains, "gender is 'constructed,' but implied in her formulation is an agent, a *cogito*, who somehow takes on or appropriates that gender and could, in principle, take on some other gender." There is nothing in Beauvoir's account, the Berkeley professor continues, "that guarantees that the 'one' who becomes a woman is necessarily female."[6] In other words, a male could opt *to be* (and not merely to identify as)

---

3 It is the "reality of the word" that makes communication possible, Josef Pieper explains, since "words convey reality. We speak in order to name and identify something that is real, to identify it for *someone*, of course—and this points to the second aspect in question, the interpersonal character of human speech." "And so, if the word becomes corrupted"—by, namely, the purposeful withholding of a "share and portion of reality" in our speech—then "human existence itself will not remain unaffected and untainted" (Josef Pieper, *Abuse of Language, Abuse of Power*, trans. Lothar Krauth [San Francisco: Ignatius, 1992], 15–16). On the specific application to gender ideology, see Gabriele Kuby, *The Global Sexual Revolution: Destruction of Freedom in the Name of Freedom*, trans. James Patrick Kirchner (Kettering, OH: LifeSite, 2015), 44.

4 Elaine Graham, *Making the Difference: Gender, Personhood and Technology* (New York: Mowbray, 1995), 84. Graham makes reference here to Salvatore Cucchiari, "The Gender Revolution and the Transition from Bisexual Horde to Patrilocal Band: The Origins of Gender Hierarchy," in Sherry B. Ortner and Harriet Whitehead, ed., *Sexual Meanings: The Cultural Construction of Gender and Sexuality* (New York: Cambridge University Press, 1981), 31–79.

5 Simone de Beauvoir, *The Second Sex*, trans. and ed. H. M. Parshley (New York: Vintage Books, 1989), 267. Similarly: "Biology is not enough to give an answer to the question that is before us: why is woman the *Other*?" (37). Donna Haraway fittingly refers to Beauvoir's famous formulation as the origin of all feminist accounts of gender. See Haraway, "'Gender' for a Marxist Dictionary: The Sexual Politics of a Word," in Donna Haraway, ed., *Simians, Cyborgs, and Women: The Reinvention of Nature* (New York: Routledge, 1992), 131. See also Michele M. Schumacher, "A Woman in Stone or in the Heart of Man? Navigating between Naturalism and Idealism in the Spirit of *Veritatis Splendor*," *Nova et Vetera* 11, no. 4 (2013): 1249–86, especially 1255–65; and Michele M. Schumacher, "The Nature of Nature in Feminism, Old and New" in *Women in Christ: Toward a New Feminism*, ed. Michele M. Schumacher (Grand Rapids, MI: Eerdmans, 2004), 17–51.

6 Judith Butler, *Gender Trouble: Feminism and the Subversion of Identity* (New York: Routledge, 1990), 8.

a "woman," just as well as (if not "better" than) a natural (natal) woman.[7] As far as Butler herself is concerned, gender is "radically independent from sex, . . . a free floating artifice, with the consequence that *man* and *masculine* might just as easily signify a female body as a male one, and a *woman* and *feminine* a male body as easily as a female one."[8] In fact, "there is no recourse to a body that has not always already been interpreted by cultural meanings," Butler reasons. Hence, sex is not to be understood "as a prediscursive anatomical facticity," that is to say, a corporeal fact existing independently of our linguistic reference to it. Rather, "sex, by definition, will be shown to have been gender [i.e., fluid] all along."[9]

As for gender, this term must not be understood as related to culture "as sex is to nature," Butler argues. Rather, gender should be recognized as "the discursive/cultural means by which 'sexed nature' or 'a natural sex' is produced and established as 'prediscursive,' prior to culture, a politically neutral surface *on which* culture acts."[10] In other words, Butler refuses to acknowledge that natal sex gives rise to a sociocultural expression thereof. Instead, it is culture that assumes this role single-handedly. That is why *gender* should not be conceived "as a

See also 111–12. Similarly, "if the distinction [between sex and gender] is consistently applied, it becomes unclear whether being a given sex has any necessary consequence for becoming a given gender" (Butler, "Sex and Gender in Simone de Beauvoir's *Second Sex*," *Yale French Studies*, no. 72 [1986]: 35).

7 Within the context of arguing for the "transferability" of the "attribute" (femininity), Judith Butler admits that certain drag queens "could do femininity much better than I ever could, ever wanted to, ever would" (*Undoing Gender* [New York: Routledge, 2004], 213). It is thus not surprising that the reputed feminist Germaine Greer objected to Caitlyn Jenner's nomination by *Glamour* as Woman of the Year in the following manner: "I think misogyny plays a really big part in all of this, that a man who goes to these lengths to become a woman will be a better woman than someone who is just born a woman" (Euan McLelland, "Feminist Germaine Greer Accuses Caitlyn Jenner of 'Wanting to Steal the Limelight' from Female Kardashians," *Daily Mail*, October 24, 2015, http://www.dailymail.co.uk/news/article-3287810/Germaine-Greer-accuses-Caitlyn-Jenner-wanting-steal-limelight-female-Kardashians.html).

8 Butler, *Gender Trouble*, 6.

9 Butler, *Gender Trouble*, 8. Butler's claim that gender precedes and produces sex is supported, at least implicitly, by history professor Thomas Laqueur, who seeks to "offer [historical] material [or accounts] for [demonstrating] how powerful prior notions of difference or sameness determine what one sees and reports about the body," and thus for "deciding what counts and what does not count as evidence" (Laqueur, *The Making of Sex: Body and Gender from the Greeks to Freud* [Cambridge, MA: Harvard University Press, 1990], 21). Laqueur thus makes "every effort," as he puts it, "to show that no historically given set of facts about 'sex' entailed how sexual difference was in fact understood and represented . . . , and I use this evidence," he continues, "to make the more general claim that no set of facts ever entails any particular account of difference" (19). As for biologist Anne Fausto-Sterling, she argues that "labeling someone a man or a woman is a social decision. We may use scientific knowledge to help us make the decision, but only our beliefs about gender—not science—can define our sex. Furthermore, our beliefs about gender affect what kinds of knowledge scientists produce about sex in the first place" (Fausto -Sterling, *Sexing the Body: Gender Politics and the Construction of Sexuality* [New York: Basic Books, 2000], 3). In other words, scientists "create truths about sexuality," which are subsequently incorporated and confirmed by our bodies (5).

10 Butler, *Gender Trouble*, 7 (emphasis original).

noun or a substantial thing or a static cultural marker," she argues, but rather as a verb: "a kind of becoming or activity," "an incessant and repeated action of some sort."[11] As for *sex*, it too is thought to have no intrinsic meaning or content that is not first given to it by culture. Indeed, even "the materiality of sex" is "constructed," Butler maintains, "through a ritualized repetition of norms."[12]

This assertion that *even the corporeal* nature of sex is constructed "is hardly a self-evident claim," Butler avows. After all, we experience our bodies as living and dying, as sleeping and eating, as feeling pain and pleasure, and subject to illness and violence; and these experiences cannot simply be dismissed "as mere constructions." "Surely," Butler admits, "there must be some kind of necessity that accompanies these primary and irrefutable experiences. And surely there is." Such necessity—even "irrefutability"—need not, however, the famous gender theorist insists, be due to what we habitually refer to as a created nature.[13] Indeed, the very concept of nature itself is, she seems to imply, merely a cultural construction.

Admittedly, the presentation of nature as a "blank and lifeless page," or as "that which is, as it were, always already dead" is, as Butler puts it, "decidedly modern, linked perhaps to the emergence of technological means of domination."[14] This accurate acknowledgement hardly betrays a preference on Butler's part, however, for a more classic understanding of nature and thus of the human body *qua natural*: an understanding of the human body as intrinsically oriented from within to its specific perfection by reason of its substantial form, namely, the human soul.[15] On the contrary, she refutes the notion of bodily sex as existing "prior to [sociocultural] construction," for there is "no access to this 'sex,'" she reasons, "except by means of its construction." Hence, bodily sex is said to be "absorbed by gender."[16] Because, in other words, the former is obliterated by the

11 Butler, *Gender Trouble*, 112. As if to build upon this insight, Martine Rothblatt maintains, "Sex should really be the sum of behaviors we call gender—an adjective, not a noun" (Rothblatt, *From Transgender to Transhuman: A Manifesto on the Freedom of Form*, ed. Nickolas Mayer [self-pub., 2011], 12).

12 Judith Butler, *Bodies That Matter: On the Discursive Limits of "Sex"* (New York: Routledge, 1993), x. Hence, as Fabienne Brugère explains, the body is understood as the "passive contents of a determined [*inexorable*] cultural law, that of gender, which operates like a sexual police" ("'Faire et défaire le genre': La question de la sollicitude," in *Trouble dans le sujet, trouble dans les normes*, ed. Fabienne Brugère and Guillaume le Blanc [Paris: Presses universitaires de France, 2009], 78 [my translation]).

13 Butler, *Bodies That Matter*, x–xi.

14 Butler, *Bodies That Matter*, 4.

15 See chapter 3 of this volume for a presentation of nature's teleological orientation to its perfection. See chapter 5 for a development of the Aristotelian-Thomistic understanding of the relation between the human body and the human soul.

16 Butler, *Bodies That Matter*, 5. "The presumption that the symbolic law of sex enjoys a separable ontology prior and autonomous to its assumption . . . is contravened by the notion that the citation of the law is the very mechanism of its production and articulation" (15).

latter—by the cultural significance that is accorded to it—cultural discourse, or human words, are said to produce material bodies.

From this perspective, it is not surprising that Butler should ask, "why is it that what is constructed is understood as [having] an artificial and dispensable character?" Or to put the question more directly, "Are certain constructions of the body constitutive in this sense: that we could not operate without them, that without them there would be no 'I,' no 'we'?" This "question" is, in fact, posed rhetorically. For after suggesting in the following sentence that we need to rethink "the meaning of construction itself," the famous professor of rhetoric and critical theory argues, "if certain constructions appear constitutive," this is due to the fact that "bodies only appear, only endure, only live within the productive constraints of certain highly gendered regulatory schemas."[17]

In short, the prerogative of nature has been assumed by culture, for "the constitutive claim" of the body and its sex, the claim that these are endowed with a specific ontology or nature, "is always to some degree performative."[18] It bears insisting that this affirmation, in turn, is not to be understood as implying—in accord with the classic metaphysical conception of human nature—that the living body possesses the principle of its own movement so as to develop, realize, and precisely in this sense (as differing from Butler's) to "act out" its own intrinsic operating powers, as we will see in chapter 5. For Butler specifies that "there is no reference to a pure body which is not at the same time a further formation of that body."[19] After all, the body—at least as far as the famous "gender" theorist is concerned—is "not a self-identical or merely factic materiality." Rather, it is a "dramatic" one: "not merely matter but a continual and incessant *materializing* of possibilities. One is not simply a body, but, in some very key sense, one does one's body,"[20] within, that is to say, the context of the possibilities accorded by cultural imperatives.

> [Social] construction has taken the place of a godlike agency which not only causes but composes everything which is its object; it is the divine performative, bringing into being and exhaustively constituting that which it names, or, rather, it is that kind of transitive

[17] Butler, *Bodies That Matter*, xi. Similarly, "the body becomes its gender through a series of acts which are renewed, revised, and consolidated through time" (Judith Butler, "Performative Acts and Gender Constitution: An Essay in Phenomenology and Feminist Theory," *Theatre Journal* 40, no. 4 [December 1988]: 523).

[18] Butler, *Bodies That Matter*, 11.

[19] Butler, *Bodies That Matter*, 10. "A performative," she specifies, "is that discursive practice that enacts or produces that which it names" (13). For that reason, it is not only "dramatic" but also "non-referential" (Butler, "Performative Acts," 522).

[20] Butler, "Performative Acts," 521 (emphasis original).

> referring which names and inaugurates at once. For something to be constructed, according to this view of construction [which is that of Butler], is for it to be created and determined through that process.[21]

FROM RESISTANCE OF THE TREND TO REVERSING THE NORM: GENDER IDEOLOGY

By way of her doctrine that the human body is socially constructed, Butler makes a parody of the creation story of Genesis, for she forthrightly denies the distinction between God who creates by his word—"God said, 'Let there be light'; and there was light" (Gen 1:3)—and Adam, who recognizes and affirms God's creation in the process of naming the animals: "God formed every beast of the field and every bird of the air, and brought them to the man to see what he would call them; and whatever the man called every living creature, that was its name" (Gen 2:19). In the end, however, the joke is on us, because the Butlerian subject (whether "woman," "man," or "other") acts under the constraint of a normative "law," namely the "heterosexual imperative," which is brought into being by its citation.[22] Hence, although Butler claims to rehabilitate "the voluntarist subject of humanism"[23]—presumably the subject who is free with respect to both nature and God—the human actor is said to operate within a sociocultural context, which sets limits to subjectivity (and thus to personal freedom) by setting "limits to intelligibility."[24]

"What I call my 'own' gender" is in fact, Butler maintains, not my own creation, for its terms lie "outside oneself, beyond oneself in a sociality that has no single author."[25] Hence, there is "no 'I' that can fully stand apart from the social conditions of its emergence."[26] More radical still, Butler claims that

---

[21] Butler, *Bodies That Matter*, 6. We are not far from Butler's presentation of Louis Althusser's "subject -constituting power of ideology through recourse to the figure of a divine voice that names, and in naming brings its subjects into being" (Judith Butler, *Excitable Speech: A Politics of the Performative* [New York: Routledge, 1997], 31). Cf. Louis Althusser, "Ideology and Ideological State Apparatuses," in *Lenin and Philosophy and Other Essays*, trans. Ben Brewster (New York: Monthly Review Press, 1971), 170–86.

[22] See Butler, *Bodies That Matter*, 14.

[23] Butler, *Bodies That Matter*, 6.

[24] Butler, *Bodies That Matter*, xi. Similarly, "The subject is constituted (interpellation) in language through a selective process in which the terms of legible and intelligible subjecthood are regulated. The subject is called a name, but 'who' the subject is depends as much on the names that he or she is never called: the possibilities for linguistic life are both inaugurated and foreclosed through the name" (Butler, *Excitable Speech*, 41).

[25] Butler, *Undoing Gender*, 1.

[26] Judith Butler, *Giving an Account of Oneself* (New York: Fordham University Press, 2005), 7.

"the 'I' neither precedes nor follows the process of this gendering, but emerges only within and as the matrix of gender relations themselves."[27] Indeed, even the desires that some theorists consider as determinative of gender "do not originate with our individual personhood," Butler maintains, but within, rather, the context of the social norms "that constitute our existence."[28] Hence, *gender* is rendered "a practice of improvisation within a scene of constraint."[29] That is to say, it is "a performative accomplishment compelled by social sanction and taboo."[30] Indeed, even "the viability of our individual personhood is fundamentally dependent on these social norms."[31]

When Butler teaches that social norms set "limits to intelligibility," and even to subjectivity, she means more specifically that the culturally *impermissible* (homosexuality, bisexuality, transsexuality, etc.) becomes, in virtue of the meditative function of discourse, *impossible to imagine* and is thus considered the "constitutive outside." Cultural construction is thus rendered "constitutive constraint": it produces "a domain of unthinkable, abject, unlivable bodies." Inversely, the so-called "heterosexual imperative"—thou shalt be straight!—operates positively to produce "the domain of intelligible bodies."[32] It determines, more specifically, which bodies "come to matter." By this phrase ("come to matter"), which is purposefully ambiguous,[33] Butler means that sociocultural pressures invest certain bodies not only with significance but *also* with materiality, while others are denied the latter precisely by the negation of the former.[34]

---

[27] Butler, *Bodies That Matter*, 7.

[28] Butler, *Undoing Gender*, 2.

[29] Butler, *Undoing Gender*, 1. Similarly, Butler argues that gender identity is "a performative accomplishment compelled by social sanction and taboo" (Butler, "Performative Acts," 520).

[30] Butler, "Performative Acts," 520.

[31] Butler, *Undoing Gender*, 2.

[32] Butler, *Bodies That Matter*, xi. Language is thus said to constitute "the subject in part through foreclosure, a kind of unofficial censorship or primary restriction in speech that constitutes the possibility of agency in speech" (Butler, *Excitable Speech*, 41). This censorship (operating hand-in-hand with compulsory heterosexuality, for example) is enforced by way of punitive measures: "those who fail to do their gender right are regularly punished," Butler explains. See "Performative Acts," 522.

[33] This form of wordplay is evident in the French translation of the one word (matter) by the two words: "une matérialiaté et une importance." See Butler, *Ces corps qui comptent: De la matérialité et des limites discursives du 'sexe,'* trans. Charlotte Nordmann (Paris: Editions Amsterdam, 2009), 38. See also the English edition, *Bodies That Matter*, 23, for explanation of how this occurs.

[34] "The historical possibilities materialized through various corporeal styles are nothing other than those punitively regulated cultural fictions that are alternately embodied and disguised under duress" (Butler, "Performative Acts," 522). It follows that "the body suffers a certain cultural construction, not only through conventions that sanction and proscribe how one acts one's body, the 'act' or performance that one's body is, but also in the tacit conventions that structure the way the body is culturally perceived. Indeed, if gender is the cultural significance that the sexed body assumes, and if that significance is codetermined through various acts and their cultural perception, then it would appear that from within the terms of culture it is not possible to know sex as distinct from gender" (523–24).

This is perhaps the most radical example to date of the "mind over matter" philosophy characterizing much of modern thought, or even the "will over mind and matter" characterizing postmodern thought.

As I put it in another context,

> The delicate balance between nature and nurture—already upset (if we accept the feminist critique) by patriarchy's reduction of the former to the [purely] physiological [material] realm—is further threatened (this time in the other direction) by feminism's insistence [willingly akin with gender theory, or ideology, on this point] upon the overbearing power of culture. For a majority of feminists [and gender "theorists"] today, human nature is no longer regarded as *human*—and thus as the seat of self-determination—except in its origin: the human being who creates himself and thus his nature. Within the context of a male- [and, again, heterosexual-] dominated society, it is reduced to a patriarchal construct designed to keep women [as well as homosexuals, bisexuals, and transsexuals] in their "place."[35]

It is thus not surprising that the Venezuelan philosopher Beatriz Vollmer de Coles regards this novel understanding of "gender" "theory" as a "new gnosis": a sort of mystical knowledge, which is not to be found in any common human experience of reality, namely, the observation (however subjective or engaged) of an objective fact (i.e., sexed being) but only in a revelation made known to a certain elect group "in the know."[36] Only those, to be more specific, who are considered as having been awakened to the "cunning tactics" of the ruling class of oppressive heterosexuals can recognize "the falsity" of the "so-called" ontological connection between biological sex and sexual identity. This connection is said, more specifically, to be merely a sociocultural construction in view of promoting the patriarchal subjection of women to men, on the one hand, and heterosexuality as the norm, on the other. The concept of a God-given nature is thus considered a man-made instrument by which "so-called" deviant sexual

---

[35] Michele M. Schumacher, "'Nature' of Nature in Feminism," 23–24. For a concrete example other than that of Butler, see Adrienne Rich, "Compulsory Heterosexuality and Lesbian Existence," *Signs* 5, no. 4 (Summer 1980): 631–60. On the connection between feminism and gender theorists, see Allen, "Gender Reality vs. Gender Ideology," esp. 14–19; and Kuby, *Global Sexual Revolution*, 42–48.

[36] See Beatriz Vollmer de Coles, "New Definition of Gender," in *Lexicon: Ambiguous and Debatable Terms Regarding Family Life and Ethical Questions*, ed. Pontifical Council for the Family (Front Royal, VA: Human Life International, 2006), 625–41; and Benjamin D. Wiker, "The New Gnosticism," *The Catholic World Report*, May 2, 2011, http://www.catholicworldreport.com/Item/514/the_new_gnosticism.aspx.

orientations and behaviors are checked, along with strong-willed women, by this same ruling class of heterosexual men.[37]

Far from calling into question the materiality of the body, however, Butler seeks "to establish the normative conditions under which the materiality of the body is framed and formed, and, in particular, how it is formed through differential categories of sex."[38] Hence, as French philosopher Sylviane Agacinski perfectly synthesizes Butler's thought, "sex has no role to play in the subject's desire before the intervention of the law [of heterosexuality], a law whose effect is the (naturalized) institution of heterosexuality, and even the production of the material body."[39] We are thus confronted with what Butler considers a "full *de*substantiation . . . from a materialist point of view" of sex by gender.[40]

Butler's purpose, however, is not merely to expose the all-pervasive role of culture upon what we understand as "sex." Ultimately, she seeks *to change the regulatory norm*: "to understand how what has been foreclosed or banished [by the so-called heterosexual imperative] from the proper domain of 'sex' [the homosexual, the transsexual, and the bisexual, for example]" might reemerge "as a troubling return": as an "*imaginary* contestation," which rearticulates "the symbolic horizon in which bodies come to matter at all."[41] Or as Fabienne Brugère explains, Butler proposes a sort of "gender game [*jeu sur le genre*]," which is transferred "from the domain of art to that of feminism [and more recently transgenderism], . . . a deviation [*un écart*] from sexual norms," likening feminism and art by way of "a common recourse to a subversion that is not . . . a forgetting of norms, but . . . a working on the norms, an artist's game on gender."[42]

In short, Butler's goal far exceeds the intention of overthrowing patriarchal schemas by exposing the social construction of gender. Ultimately, she seeks to enthrone her own interpretative schema as an absolute norm by which to judge

---

37 Hence Monique Wittig, for example, is reported by Judith Butler as understanding "'sex' to be discursively produced and circulated by a system of significations oppressive to women, gays, and lesbians. She refuses to take part in this signifying system or to believe in the viability of taking up a reformist or subversive position within the system; to invoke a part of it is to invoke and confirm the entirety of it. As a result, the political task she formulates is to overthrow the entire discourse on sex, indeed, to overthrow the very grammar that institutes 'gender'—or 'fictive sex'—as an essential attribute of humans and objects alike (especially pronounced in French)" (Butler, *Gender Trouble*, 113).

38 Butler, *Bodies That Matter*, 17.

39 Sylviane Agacinski, *Femmes entre sexe et genre* (Paris: Editions du Seuil, 2012), 115 (my translation).

40 Emphasis original. While gender is thus said to "absorb and displace 'sex,'" the latter "becomes something like a fiction, perhaps a fantasy, retroactively installed at a prelinguistic site to which there is no direct access" (Butler, *Bodies That Matter*, 5).

41 Butler, *Bodies That Matter*, 23 (emphasis original).

42 Brugère, "'Faire et défaire le genre,'" 81.

all other attempts to come to terms with the notion of "gender." In this way, her position again approaches that of Jean-Paul Sartre, for "in creating the man that we want to be, there is not a single one of our acts," the French philosopher maintains, "which does not at the same time create an image of man as we think he ought to be."[43] In fact, this is how the so-called heterosexual imperative was created in the first place, Sartre seems to admit. "If I want to marry, to have children; even if this marriage depends solely on my own circumstances or passion or wish, I am involving all humanity in monogamy and not merely myself," he explains. "Therefore, I am responsible for myself and for everyone else. I am creating a certain image of man of my own choosing. In choosing myself, I choose man."[44] Or, to put it still more straightforwardly, it is the individual self who creates the essence of the human: "there is a universality of man; but it is not given, it is perpetually being made. I build the universal in choosing myself; I build it in understanding the configuration of every other man."[45]

Ultimately, therefore, this philosophy is much more radical than the culturally prevalent relativist position, which holds that each individual is "faced with his own truth, different from the truth of others."[46] For as Sartre would have it, *his* (subjectively determined) "truth" is true *for everyone*: "if we grant [in holding to a profoundly atheist position] that we exist and fashion our image at one and the same time, the image is valid for everybody and for our whole age. Thus, our responsibility is much greater than we might have supposed, because it involves all mankind."[47]

A great responsibility indeed! For "to choose" means, in Sartre's system, to make right, or to create values. "To choose to be this or that is to affirm at the same time the value of what we choose, because we can never choose evil," he reasons. "We always choose the good, and nothing can be good for us without being good for all."[48] Again, this does not mean that we simply agree to a timeless truth, because Sartre holds as the "starting point" of his atheistic position that "man is forlorn": "neither within him nor without does he find

[43] Jean-Paul Sartre, *Existentialism and Human Emotions*, trans. Bernard Frechtman and Hazel E. Barnes (New York: Philosophical Library, 1957), 17–18.

[44] Sartre, *Existentialism and Human Emotions*, 17–18.

[45] Sartre, *Existentialism and Human Emotions*, 39.

[46] John Paul II, Encyclical Letter *Veritatis Splendor* (August 6, 1993), no. 32.

[47] Sartre, *Existentialism and Human Emotions*, 17.

[48] Sartre, *Existentialism and Human Emotions*, 17. Or, as Andrew N. Leak explains of Sartre's position, "If I am by definition free to 'choose myself,' my responsibility consists in my awareness that I alone am answerable for the acts I do choose to commit. By extension, I have a responsibility to all other human beings, in that the acts I commit thereby become universal human possibilities" (Leak, *The Perverted Consciousness: Sexuality and Sartre* [London: Macmillan, 1989], 157).

anything to cling to." Hence, everything is both "possible" and "permissible."[49] In subscribing to this philosophy, Simone de Beauvoir is not refusing the freedom to choose motherhood but rather: the freedom to choose a certain form of motherhood. "No woman should be authorized to stay at home to raise her children," she holds. "Society should be totally different. Women should not have that choice, precisely because if there is such a choice, too many women will make that one."[50]

In short, "what existentialism shows"—not only as it is proposed by Sartre but also as it is adopted by Simone de Beauvoir and finally by Butler—"is the connection between the absolute character of free involvement, by virtue of which every man [or woman] realizes himself [or herself] in realizing a type of mankind, and the relativeness of the cultural ensemble which may result from such a choice."[51] Individual human freedom is thus said to reign over *both nature and culture*. In the words of Beauvoir, "It is male activity that in creating values has made of existence itself a value," a value "which prevailed over the confused forces of life" in order to subdue both "Nature and Woman."[52] It is thus not surprising that Heather Brunskell-Evans recognizes existentialism, along with queer theory, as foundational for the transactivist organization Gendered Intelligence.[53] In the words of its trans-identifying CEO, Jay Stewart, "Our human rights should not be based upon that which is biologically determined. Our human rights should be based upon the idea of pursuing that which we wish to become. It is about the freedom to act that is important in terms of gaining our human rights. . . . This is about agency. This is about being able to make choices and to express ourselves."[54] And this in turn means, as Sartrian doctrine suggests, changing norms; for as Brunskell-Evans also points out

---

[49] Sartre, *Existentialism and Human Emotions*, 22–23. This means, as Deniz Durmus explains of Beauvoir's thought, that all pre-established rules must be denounced and that one must "continually create one's own and assume responsibility for the self-created moral codes" (Durmus, "Existentialist Roots of Feminist Ethics," 140). Cf. Beauvoir, *The Ethics of Ambiguity*, trans. Bernard Frechtman (New York: Open Road Integrated Media, 2018), 153–54.

[50] Simone de Beauvoir, "Sex, Society, and the Female Dilemma: A Dialogue between Betty Friedan and Simone de Beauvoir," *Saturday Review*, June 14, 1975, 12–21, at 18.

[51] Sartre, *Existentialism and Human Emotions*, 40.

[52] De Beauvoir, *Second Sex*, 65.

[53] See Heather Brunskell-Evans, "The Medico-Legal 'Making' of 'The Transgender Child,'" *Medical Law Review* 27, no. 4 (June 25, 2019): 647–48.

[54] Jay Stewart, "We Are Living on the Cusp of a Gender Revolution," February 23, 2015, https://www.youtube.com/watch?v=UpQd-VrKgFI. Also worth noting is the connection between Stewart's notion of a "gender revolution" and Judith Butler's *Notes Toward a Performative Assembly* (Cambridge, MA: Harvard University Press, 2015), which Stewart cites to strengthen his argument. See Jay Stewart, "Trans Youth Are Real," Gendered Intelligence (website), January 20, 2017, https://genderedintelligence.wordpress.com/2017/01/20/trans-youth-are-real/.

with regret, "it is now firmly established as incontrovertible that transgender people are oppressed by traditional social norms, an injustice which needs to be rectified by the official knowledges of psychology and psychiatry."[55]

[55] Brunskell-Evans, "Medico-Legal 'Making' of 'The Transgender Child,'" 645. For a development of this insight, see our final chapter.

CHAPTER 3

Nature and Art: Imitating or Supplanting the Divine Artist?

This strategy of changing norms by way of our personal or cultural choices and behaviors presupposes what Georges Cottier observes as the blurring of the distinction between what the ancient and medieval traditions referred to as *praxis*—namely, the action whereby the human subject governs him- or herself in the movement toward his or her end (that is to say, ethical action)—and *technè* (or art): the action whereby he or she modifies things and produces technical objects.[1] Missing, in fact, is an appreciation for the natural qualities (and thus the natural norms) of human nature itself, which in turn is far too often reduced in our present cultural situation to behaviorism or, worse, sacrificed to the "god" of subjective human freedom.[2] In Sartre's own very matter-of-fact formulation, which bears repeating in this context, "there is no human nature, since there is no God to conceive it."[3]

> When we conceive God as the Creator, He is generally thought of as a superior sort of artisan. Whatever doctrine we may be considering, . . . we always grant . . . that when God creates He knows exactly what He is creating. Thus, the concept of man in the mind of God is comparable to the concept of paper-cutter in the mind of the manufacturer, and, following certain techniques and a conception,

1 See Georges Cottier, "Nature et nature humaine," *Nova et Vetera* 4 (1991): 57–74, at 69. Hence, as Cottier diagnoses the situation, "man affirms himself in creating and he creates himself in dominating the world and society" (70) (my translation).

2 Thus is signaled an additional confusion: that of the so-called "normal" and the normative. When, as Georges Cottier explains more specifically, certain behaviors or manners of acting are observed with frequency among a given population, they are considered within "the norm," regardless of the consequences that they have upon the social order and human lives. Such, the Swiss philosopher suggests, is the result of the uprooting of cultural norms from human nature so as to be placed instead under the sway of public opinion. See Georges Cottier, *Défis éthiques* (Saint-Maurice, Switzerland: Editions Saint-Augustin, 1996), 90–92.

3 Jean-Paul Sartre, *Existentialism and Human Emotions*, trans. Bernard Frechtman and Hazel E. Barnes (New York: Philosophical Library, 1957), 15.

> God produces man, just as the artisan, following a definition and a technique, makes a paper-cutter. Thus, the individual man is the realization of a certain concept in the divine intelligence.[4]

From this point of view, it is obvious that once God is abandoned, the role of crafting man is accorded to man himself, with the result that ethics is likewise understood as a human work in the making. "Let us say that moral choice is to be compared to the making of a work of art," Sartre suggests. "I ask whether anyone has ever accused an artist who has painted a picture of not having drawn his inspiration from rules set up *a priori*? Has anyone ever asked, 'What painting ought he to make?' It is clearly understood that there is no definite painting to be made." Similarly, "It is clearly understood that there are no *a priori* aesthetic values, but that there are values which appear subsequently in the coherence of the painting, in the correspondence between what the artist intended and the result."[5] In short, as Simone de Beauvoir would have it, "Ethics does not furnish recipes any more than do science and art."[6]

THE NORMATIVE VALUE OF ART

Before we entertain Sartre's analogy between art and ethics, we might examine more carefully the question of the normative value of art. For, although it might well be the case that the modern conception of art is as Sartre describes it—without *a priori* values—the classic tradition *did* in fact recognize normative

---

4 Sartre, *Existentialism and Human Emotions*, 14. We are not far from the logic of St. Thomas when he teaches that "God is the first exemplar cause of all things. In proof whereof we must consider that if for the production of anything an exemplar is necessary, it is in order that the effect may receive a determinate form. For an artificer [*artifex*, meaning craftsman or artist] produces a determinate form in matter by reason of the exemplar before him, whether it is the exemplar beheld externally, or the exemplar interiorly conceived in the mind. Now it is manifest that things made by nature receive determinate forms. This determination of forms must be reduced to the divine wisdom as to its first principle, for divine wisdom devised the order of the universe, which order consists in the variety of things. And therefore we must say that in the divine wisdom are the types of all things, which types we have called ideas—i.e., exemplar forms existing in the divine Mind" (*Summa theologiae*, trans. Laurence Shapcote, ed. John Mortensen and Enrique Alarcón, vols. 13–20 of The Works of St. Thomas Aquinas [Lander, WY: The Aquinas Institute for the Study of Sacred Doctrine, 2012], I, q. 44, a. 3 [hereafter, *ST*]). "And these ideas, though multiplied by their relations to things, in reality are not apart from the divine essence, according as the likeness to that essence can be shared diversely by different things. In this manner therefore God Himself is the first exemplar of all things" (*ST* I, q. 44, a. 3; cf. q. 45, a. 6; q. 15, a. 1).

5 Sartre, *Existentialism and Human Emotions*, 42.

6 Simone de Beauvoir, *The Ethics of Ambiguity*, trans. Bernard Frechtman (New York: Open Road Integrated Media, 2018), 145. To ask the question of which actions are good or bad is, Beauvoir claims, "to fall into a naïve abstraction. We don't ask the physicist, 'Which hypotheses are true?' Nor the artist, 'By what procedures does one produce a work whose beauty is guaranteed?' . . . One can merely propose methods" (144–45).

qualities by which to judge art,[7] and it faulted the artist who practiced it with excess or defect[8] or who did not attain the end that he sought thereby.[9] Hence, we are reminded of Lewis's statement, cited in our introduction, that "until quite recently . . . the business of the artist was to delight and instruct his public." The drastic change in public attitudes toward art's purpose is due, Lewis argues, to "our changed attitude to work." After all, there was a growing "tendency," already in his lifetime, "to regard every trade as something that exists chiefly for the sake of those who practice it."[10] In short, the evolution in the socially prevalent attitude toward art, not unlike that toward work, is such that it is now—and only recently, Lewis reminds us—thought to be *without objective norms* beyond those dictated by the subjective interests or desires of the one practicing it.

Lewis's likening of our attitude toward art and our attitude toward work is of particular importance given the unity of the two in the classic (ancient and medieval) sense of the term art (*ars*), by which was understood "not so much every sort of symbolic representation of reality" as instead "craftsmanship." Hence pharmaceutics and shipbuilding were considered art forms just as much as were the "liberal arts," and these in turn were "philosophical disciplines" to be studied.[11] From this point of view, the arts were obviously not considered to be produced haphazardly or by chance but were carefully—that is to say, *intelligently*—directed in view of a purpose or an end conceived in the artist's mind in accord with the rules of his art.[12] In the classic formulation of St. Thomas

7 "For just as a flute-player, a sculptor, or any artist, and, in general, for all things that have a function or activity, the good and the 'well' is thought to reside in the function" (Aristotle, *Ethica* Nico*machea* [Nicomachean Ethics], trans. W. D. Ross, rev. J. O. Urmson, in *The Complete Works of Aristotle: The Revised Oxford Translation*, vol. 2, ed. Jonathan Barnes [Princeton, NJ: Princeton University Press, 1984], 1.7.1097b25–28 [p. 1735] [hereafter, *Ethic. Nic.*]).

8 Cf. Aristotle, *Ethic. Nic.*, 2.6.1106b23–28 (Barnes, 1747–48).

9 "Now mistakes come to pass even in the operations of art: the literate man makes a mistake in writing and the doctor pours out the wrong dose" (Aristotle, *Physica* [*Physics*], trans. R. P. Hardie and R. K. Gaye, in *The Complete Works of Aristotle: The Revised Oxford Translation*, vol. 1, ed. Jonathan Barnes [Princeton, NJ: Princeton University Press, 1984], 2.8.199a35 [p. 340] [hereafter, *Phys.*]). Here, of course, the meaning of art (*ars*) is taken in a large sense to include, as we shall see in what follows, what is commonly known as craftsmanship.

10 C. S. Lewis, "Good Work and Good Works," in *The World's Last Night and Other Essays* (San Diego: Harcourt and Brace, 1987), 78–79. Lewis's lifetime spans slightly more than the first half of the past century (1898–1963).

11 Otto Hermann Pesch, *Thomas von Aquin: Grenze und Grösse mittelalterlicher Theologie: Eine Einführung* (Mainz: Matthias-Grünewlad-Verlag, 1988), 345–46.

12 It seemed obvious enough to St. Thomas, for example, that "every artist intends to give to his work the best disposition; not absolutely the best, but the best as regards the proposed end" (Aquinas, *ST* I, q. 91, a. 3).

Aquinas, "all things wrought by art are subject to the order of that art."[13] Hence, the gifted artist of antiquity was one capable not only of conceiving an artistic idea (the concept of the paper-cutter in Sartre's example above) with brilliant imagination but also of effectively introducing into matter (marble, clay, canvas, or wood, for example) the image thus conceived.[14]

To do so—to effectively introduce a creative form into matter—required that the artist or craftsman be trained according to the norms of his discipline, which de facto included an understanding of the natural properties of the materials employed by his discipline: those of wood for the carpenter or iron for the blacksmith, for example. Hence, to draw an illustration, the trained carpenter knows which wood best serves the goal of creating a chair or of building a house, a nuance that need not be evident to one who has not been initiated into the art of carpentry. This double requirement of ancient and medieval art or craftsmanship—that creative ingenuity be matched by practical knowledge of one's art, including knowledge of the natural properties of the materials employed therein—thus points to natural limitations. The forms invented by man are, after all, limited by the forms created by God; whence the classic distinction between *res artificiales* and *res naturales*: between artificial and natural things. "If you planted a bed and the rotting wood acquired the power of sending up a shoot," Aristotle explains by way of an example, "it would not be a bed that would come up, but *wood*." This, he suggests, demonstrates that the organization that is affected by the rules of art "is merely an accidental attribute," whereas the order attributable to nature "persists continuously through the process."[15] In short, whereas "art imitates nature," the reverse is not the case.[16] Nature does *not* imitate art. Both human art and ethical action are necessarily—that is to say, *naturally*—limited by divine art; for God "alone can produce a form in matter, without the aid of any preceding material form."[17]

THE ANALOGY OF ART AND NATURE

In keeping with the distinctions exposited above, it is evident that the things of nature and the things of art are not only distinguished in classic philosophy

[13] Aquinas, *ST* I, q. 22, a. 2.

[14] Hence Aristotle argues that "it is the part of the same discipline to know the form and the matter up to a point." *Phys.* 2.2.194a22 (Barnes, 331). This also serves as the distinction between material and formal causality. See *Phys.* 2.2.194b (Barnes, 331–32).

[15] Aristotle, *Phys.* 2.1.193a17 (Barnes, 330).

[16] See, for example, *Phys.* 2.2.194a22 (Barnes, 331).

[17] Aquinas, *ST* I, q. 91, a. 2.

by their matter but also by their forms: by their specific orientations, directedness, or purposefulness, and more specifically by the manner in which these orientating forces are exerted or realized.[18] The human artist, to be more specific, is one who introduces a form into matter *from without* (and thus with more or less violence), whereas the divine Artist does so *from within*. As the Creator of natures,[19] he directs things according to nature's own direction.[20] "If the ship-building art were in the wood, it would produce the same results *by nature*," Aristotle maintains.[21] It follows, in due respect for this analogy, that "art in some cases completes what nature cannot bring to a finish [by working upon it from without], and in others imitates nature."[22]

Therefore, the most talented artists of the classic tradition were those who not only conceived marvelous new forms by way of their imaginations but who also introduced these imaginative forms into matter in the most natural possible way: in a manner respecting nature's *own* forms. In the words of the Swiss philosopher Pierre-Marie Emonet:

> The divine artist does not work "on" matter, as if this divine cause were somehow external to it. . . . As the greatest of all artists, this one brings forth the forms corresponding to the divine ideas from "within" matter itself, matter with its limitless capacity to be shaped and molded. What is beautiful in God's activity, and in the work of the greatest artists [whence the continuation of the classic analogy], is that they do not superimpose a form on matter as one forces clay into a ready-made mold. No, the art of both is to invite a form by which the matter becomes intelligible and sensible to the mind.[23]

---

18 "Upon the form follows an inclination to the end, or to an action, or something of the sort; for everything, in so far as it is in act, acts and tends towards that which is in accordance with its form" (Aquinas, *ST* I, q. 5, a. 5).

19 "All natural things were produced by the Divine art," St. Thomas holds, "and so may be called God's works of art" (Aquinas, *ST* I, q. 91, a. 3).

20 "For those things are natural which, by a continuous movement originated *from an internal principle*, arrive at some end" (Aristotle, *Phys.* 2.8.199b16–17 [Barnes, 340] [emphasis added]). On the violent manner of the moving things, see, for example, Aquinas, *ST* I, q. 105, a. 7, ad 1.

21 Aristotle, *Phys.* 2.8.199b27–28 (Barnes, 341) (emphasis added).

22 Aristotle, *Phys.* 2.8.199a16–17 (Barnes, 340).

23 Pierre-Marie Emonet in *The Dearest Freshness Deep Down Things: An Introduction to the Philosophy of Being*, trans. Robert R. Barr (New York: Crossroad, 1999), 54. Similarly, as Servais Pinckaers would have it: "The ideal, in the arts, is to achieve the natural. We do not appreciate a work that seems contrived and artificial and is not inspired by natural sense of beauty. Condillac wrote, 'The natural . . . is art become habitual. The poet and dancer are each natural when they achieve that degree of perfection where their conformity to the rules of art appears effortless.' And again, 'Natural means everything that is not inhibited, strained, artificial, pretentious'" (*The Sources of Christian Ethics*, trans. Sr. Mary Thomas Noble [Washington, DC: The Catholic University of America Press, 1995], 403).

The human artist is thus invited by the classic tradition "to imitate nature" also in this: that he or she respect nature's characteristic properties in employing them. In this way, he or she capitalizes on nature's *own* (i.e., intrinsic) orientation or purposefulness. In short, the artist of antiquity, and even of much of the medieval and romantic periods, does not only act with purpose, or intent, he or she also recognizes nature's *own* purpose at work within things so as to collaborate with her. The human being, after all, "is not the author of nature," as St. Thomas observes, "but he uses natural things in applying art and virtue to his own use."[24] And in so doing, he himself remains a work of the divine Artist, so as to be simultaneously "artist and artifact."[25]

The implication of this statement is, of course, that the human person likewise has a nature with a specific end, wherein resides his or her perfection.[26] Indeed, his or her causality—artistic or otherwise—is never exercised in the absence of the divine causality.[27] Like all created things, we too are subject to divine providence, not excepting the most "excellent manner" of being subjected: namely "by being provident" both for ourselves and for others. We too have, more specifically, received on our very being the imprint of that law whereby all things "derive their respective inclinations to their proper acts and ends."[28]

---

[24] Aquinas, *ST* I, q. 22, a. 2, ad 3. Or, as Pope John Paul II has put it, "everything that comes from man throughout the whole process of economic production, whether labour or the whole collection of means of production and the technology connected with these means (meaning the capability to use them in work), presupposes these riches and resources of the visible world, riches and resources *that man finds* and does not create. In a sense man finds them already prepared, ready for him to discover them and to use them correctly in the productive process. In every phase of the development of his work man comes up against the leading role of *the gift made* by 'nature,' that is to say, in the final analysis, by *the Creator.* At the beginning of man's work is the mystery of creation" (Encyclical Letter on Human Work *Laborem Exercens* [September 14, 1981], no. 12). As for God, he creates *ex nihilo*: out of nothing. See Aquinas, *ST* I, q. 45, a. 5.

[25] Hans Urs von Balthasar, *The Glory of the Lord: A Theological Aesthetics*, vol. 1, *Seeing the Form*, trans. Erasmo Leiva-Merikakis, ed. Joseph Fessio and John Riches (San Francisco: Ignatius, 1989), 221.

[26] "Have the carpenter, then, and the tanner certain functions or activities, and has man none?" Aristotle asks. "Is he naturally functionless? Or as eye, hand, foot, and in general each of the parts evidently has a function, may one lay it down that man similarly has a function apart from all these?" The answer, the Greek philosopher suggests, is not surprisingly that which is supplied by the particular form specifying the human being as such: "Human good turns out to be activity of soul in conformity with excellence, and if there are more than one excellence, in conformity with the best and most complete," for the duration, he adds, of "a complete life[time]" (Aristotle, *Eth. Nic.* 1.7.1097b29–33, 1098a17–19 [Barnes, 1735]).

[27] As St. Thomas affirms, "God works in every agent" because God "not only gives things their form, but He also preserves them in existence, and applies them to act [as, he specifies in the corpus of the article, 'the workman applies the axe to cut'], and is moreover the end of every action" (*ST* I, q. 105, a. 5, ad 3). Similarly, "not only is every motion from God as from the First Mover, but all formal perfection is from Him as from the First Act. And thus the act of the intellect or of any created being whatsoever depends upon God in two ways; first, inasmuch as it is from Him that it has the form whereby it acts; second, inasmuch as it is moved by Him to act" (*ST* I–II, q. 109, a. 1).

[28] Aquinas, *ST* I–II, q. 91, a. 2.

It follows as a consequence of our own subjection to eternal (divine) law—however unique the manner—that we cannot simply project upon nature "the process of finalization proper to human actions."[29] In other words, we must guard against thinking that nature (God's work) imitates art (our work). On the contrary, it is human reason that follows and imitates nature in its intelligent design and thus also in its specific orientation to an end.[30] "Now [intelligent] action is for the sake of an end," Aristotle reasons; "therefore the nature of things also is so. Thus, if a house, e.g., had been a thing made by nature, it would have been made in the same way as it is now by art; and if things made by nature were made also by art, they would come to be in the same way as by nature."[31]

Rather than conceive of the Creator "as a super engineer" (as in the mocking attitude of Sartre), we should thus recognize, Jean-Hervé Nicolas argues, the human engineer as attempting, ever so "distantly and awkwardly, to walk in the Creator's footsteps."[32] Or, to express this same insight from the perspective of St. Thomas as he is read by Josef Pieper, "creative knowledge of God gives measure but receives none (*mensurans non mensuratum*)." As for natural reality, it is simultaneously "measured and itself measuring (*mensuratum et mensurans*)," while human knowledge is "measured and does not give measure (*mensuratum non mensurans*)": at least, that is to say, "it is not what gives measure with respect to natural things, although it does so with regard to *res artificiales*, artificial things."[33] Or, again, as the Swiss theologian Hans Urs von Balthasar puts it still more straightforwardly, "God alone primarily possesses knowledge that is not an image but the archetype of reality whose truth is not measured by things."[34]

---

[29] Jean-Hervé Nicolas, *Synthèse dogmatique: Complément: De l'Univers à la Trinité* (Paris: Editions Beauchesne, 1993), 49.

[30] As James V. Schall has put it, "bricks and stones are necessary for the house to be, but the house, the end, is only present because someone chose it and knows what a house is" ("Nature and Finality in Aristotle," *Laval théologique et philosophique* 45, no. 1 [1989]: 79). Cf. Aristotle, *Phys.* 2.9.200a25–27 (Barnes, 341).

[31] Aristotle, *Phys.* 2.8.199a11–15 (Barnes, 340).

[32] Jean-Hervé Nicolas, *Synthèse dogmatique*, 49. Cf. Aquinas, *ST* I, q. 4, a. 3, ad 4: "a statue is like a man, but not conversely; so also a creature can be spoken of as in some sort like God; but not that God is like a creature."

[33] Josef Pieper, *The Silence of St. Thomas*, trans. John Murray and Daniel O'Connor (South Bend, IN: St. Augustine's Press, 1999), 54. Cf. Aquinas, *Quaestiones Disputatae de Veritate*; English translation by Robert W. Mulligan, S.J., *Truth* (Chicago: Henry Regnery Company, 1952), q. 1, a. 8 (hereafter, *De Ver.*). "The concept of measure is represented and actualized in three realms of reality, or, rather, three relations of reality: the relation of God and creature, the relation of the artist to his work and the relation between the objective world of being and human knowledge" (Josef Pieper, *Reality and the Good*, in *Living the Truth*, trans. Stella Lange [San Francisco: Ignatius, 1989], 121). See also Josef Pieper, "Things Are Unfathomable Because They Are Created," in *Josef Pieper: An Anthology*, trans. Lothar Krauth (San Francisco: Ignatius, 1989), 98–99.

[34] Hans Urs von Balthasar, *Theo-Logic: Theological Logical Theory*, vol. 1, *Truth of the World*, trans. Adrian J. Walker (San Francisco: Ignatius, 2000), 119.

If there is anyone who understood the important implications of this thinking, it is, ironically enough, Pieper suggests, Jean-Paul Sartre.

> From Sartre's radical negation of the idea of creation (he declares, for example that "Existentialism is nothing more than an attempt to draw all the conclusions from a consistently atheistic position") it is suddenly made evident how and to what extent the doctrine of creation is the concealed but basic foundation of classical Western metaphysics. If one were to compare the thought of Sartre and St. Thomas and reduce both to syllogistic form, one would realize that both start with the same "major premise," namely from this principle: things have an essential nature only in so far as they are fashioned by thought. Since man exists and has a constructive intellect, which can invent and has in fact invented, for instance, a letter opener, therefore, and for no other reason, we can speak of the "nature" of a letter opener. Then, Sartre continues, because there exists *no* creative intelligence which could have designed man and all natural things—and could have put an inner significance into them—therefore there is *no* "nature" in things that are not manufactured and artificial. . . . St. Thomas, on the contrary, declares: Because and in so far as God has creatively thought things, just so and to that extent have they a nature.[35]

When, on the other hand, one is unwilling, as was Sartre, to admit to God and thus to the purposefulness, or directedness, of nature, the world itself becomes disenchanted.[36] Hence, as Emonet describes the vision of Sartre:

> [He] begins by emptying things of their dynamic, of the surge that carries them to their purposes. He [Sartre] has no use for their youthful energies. He blinds himself to the happy thrust that leads them to their flowers and their fruits. But this radical evacuation

[35] Pieper, *Silence of St. Thomas*, 52–53. Reference is made to Sartre, *Existentialism and Human Emotions*, 51: "Existentialism is nothing else than an attempt to draw all the consequences of a coherent atheistic position." As for St. Thomas, he holds that "God knows all things, both universal and particular. And since His knowledge may be compared to the things themselves, as the knowledge of art to the objects of art, all things must of necessity come under His ordering; as all things wrought by art are subject to the order of that art" (Aquinas, *ST* I, q. 22, a. 2). See also *ST* I, q. 9, a. 2, ad 2. Pieper's insight is proof of the fact, as Robert Sokolowski observes, that "the denial of Christian belief is to some extent defined by Christian notions and permeated by them" and that "many of the teachings we find in modernity could hardly be understood except as subsequent to Christian belief" (Sokolowski, *The God of Faith and Reason: Foundations of Christian Theology* [Notre Dame, IN: University of Notre Dame Press, 1982], 21–22).

[36] See the long reflection to this end in Charles Taylor, *A Secular Age* (Cambridge, MA: The Belknap Press of Harvard University Press, 2007).

of essences leads him fatally to underestimate existence: "These trees—they had no desire to exist; they simply could not prevent it. There you have it. Yes, they did all their little recipes quietly, without zest. The sap runs slowly in their ducts, and reluctantly." In Sartre's kitchen, unlike that of Heraclitus, we never meet the gods![37]

THE "ART" OF ETHICS

In short, because Sartre's "kitchen" is not enchanted, it cannot supply the "magical" forces that the ancients call *forms*: those directive powers which work *from within* matter—as differing from the man-made version which work upon matter *from without*—pushing each nature to its proper perfection and thus also to its growth, maturity, and reproduction, when that nature is living. Nor—and this is perhaps still more fundamental—can it supply the notion of ends or goods, which define both nature and the art of antiquity.[38] "Every art and every inquiry, and similarly every action and choice," Aristotle writes at the beginning of his *Nicomachean Ethics*, "is thought to aim at some good; and for this reason the good has rightly been declared to be that at which all things aim."[39]

It is thus perhaps not surprising that St. Thomas, in his appropriation of this teaching,[40] should present sin (*peccatum*) as "a departure from the order to the end," whence also his distinction between *a bad artist* and *a bad man*:

> Sin may occur in two ways, in a production of art. First, by a departure from the particular end intended by the artist: and this sin will be proper to the art; for instance, if an artist produce a bad thing, while intending to produce something good; or produce something good, while intending to produce something bad. Second, by a departure from the general end of human life: and

---

37 Pierre-Marie Emonet, *Dearest Freshness Deep Down Things*, 84–85. The reference is to Jean Paul Sartre, *La nausée* (Paris: Gallimard, 1938), 133. Hence, as Karl Stern appropriately remarks, "What Sartre said about Baudelaire we may say about Sartre himself: '[Nature] is something huge, lukewarm which penetrates everything. Of that warm dampness, of that abundance, he was in perfect horror. Prolific Nature, which produces one single model in millions of copies, was bound to hurt his love for the rare. He, too, could say: I love everything which one can never see twice. By this he praises absolute sterility" (Karl Stern, *The Flight from Woman* [London: Farrar, Strauss, and Giroux, 1965; St. Paul, MN: Paragon, 1985], 141). Citations refer to the Paragon edition.

38 For a succinct presentation, see James V. Schall, "Nature and Finality in Aristotle." See also Thomas Aquinas, *Summa contra Gentiles* III, c. 1, c. 2; English trans. Anton C. Pegis, Janes F. Anderson, Vernon J. Bourke, and Charles J. O'Neil (Notre Dame, IN: University of Notre Dame Press, 1997) (hereafter cited as *SCG*).

39 Aristotle, *Eth. Nic.* 1.1.1094a1–3 (Barnes, 1729).

40 See, for example, Aquinas, *SCG* I, c. 37; *ST* I, q. 5, a. 4; q. 6, a. 1; I–II, q. 94, a. 2.

> then he will be said to sin, if he intend to produce a bad work, and does so in effect, so that another is taken in thereby. But this sin is not proper to the artist as such, but as man.[41]

Corresponding to this distinction—that of the good artist and the good man—is thus the distinction between two disciplines, each with its own governing principle: art and ethics. Whereas the former provides "right reason" with respect to *things that are made*, the latter provides "right reason" about *things to be done.* As such, ethics necessarily solicits the virtue of prudence, providing the rectitude of the agent's will—a rectitude that is not necessary to the production of art.[42] Hence, unlike the good of art that is found in its product (the book, the chair, or the painting, for example) and not in its producer (the craftsman or the artist), the goods of ethics and prudence concern the actor as such. It is necessary so that he or she might "lead a good life" and ultimately be a good man or woman.[43] As such, ethics qualifies the person "comprehensively" in contrast to art, which qualifies him or her "only partially," namely, within the context of practicing his or her art. One might be a fine musician, a great poet, or a gifted carpenter and still remain an unjust and dishonest human being.[44] In both cases, however—that of the actor considered as an artist and that of the actor considered as simply human—we might judge him or her as more or less "disposed with regard to the [predetermined] ends" and in this sense as good or bad.[45]

A PLEA FOR NORMALCY: NATURE AS NORM

The point that I wish to emphasize from the foregoing—contra Sartre, Beauvoir, and Butler—is that human nature, like human art, really *is* normative and was considered as such—even in an ethical sense—throughout much, if not most, of the philosophical tradition.[46] For those of the Judeo-Christian tradition, this

---

41 Aquinas, *ST* I–II, q. 21, a. 2, ad 2. In short, "to sin is nothing else than to fail in the good which belongs to any being according to its nature" (q. 109, a. 2, ad 2).

42 See Aquinas, *ST* I–II, q. 57, a. 4. Such is also the idea of Aristotle, as he is summarized by Yves Simon on this point: "When you have art, you still need virtue to make a good human use of it; but if you have prudence, you do not need an extra virtue to make good use of it, because prudence, being a moral as well as an intellectual virtue, supplies this good use of itself. And that is also why practical wisdom depends directly on a person's inclinations and disposition" (Simon, *The Definition of Moral Virtue* [New York: Fordham University Press, 1986], 98). Cf. Aristotle, *Eth. Nic.* 6.5.1140a–1140b (Barnes, 1800–1801).

43 See Aquinas, *ST* I–II, q. 57, a. 5, ad 1.

44 See Pinckaers, *Sources of Christian Ethics*, 84.

45 Cf. Aquinas, *ST* I–II, q. 57, a. 4.

46 Servais Pinckaers argues that the principle *sequi naturam* was a "common basis for discussions between Peripatetics, Stoics, Academicians, Epicureans and others" (*Sources of Christian Ethics*, 334). As for the natural law, this was traditionally considered "the first foundation of the moral life" (Servais Pinckaers,

was understood to be the case because nature was said to reveal the Creator's mind and thus also his intentions for the creatures whom he has made. As for the ancients, once they had dismissed their mythical gods as mere human projections, they attributed necessity to nature: to "the way things were born to be." The deity nonetheless remained responsible for governing nature, insofar as he ruled by causation. That is to say, the deity set things into motion and development and drew other beings "to imitate, in their own appropriate ways, its permanence and independence."[47] Unlike the Greek deity, however, who moved other beings in an external manner, the Christian Creator was understood as moving each being from within, by way of the creature's natural appetites or inclinations, to specific ends that simultaneously define and perfect nature itself, including human nature.[48] In this way, nature is viewed as normative not so much in the negative sense of *constraint*—such that natural law might be understood as setting limits from without—but rather in the positive sense of *attraction*. Natural law is thus envisioned as exercising its influence by way of the creature's *own* inclinations to its own (proper) end, or perfection, as we will investigate more fully in chapter 4.[49] Indeed, St. Thomas could hardly be more explicit when he writes, "all those things to which man has a natural inclination are naturally apprehended by reason as being good, and consequently as

---

Morality: The Catholic View, trans. Michael Sherwin [South Bend, IN: St. Augustine's Press, 2001], 96). Or, as Aristotelian ethics is summarized by Louis Dupré, "The more virtuous (that is, 'excellent') we grow, the more we allow ourselves to be guided by nature and the more aptly we discern the course of action appropriate in each particular instance. Ultimately what ought to be coincides with what a person or any organic being is according to its true, fully developed nature" (Dupré, *Passage to Modernity: An Essay in the Hermeneutics of Nature and Culture* [New Haven: Yale University Press, 1993], 26).

47 Sokolowski, *God of Faith and Reason*, 15. See also Sokolowski, 81, for more explanation of the differences between the ancient Greek and the Christian understandings of teleology. As for James Schall, he argues that Aristotle "did suggest the possibility of the origin of the universe from a cause which stands to the universe as the human artist to the work of art, that is, as creator of the ends and means of the created product, which then continues to exist in its own right with its own capacities" (Schall, "Nature and Finality in Aristotle," 83). Similarly, Louis Dupré points to the "axiomatic quality" of Aristotle's "belief in the rightness of nature," which the Belgian philosopher attributes to "an ontological vision of the real. No less than Plato, he [Aristotle] supports his metaphysics by the assumption that beings owe their intrinsic meaningfulness to the divine quality of the *kosmos*" (Dupré, *Passage to Modernity*, 27).

48 This precision is of capital importance in light of the Nominalist challenge, which would have us believe that there is no correspondence between God's creative will and the good as such. For what was willed by the capricious God of Nominalism "was necessarily just and good precisely because [and only because] he willed it," and there was "no guarantee that the divine will might not change tomorrow" (and with it, the designation of the good) (Pinckaers, *Source of Christian Ethics*, 246–47). We are far from the Aristotelian presentation of the good as that toward which "all things aim." For a very thorough development of Nominalist principles and their influence upon the Western philosophical tradition, see Michael Allen Gillespie, *The Theological Origins of Modernity* (Chicago: University of Chicago Press, 2008).

49 See also International Theological Commission, "In Search of a Universal Ethic: A New Look at the Natural Law" (2009), no. 43, http://www.vatican.va/roman_curia/congregations/cfaith/cti_documents/rc_con_cfaith_doc_20090520_legge-naturale_en.html.

objects of pursuit, and their contraries as evil, and objects of avoidance."[50] And, respectively, a thing is considered good for St. Thomas not "simply because it is an end, or because it has achieved the end," but also because it is "ordered to the end," that is to say, "precisely because of this relation [of inclination, or orderedness, to the end]."[51] After all, Aquinas reasons that the "good of order existing in things created, is itself created by God,"[52] and that is why "nothing except a good thing desires the good."[53]

Of course, this does not mean that natural law might simply be reduced to desire, even if the latter is employed interchangeably by the Aristotelian-Thomistic tradition with the notions of appetite and inclination. For, although the concupiscible and irascible appetites are said by Aquinas to belong to natural law, this is the case "in so far as they are ruled by reason."[54] The latter, in turn, is said to "direct all things regarding man, so that whatever can be ruled by reason, is contained under the law of reason."[55] When, therefore, St. Thomas explains that the precepts of the natural law are ordered according to the order of the natural inclinations,[56] he would have us understand that the higher inclinations rule over the lower: that those which are proper to the human being as spiritual (such as the desire to know God and to live in society) give direction to those which we share with all material creatures (such as the inclination to preserve our being and thus to ward off danger) and those which we share with other animals (such as the inclination to reproduce and to raise offspring).[57] If, then, the higher inclinations rule the lower, this is due not only to the fact that God profoundly respects human liberty and gives us dominion over our own acts[58] but also to the fact that the spiritual inclinations to truth and goodness render us capable of ordering or directing all of our inclinations toward the properly human good: the good of the person as such.[59]

---

50 Aquinas, *ST* I–II, q. 94, a. 2.

51 Aquinas, *SCG* III, c. 20, 5; cf. *ST* I, q. 21, a. 4.

52 Aquinas, *ST* I, q. 22, a. 1.

53 Aquinas, *SCG* III, c. 20, 5.

54 Aquinas, *ST* I–II, q. 94, a. 2, ad 2. See also *ST* I–II, q. 17, a. 7.

55 Aquinas, *ST* I–II, q. 94, a. 2, ad 3.

56 See Aquinas, *ST* I–II, q. 94, a. 2, ad 3, corpus.

57 See Aquinas, *ST* I–II, q. 94, a. 2; q. 17, a. 7. See also my application of this reasoning in Michele M. Schumacher, "Woman's Self-Interest or Sacrificial Motherhood: Personal Desires, Natural Inclinations and the Meaning of Love," *The Thomist* 77, no. 1 (January 2013): 71–101.

58 Rational creatures "are so controlled by God," St. Thomas teaches, "as objects of care for their own sakes; while other creatures are subordinated, as it were, to the rational creatures" (*SCG* III, c. 112).

59 See, for example, Aquinas, *ST* I–II, q. 10, a. 1, ad 3.

To speak of nature as normative thus means that there is a built-in harmony between nature's end and its specific inclinations to (or desires for) that end, because these are of the essence of nature itself.[60] Indeed, nature, in the traditional sense of the term, "does not exist without interiority"—without natural inclinations that act as "intimate springs . . . water[ing] the human mind and heart," which in turn lead the human person to his or her natural fulfillment. Natural inclinations are thus "like a primal spontaneity that we can discern in the intuitive flashes of our minds or in the original vitality of our loves," as Servais Pinckaers puts it, and it is as such that they are also foundational with respect to freedom.[61] It is thus not surprising that Aquinas's entire moral theology is "based largely on his teaching on natural inclinations and on the freedom for the good that activated them."[62] To the spiritual nature of the human person was thus accredited "the very source of free and moral actions."[63]

To be sure, this is not to say that nature might be thought of as dictating morality. It *is*, however, as Marie-Joseph Nicolas notes with respect to the Aristotelian-Thomistic tradition, the only criterion whereby it might be discovered and applied.[64] "Every free action has a rule, a criterion of rectitude (*justesse*), and that criterion is the end, the objective end of the free nature, and not the end chosen by [the will] itself."[65] Because, in fact, reason is able to discern the natural ends of created things and thus also God's purpose for them (including our own human nature, short of its supernatural end[66]), it also belongs to reason to command the will.[67] Because the will in turn "relates to the end as to its proper object," it is also by the will that we employ the other

60 When, therefore, we speak of inclinations, desires, or appetites, these are not to be understood as special faculties, Michel Labourdette explains with regard to the Aristotelian-Thomistic tradition. Nor are they operations. Rather, they are "the form itself, precisely as orientated, as inclined to its end" (Michel Labourdette, *Cours de théologie morale*, vol. 1, *Morale Fondamentale* [Paris: Editions Parole et Silence, 2010], 83). See also Marie-Joseph Nicolas, "L'idée de nature dans la pensée de saint Thomas d'Aquin," *Revue thomiste* 74, no. 4 (1974): 544, 566; and Georges Cottier, "Le concept de nature chez Saint Thomas," in *Le désir de Dieu: Sur les traces de Saint Thomas* (Paris: Editions Parole et Silence, 2002), 149–72.

61 Pinckaers, *Morality: The Catholic View*, 97. See also Pinckaers, "Aquinas on Nature and the Supernatural," in *The Pinckaers Reader: Renewing Thomistic Moral Theology*, ed. John Berkman and Craig Steven Titus, trans. Sr. Mary Thomas Noble (Washington, DC: The Catholic University of America Press, 2005), 361.

62 Pinckaers, *Sources of Christian Ethics*, 405.

63 Pinckaers, "Aquinas on Nature and the Supernatural," 362. Cf. *ST* I–II, q. 63, a. 1.

64 See Nicolas, "L'idée de nature," 569.

65 Marie-Joseph Nicolas, "Introduction à la Somme théologique," in Thomas Aquinas, *Somme théologique*, trans. Albert Raulin (Paris: Cerf, 1984), 41.

66 For as St. Paul would have it, "no eye has seen, nor ear heard, nor the heart of man conceived, what God has prepared for those who love him" (1 Cor 2:9).

67 See Aquinas, *ST* I–II, q. 17, a. 5.

powers that nature has bequeathed upon us. That is why, St. Thomas reasons, "a man is said to be good, not by his good understanding; but by his good will."[68] Such, of course, is a moral specification: one that is determined by the choices a man makes but one that is nonetheless judged according to the standard of the perfection (or corruption) of his own nature, wherein is rooted both his will and the fundamental, or innate, inclinations that the will is charged to direct. Hence the correlation between the end natural to man and his freely willed action is viewed by the Aristotelian-Thomistic tradition as the very foundation of morality.

As differing, therefore, from Judith Butler, who holds that nature "assumes its value [and its intelligibility] at the same time that it assumes its social character,"[69] the Aristotelian-Thomistic tradition holds that nature does have a value—a value which is defined by its specific perfecting end[70]—*prior* to the influence of human culture and even prior to the operation of the human will. For St. Thomas, in fact, being, which is proper to nature, necessarily precedes the act of the will precisely because the will is grounded in human nature. That is why "it is necessary that the movement proper to nature be shared by the will, to some extent: just as what belongs to a previous cause is shared by a subsequent cause."[71] It follows that the rectitude of any given human action is not simply the end chosen by the human will but rather the end, or perfection, of the creature as implied by his nature.

ONTOLOGICAL GOODNESS AND MORAL GOODNESS

To summarize the foregoing in terms borrowed from St. Thomas, "every appetite," or "inclination of a person desirous of a thing towards that thing, . . . is only of something good"[72]—good primarily in the *ontological sense* and only secondarily, or analogically, in the moral sense, in accord with the principle that

---

[68] Aquinas, *ST* I, q. 5, a. 4, ad 3. The first part of this affirmation is not to deny that "we have free-will with respect to what we will not of necessity, nor by natural instinct" (*ST* I, q. 19, a. 10).

[69] Butler, *Bodies That Matter: On the Discursive Limits of "Sex"* (New York: Routledge, 1993), 5. Butler specifies that there is "no access" to nature "except by means of its construction." The Berkley professor thus continues the Nominalist understanding of meaning as "first established by the mind and subsequently expressed in conventional signs," as well as the trend—recognized by Louis Dupré as belonging to the early humanists—of regarding "language itself as creative of meaning. Reversing the traditional order of reference, they began to envision reality itself through the prism of language" (Dupré, *Metaphysics and Culture*, The Aquinas Lecture, 1994 [Milwaukee, WI: Marquette University Press, 1994], 7).

[70] "Nature," writes Aristotle, "is the end or that for the sake of which" (*Phys.* 2.2.194a29 [Barnes, 331]).

[71] Aquinas, *ST* I–II, q. 10, a. 1, ad 1.

[72] Aquinas, *ST* I–II, q. 8, a. 1.

goodness and being are convertible.[73] We speak of good and evil actions, just as we speak of good and evil things, "because such as everything is, such is the act that it produces."[74] This means that sin and evil are characterized not by a simple negation but by a privation of what a creature *ought* to have in virtue of what it is.[75] Such, in other words, is a privation of what belongs to it by nature, such as a natural power or a naturally perfecting or connatural good. Hence, for example, a blind man might be said to have suffered an evil precisely because he lacks a power (vision) that is proper to his nature. Similarly (or analogically), an action is said to be evil or sinful to the extent that it lacks something due to its perfection: "for instance if it lacks the quantity determined by reason, or its due place, or something of the kind."[76] Such an act is thus qualified by St. Thomas as inordinate.[77]

Because, in fact, the human person like all other creatures is thought of as naturally equipped with an appetite for the good that serves or even constitutes his perfection, it follows that if the appetite is inclined to an evil instead, this must be due to a corruption or a disorder in some aspect of his nature, such as the intellect, the sensitive appetite, or the will. Such a corruption or disorder is in fact of primordial significance for Aquinas's treatment of *peccatum* in the actions of natural things: a word that might be translated not only in the moral sense of "sin" but also—to return to an insight touched upon above—in the ontological sense of "error" or "fault."[78] Hence, without changing nature per se, sin adversely affects nature's inclination to its perfecting end (*ordinatur ad terminum*).[79] When, moreover, the appetite is repetitively inclined toward evil, there may well result what St. Thomas identifies as a corruption in one's habitual manner of acting and a sort of perversion of one's taste that he calls "malice."[80]

By reason of such sinful or vicious inclinations, human beings are said to be less (and not more) free, to anticipate the theme of our next chapter. After all, human persons are endowed, in virtue of their rational souls, with naturally known principles of knowledge and action, which St. Thomas qualifies as "nurseries of intellectual and moral virtues," and likewise with a "natural appetite for

---

73 See Aquinas, *ST* I, q. 5, aa. 1, 3.

74 Aquinas, *ST* I–II, q. 18, a. 1.

75 See Aquinas, *ST* I–II, q. 75, a. 1.

76 Aquinas, *ST* I–II, q. 18, a. 1.

77 See Aquinas, *ST* I–II, q. 75, a. 1, ad 1. See also the thorough treatment of the inordinate character of human sin in Josef Pieper, *The Concept of Sin*, trans. Edward T. Oakes (South Bend, IN: St. Augustine's Press, 2001).

78 See Aquinas, *ST* I–II, q. 78, a. 1.

79 See Aquinas, *ST* I, q. 83, a. 2, obj. 3; and q. 98, a. 2.

80 See Aquinas, *ST* I–II, q. 78; and *De Malo* q. 3, a. 12.

good in accordance with reason."[81] These seeds of virtue are, however, negatively affected by sin, which creates a contradiction within the human heart between, on the one hand, the choice for a temporal good or pleasure deviating from the good *specific to human nature* and, on the other hand, one's natural aspiration for this same good.[82] To be sure, sin cannot remove the general principle of the natural law from men's hearts—the recognition that good must be done and evil avoided—but it can remove "secondary precepts," such as the injunction against murder or adultery, because of concupiscence or "evil persuasions" or "vicious customs and corrupt habits."[83] Due to such corrupt habits, whereby one cleaves to objects "against the light of reason," the vicious person tends almost "connaturally" *away* from the good perfective of human nature.[84] It is, in fact, as contrary to the good of reason, to which human nature is naturally inclined, that *every* sin is considered "contrary to nature (*contra naturam*)."[85] That is why "to sin is nothing else than to fail," Aquinas summarizes, "in the good which belongs to any being according to its nature."[86]

To acknowledge, moreover, that an appetite might be ascribed to a human *person* does not entail—to return to the subject at hand—that sexual orientations might escape the normative structure bound up with human *nature*, as certain moralists would have us believe, even with regard to Thomistic doctrine.[87] When, in fact, Aquinas reasons that an inclination is to "something like and suitable to the thing inclined," he explicitly evokes the correspondence between the inclination and the "being and substance" of the thing thus

---

[81] Aquinas, *ST* I–II, q. 63, a. 1.

[82] That is why sin is said to lead to "a diminution of that good of nature, which is the inclination to virtue" (Aquinas, *ST* I–II, q. 85, a. 1).

[83] Aquinas, *ST* I–II, q. 94, a. 6.

[84] Aquinas, *ST* I–II, 86, a. 1. St. Thomas therefore likens the "stain" (*macula*) of sin on the soul to a "shadow" caused by an object obstructing the light (ad 2).

[85] Aquinas, *ST* I–II, q. 78, a. 3; cf. q. 94, a. 3, ad 2. See also the well-developed argument to this effect by Josef Pieper in his *Concept of Sin*.

[86] Aquinas, *ST* I–II, q. 109, a. 2, ad 2.

[87] Hence, for example, Andriano Oliva—member of the Leonine Commission, responsible for the critical edition of the works of St. Thomas—argues, "There cannot exist a natural principle which renders the homosexual inclination illicit as such, for it is connatural to the homosexual individual and has as its end the love of a person" (Andriano Oliva, *Amours: L'Eglise, les divorcés remariés, les couples homosexuels* [Paris, Cerf, 2015], 92). Similarly, Todd A. Salzman and Michael G. Lawler maintain that because "people with a permanent homosexual orientation . . . do not choose that orientation . . . a homosexual orientation *is* normative" (Salzman and Lawler, *The Sexual Person: Toward a Renewed Catholic Anthropology* [Washington, DC: Georgetown University Press, 2008], 108). In other words, "*Homosexual* and *heterosexual* are *further* specifications of *sexual* orientation, and this further specification constitutions what is normative for homosexual or heterosexual persons" (109). In response to this challenge, see Michele M. Schumacher, "The Reunification of Naturalism and Personalism in the Conjugal Act: A Contribution by Servais Pinckaers," *The Thomist* 84, no. 3 (2020): 435–66.

inclined, thereby implying an additional correspondence between a nature and its specific good, resulting "from a form existing in the nature of things."[88] After all, it is the form that makes a thing to be what it is and that likewise provides it with its specific principles of action. Underlying a natural inclination is therefore, as Jan Aertsen explains of Aquinas's thought, "an anticipatory unity of the nature in which it is rooted and of the end towards which it tends."[89] And this in turn means that such an inclination presupposes a sort of affinity, or connaturality,[90] between the desiring subject and the objective good that befits, or is appropriate to, him. For not every good is actually good nor desirable for every nature. However, "whatever is desired has the nature of good."[91] In other words, it is desired precisely insofar as it is considered (whether by the appetite or the reason or both) as an *objective* (ontological) good: a thing that is *good in itself*, and/or as a *subjective* (relative) good: a thing that is *good for me*. Even in the latter sense, however, a thing might be considered ontologically, for a thing is *good for me* to the extent that it *contributes to my fullness or perfection*, again, as determined by my (human) nature.

In this way, we are invited to remove all ambiguity from the term *perfection*. For St. Thomas at least, it always designates a creature's *actuality* and thus its "*ontological* richness,"[92] or the fullness of its being, the accomplishment of its powers—including most particularly, in the case at hand, its procreative powers—and, ultimately, the plenitude of its nature. As for the human being, like all creatures, it is good, or perfect, to the extent that its potencies, or powers, are actualized: "to be in act constitutes the nature of the good," St. Thomas explains.[93] And this in turn entails that it achieves the end for which it was created.

The perfection of nature is thus conceived by the Aristotelian-Thomistic tradition as consisting in the good that is already contained within the natural form of the species, whence the depiction of a being's form as its *entelecheia*: as that whereby it literally bears its end (*telos*) within itself.[94] Because, to explain, the natural form of each creature is the seat of its natural powers or potencies

---

88 Aquinas, *ST* I–II, q. 8, a. 1.

89 Jan Aertsen, *Nature and Creature: Thomas Aquinas's Way of Thought* (New York: Brill, 1988), 343.

90 Literally, that which corresponds ("con" = with) to nature. See, for example, Aquinas, *ST* I–II, q. 26, a. 2, c. et ad 3.

91 Aquinas, *ST* I, q. 6, a. 2, ad 2.

92 Jean-Hervé Nicolas, footnote 3 to *ST* I, q. 6, a. 1, in Thomas d'Aquin, *Somme théologique*, vol. 1 (Paris: Cerf, 1984), 193 (emphasis added).

93 Aquinas, *SCG* I, c. 37, 4.

94 See William E. Ritter, "Why Aristotle Invented the Word Entelecheia," *The Quarterly Review of Biology* 7, no. 4 (December 1932): 377–403.

(that in virtue of which it acts), its proper end might be thought of as the blossoming of what is already contained within the bud, the sprouting of what is already programmed within the seed, or the development of the powers and potencies that are already present within the human soul, as we will treat more extensively in chapter 5.[95] For as Aquinas reasons, "Upon the form follows an inclination to the end, or to an action, or something of the sort; for everything, insofar as it is in act, acts and tends towards that which is in accordance with its form."[96]

One need only observe the growth of the early embryo:

> Tissues and organs do not result from the agglomeration of cells, as if these cells were givens, like a child's building blocks. The cells for the morula did not previously exist and therefore cannot be "added" to the fertilized egg, or zygote. *The zygote is already the whole.* Instead of joining part to part in an additive manner, it develops and differentiates from within. It divides, reorganizes, and transforms itself; no one and no force is piling up pre-existing building blocks.[97]

Because, moreover, each natural being—a child, a plant, an animal, or an insect, for example—is further ordained to its operation or to that which is obtained thereby,[98] it naturally passes from one degree of perfection to another.[99] In this way, nature nurtures her own. To address the nature of a thing—in accord with the etymological significance of the term ("nature" coming from *nascor*, meaning "to be born")—is thus to address that which it is *born to be.* Indeed, as senior researcher at the Nature Institute Stephen Talbott explains from a purely biological standpoint, *telos* might be thought of as "the organism's own completeness and wholeness—the fullness of its self-expression under all life conditions that present themselves": its "being-at-work-staying-itself."[100] This

95 "The form which makes a thing actual is a perfection and a good," Aquinas teaches; "and thus every actual being is a good; and likewise every potential being, as such, is a good, as having a relation to good. For as it has being in potentiality, so has it goodness in potentiality" (*ST* I, q. 48, a. 3).

96 Aquinas, *ST* I, q. 5, a. 5.

97 Stephen L. Talbott, "The Embryo's Eloquent Form," The Nature Institute, Biology Worthy of Life, May 22, 2008, updated March 18, 2013, https://bwo.life/mqual/embryo.htm.

98 Cf. Aquinas, *ST* I–II, q. 49, a. 3.

99 Again, this is not to deny that there might be a certain "corruption" of nature when it is set off its course in search of goods that do not correspond to its own good. Such is the "missing of the mark," a deviance from the moral norm that leads to fullness or perfection; see Pieper, *Concept of Sin*, 16–33. Particularly important for understanding this deviation is the distinction between moral and technical failure. In the first case, Pieper explains, the deviation is willed and intentional. See Pieper, *Concept of Sin*, 41.

100 Stephen L. Talbott, "Evolution and the Purposes of Life. On Biology's Unasked Questions about the Goal

fullness is thus not to be conceived as some sort of static preservation that would "freeze all existence in an unnatural stasis." On the contrary, it points to "the urge toward self-transcendence, at the world's heart."[101]

From this perspective, the term (or goal) of a natural inclination is not so much the attractive good, which is the object of an appetite, but rather the being itself that is perfected thereby. "For the good of anything whatsoever consists in its perfect operation."[102] Hence, as David Gallagher summarizes, "Goodness is said with reference to perfection, and perfection always implies completion, and so a thing is said to be good simply when it is simply complete, that is to say, when it has its full completion."[103]

-Directed Activities of Organisms," *The New Atlantis* 51 (Winter 2017), https://www.thenewatlantis.com/publications/evolution-and-the-purposes-of-life. The latter phrase is accredited by Talbott to Joe Sachs without reference.

[101] Stephen L. Talbott, "A Conversation with Nature," *The New Atlantis* 3 (Fall 2003), https://www.thenewatlantis.com/publications/a-conversation-with-nature.

[102] Aquinas, *De Ver.* I, a. 8.

[103] Gallagher, "Goodness and Moral Goodness," in *Thomas Aquinas and His Legacy*, ed. David M. Gallagher (Washington, DC: The Catholic University of America Press, 1994), 46. See also Oliva Blanchette, "The Logic of Perfection in Aquinas," in Gallagher, *Thomas Aquinas and His Legacy*, 107–30.

CHAPTER 4

Freedom as Created or as Self-Determined?

To view perfection as the completion of a natural process—to summarize a key aspect of our previous chapter—is not to call into question the compatibility of nature and human freedom. On the contrary, it is to provide a natural foundation for freedom. Because, in fact, the free will is presented by St. Thomas as a "faculty formed by the conjunction of the intellect and the will," it is understood by him as *proceeding from* (as an essential fruit of) the reason and the will, as differing from the popular understanding, akin to Sartrian doctrine, of the human will as a sort of first faculty *preceding* human reason and will. In fact, from the Thomistic perspective, the primary source of our free action is understood as lying within "the two natural inclinations that move our spiritual faculties: the sense of truth and the attraction to the good."[1]

CREATED FREEDOM AND THE NATURAL INCLINATION TO GOODNESS

It thus bears insisting that Aquinas proposes a very different understanding of freedom than that of the conventional, essentially negative conception thereof, namely, as untethered or unconstrained: as, in other words, escaping both external and internal influences.[2] Far beyond this minimalist conception of

---

1 Servais Pinckaers, "Aquinas on Nature and the Supernatural," trans. Sr. Mary Thomas Noble, in *The Pinckaers Reader: Renewing Thomistic Moral Theology*, ed. John Berkman and Craig Steven Titus (Washington, DC: The Catholic University of America Press, 2005), 361–62. See also Pinckaers, *The Sources of Christian Ethics*, trans. Sr. Mary Thomas Noble (Washington, DC: The Catholic University of America Press, 1995), 245; and Pinckaers, *Morality: The Catholic View*, trans. Michael Sherwin (South Bend, IN: St. Augustine's Press, 2001), 68–69.

2 As Pinckaers acknowledges, "Our chief difficulty is caused by our habit of considering nature and freedom as contraries. If we think of freedom as something dependent only on our voluntary decision, and totally indeterminate before we take that decision, then we will be led to think of the natural as something necessarily predetermined. In this view, it is hard to see how we can reconcile the natural and the free. We will see the natural inclinations of both intellect and will as tendencies both blind and coercive" (*Sources of Christian Ethics*, 400–401).

freedom as one of "indifference" with regard to ends—a freedom which is manifest in the act of choosing between contraries or of resisting natural inclinations—Aquinas's presentation of freedom is essentially positive: freedom *for the good* and not simply freedom *from constraint*.[3] The former, which Pinckaers designates "freedom for excellence," is one that aims high, because it is guided by man's natural orientation, or inclination, to that which is fundamentally transcendent to him and yet proper to his perfection, or happiness: goodness, truth, and being.[4] This in turn means that predominance is accorded to the good that attracts rather than to the evil that repels.[5] Because, moreover, these inclinations to transcendent values are proper to man as such—as rational and free—Pinckaers argues that "we are free not in spite of our natural inclinations, but because of them."[6]

Freedom for excellence is thus none other than the natural human capacity to reach the fullness of man's own being, to achieve his natural and personal perfection, or to obtain the end befitting his nature by way of his own actions, as we saw in our previous chapter. After all, the human person is not simply moved to his end, as are creatures who lack freedom. Rather, he really moves himself. Such, moreover, is the origin of Aquinas's distinction between a properly human act (*actus humanus*), which is willed and thus moral—an act which, in other words, follows upon deliberation so as to be conducted with purpose or intention—and an act that is merely performed by a human being (*actus humanis*) under the influence of a natural impulse (such as the desires to eat, to sleep, or to engage in sexual intercourse) in the absence of freedom's intervention. That is why it is said to lack moral value.[7] Such is also the origin of the

---

3 As Pinckaers explains the concept, under the influence of Nominalism, this conception of freedom is one which "turns away from spiritual interiority and from the life that flows from it as a vital yearning for truth, goodness, and happiness" (*Morality*, 97).

4 See Pinckaers, *Sources of Christian Ethics*, 354–78.

5 For Aquinas, the good acts as "the cause of causes" because, in the absence of its attractive force, there is no efficient causality—no incentive to act—and thus no movement (*ST* I q. 5, a. 2, ad 1). Of course, this is not to deny that the human person is also naturally inclined *away* from evil or danger. However, St. Thomas recognizes natural inclinations as tending more to what is suitable to nature than as receding from what is unsuitable. See Aquinas, *ST* I–II, q. 35, a. 6, ad 2.

6 Pinckaers, *Sources of Christian Ethics*, 245. In contrast, for William Ockham, the father of Nominalism who influenced much of modern philosophy and thus indirectly Sartre, "freedom dominated the natural inclinations and preceded them, because of its radical indetermination and its ability to choose contraries in their regard. From this point of view, it could be said that freedom is more apparent when it resists natural inclinations" (Pinckaers, *Sources of Christian Ethics*, 245). "Here in brief are the two interpretations: according to Aquinas, free will *proceeds from* reason and will; according to Ockham, free will *precedes* reason and will, like a first faculty" (Pinckaers, "Aquinas on Nature and the Supernatural," 361). See also Pinckaers, *Morality*, 68–69.

7 See Aquinas, *ST* I–II, q. 1, aa. 1–3. Of course, this is not to admit that the decision to engage in the act is necessarily devoid of moral value. To that effect, see Michele M. Schumacher, "The Reunification of

distinction between the two manners in which *nature* may be ascribed to the human person: (1) as that which *specifies our humanity* as rational—hence, for example, it is "natural to man to take pleasure in contemplating the truth and in doing works of virtue"—and (2) as that which *we share with other animals*. "And in this [latter] sense, that which pertains to the preservation of the body"—whether that of the individual (by means of food, drink, and sleep) or that of the species (by means of sexual intercourse)—are said by St. Thomas "to afford man natural pleasure."[8] Because such an act (*actus humanis*) does not entail the use of reason, it is not a specifically human act (*actus humanus*), but that does not make it unreasonable nor inhumane. After all, it is in accord with reason that the act of reason might be interrupted during the sexual act, for example. If such were not the case, it would be unreasonable to sleep.[9] Nor is the "exceeding" pleasure of the sexual act opposed to virtue. On the contrary, this act is pleasurable *precisely because* the Creator has ordained it to the great good of preserving the human species.[10]

As these examples serve to illustrate, human freedom is not any less free because it is subject to the creative intentions of its Author. On the contrary, it is precisely as created that freedom is understood to operate for the good of both the individual and the species in accord with natural inclinations that are—as we saw in our previous chapter—foundational with respect to natural law. It is thus not surprising that Pinckaers recognizes natural inclinations and the natural law as "God's most precious work in the human person, a direct, unique participation in his own wisdom, goodness, and freedom and the emanation of the eternal law."[11] Human causality and human creativity might thus be understood as participating in divine causality and divine creativity; for God works in things in such a way that they have their proper operation.[12] Although, in fact, every operation of every creature, as well as every created inclination toward any sort of acting or moving, is radically dependent upon God, these operations and inclinations are nonetheless also attributable to the creature. Aquinas thus admits "no difference" between the acknowledgement that things "seek [*appetere*] the good by a natural appetite" and that they "seek . . . their

Naturalism and Personalism in the Conjugal Act: A Contribution by Servais Pinckaers," *The Thomist* 84, no. 3 (2020).

8 Aquinas, *ST* I–II, q. 31, a. 7.

9 See Aquinas, *ST* II–II, q. 153, a. 2, ad 2.

10 See Aquinas, *ST* II–II, q. 153, a. 2, ad 2, corpus; and q. 151, a. 3, ad 3.

11 Pinckaers, *Sources of Christian Ethics*, 405.

12 See, for example, Aquinas, *SCG* III, c. 70, 8; *ST* I, q. 105, a. 5; I–II q. 109, a. 1; and *De Pot.* q. 3, a. 7.

own perfection. . . . For, by the fact that they tend to their own perfection they tend to the good, since a thing is good to the extent that it is perfect."[13]

It follows from this profoundly positive understanding of human freedom—of freedom as created—that the good proper to man cannot simply be understood as a "preformed idea" wherein his actions are molded, nor as "a pre-established plan" to be simply executed according to instructions. On the contrary, the particularly human good is a "fullness" befitting one who is capable of acting in virtue of his own initiative, of drawing from his own inner depths, of "somehow inventing and creating his action and his perfection."[14] And this in turn means that we cannot simply transpose physical or biological accounts of goodness (such as health, for example) to the moral plane.[15] The particularly human "instinct" for truth and goodness must, rather, be understood as differing radically from the animal instinct that is more readily associated with the term, namely, "impulses of a lower order" that exist on the psychosomatic plane.[16] Indeed, the specifically human instinct for truth and goodness is designated by Pinckaers as essentially (*au fond*) an "instinct for God."[17]

THE INVENTION OF ETHICS AND DESIRE: SARTRE'S SELF-MADE MAN

We could hardly be further from the vision proposed by Simone de Beauvoir's appropriately entitled *Ethics of Ambiguity*. For "a being, who from the very start would be an exact co-incidence of himself, in a perfect plenitude, the notion of having-to-be would have no meaning," she reasons. After all, the absolute correspondence of subjectivity and objectivity, or the identity of essence and existence, is a prerogative reserved for God, to whom "one does not offer an ethics." That is why Beauvoir concludes that it is "impossible to propose any [ethics] to man if one defines him as a nature, as something given."[18] Because—as the famous French feminist insinuates in this passage—the end of nature is fixed or determined from the outset, the natural man is subject to nature's dictates,

[13] Aquinas, *SCG* III, c. 24, 6.

[14] Servais Pinckaers, "Appendice I: Notes explicatives," in Thomas d'Aquin, *Somme théologique*, I–II, qu. 6–17: *Les actes humains*, trans. Servais Pinckaers, vol. 2, Editions de la revue des jeunes, nouvelle édition (Paris: Cerf, 1997), 164.

[15] See Pinckaers, "Appendice I," 165.

[16] Pinckaers, *Sources of Christian Ethics*, 333. For a more extensive development of these ideas, see Schumacher, "Reunification of Naturalism and Personalism," and Stephen J. Heaney, "Fundamental Inclinations and Sexual Desires," *Nova et Vetera* 15, no. 1 (2017): 37–52.

[17] Pinckaers, *Sources of Christian Ethics*, 404.

[18] De Beauvoir, *Ethics of Ambiguity*, trans. Bernard Frechtman (New York: Open Road Integrated Media, 2018), 10.

and this in turn is thought to severely limit his self-determining freedom, which is deemed "the source of all values" and thus also of moral action.[19] "To will oneself moral and to will oneself free are one and the same decision," Beauvoir maintains.[20] After all, for one adhering—as does Beauvoir—to the Sartrian doctrine that there is no human nature, there can be no predetermined end, "no absolute value," or goodness, directing the human person if not for freedom itself and the "projects and the ends he sets up" for himself, including that of his own being.[21] For, as Sartre would have it, man "makes himself be."[22] The human person is thus "free to define for himself the conditions of a life which is valid in his own eyes,"[23] and this in turn means that morality is nothing other than an "adhesion to the self"[24] and to the ends determined by the self for the self.[25] That is why we should not be surprised by Beauvoir's acknowledgement that "freedom will never be given; it will always have to be won."[26]

It is with respect to this radically unanchored understanding of human freedom that Sartrian existentialism is judged by Beauvoir as "the only philosophy in which an ethics has its place."[27] It is "not a matter of being right in the eyes of a God, but of being right in [one's] own eyes."[28] Human freedom is "the ultimate, the unique end to which man should destine himself."[29] To refuse to acknowledge this inescapable curse of human existence—namely, the nonidentity of its existence and its essence—is to live "under the eyes of the gods" in an "infantile world," where values are already given.[30] And this in turn means living either as a "sub man," who rejects the confrontation with "the agonizing consciousness of himself" as a self-founding freedom, or as a tyrant, who "ignores the value

19 De Beauvoir, *Ethics of Ambiguity*, 16. Cf. Jean-Paul Sartre, *Existentialism and Human Emotions*, trans. Bernard Frechtman and Hazel E. Barnes (New York: Philosophical Library, 1957), 49.

20 De Beauvoir, *Ethics of Ambiguity*, 24.

21 De Beauvoir, *Ethics of Ambiguity*, 10.

22 Sartre, *Existentialism and Human Emotions*, 52.

23 De Beauvoir, *Ethics of Ambiguity*, 14–15.

24 De Beauvoir, *Ethics of Ambiguity*, 34.

25 They do so, Beauvoir explains, "on the basis of situations whose particularity is as radical and as irreducible as subjectivity itself" (*Ethics of Ambiguity*, 17).

26 De Beauvoir, *Ethics of Ambiguity*, 128.

27 De Beauvoir, *Ethics of Ambiguity*, 34.

28 De Beauvoir, *Ethics of Ambiguity*, 13. Because in the Thomistic tradition, in contrast, "the concept 'nature' contains within itself an element of binding directedness [*verbindlicher Richtweisung*]," it follows, as Pieper explains, that "a formal lapse [*Verfehlung*] against nature is at the same time and for that reason an infringement against a superhuman norm and thus is guilt before God the Creator" (Pieper, *The Concept of Sin*, trans. Edward T. Oakes [South Bend, IN: St. Augustine's Press, 2001], 38–39).

29 De Beauvoir, *Ethics of Ambiguity*, 52.

30 De Beauvoir, *Ethics of Ambiguity*, 50–51.

of the subjectivity and the freedom of others."[31] A "tyrant," more specifically, is one who "imposes a credo," whereby he enslaves both himself and others to an end whose value he refuses to call into question.[32] Any such acknowledgement of transcendent values beyond human freedom is designated by Sartre as a "spirit of seriousness," whereby the human subject is reduced to nothing but "passive obedience" to the "mute demands" of objects.[33] The "genuine man" avoids this trap by refusing to admit "any foreign absolute," that is to say, any transcendent goal that has not been projected by man himself.[34]

Sartrian freedom thus distinguishes itself from the classic metaphysical version thereof by its radical uprootedness from human nature, which is to say that it is both unmoored and unoriented, like a ship without a compass. For, as was pointed out in our general introduction, to admit that man is free means for Sartre that "man is freedom."[35] It follows from this profoundly atheistic vision that human passions—in contradistinction to the human will, which Beauvoir and Sartre regard in the voluntarist fashion as assertive, rather than passive—are "useless," because, as Beauvoir reasons, man "has no means for becoming the being he is not."[36] The authentically free man is one who affirms, or chooses, himself anew at every instant, an act that Josef Pieper recognizes as a choice for the self over God.[37] By dissociating himself from his own past—which for Sartre also, even primordially, implies a denial of his creation—and by differentiating himself from the objective world of things, man as a conscious being is said by Sartre to "nihilate" his own objectivity: the givenness or facticity that is the fate of unconscious beings, who are mere objects. In so doing, he projects himself toward the being whom he is not yet, so as to assume "the anguish of freedom":[38]

31 De Beauvoir, *Ethics of Ambiguity*, 47–48.

32 De Beauvoir, *Ethics of Ambiguity*, 53.

33 Sartre, *Being and Nothingness: A Phenomenological Essay on Ontology*, trans. Hazel E. Barnes (New York: Washington Square Press, 1984), 796.

34 De Beauvoir, *Ethics of Ambiguity*, 13.

35 Sartre, *Existentialism and Human Emotions*, 23; cf. Jean-Paul Sartre, *L'existentialisme est un humanisme* (Paris: Nagel, 1946), 36–37: "l'homme est liberté."

36 De Beauvoir, *Ethics of Ambiguity*, 10. Assuredly, the idea comes from Sartre. See his *Being and Nothingness*, 784. In short, as Judith Butler summarizes, desire is said to be a useless passion for Sartre because it is "without a final destination in being" (Butler, *Subjects of Desire: Hegelian Reflections in Twentieth-Century France* [1987; repr., New York: Columbia University, 2012], 161).

37 "As Jean-Paul Sartre realized, we are faced with either a clear Yes or a clear No. All intermediate positions eventually prove to be compromises. What is specific to man's creatureliness lies in the fact that he, unlike a crystal, a tree or an animal, can say 'I myself.' As soon as he does this, in the very moment when he recognizes that his status as a rational animal is unique (on the one hand, he is a creature; on the other, he can either accept or reject this fact), at just that moment he stands before the alternative: he can either choose himself or God" (Pieper, *Concept of Sin*, 64).

38 De Beauvoir, *Ethics of Ambiguity*, 39. As understood by Sartre, *anguish* is conscious awareness that I make

the recognition of human freedom as groundless because it is no longer conceived in terms of the natural inclinations to goodness and truth.[39] In short, the Sartrian man is one who owns up to the intrinsic void marking his personal existence, in view of charging it with meaning.[40] "Every man casts himself into the world by making himself a lack of being; he thereby contributes to reinvesting it with human signification," Beauvoir explains in typically Sartrian fashion.[41]

In this way the conscious subject, whom Sartre names a *pour-soi* (literally a being *for-self*), is caught up in the dichotomy between nature (*what* he is: ontology) and existence (*that* he is: facticity). Such is a dichotomy denied of an unconscious being (whom Sartre calls an *en-soi*, literally a being "in-itself"), which is epitomized by complete self-coincidence: it is simply what it is. A conscious (or free) being, in contrast, is defined as noncoincidence: it is what it is not, and it is not what it is.[42] That is why the conscious subject (the *pour-soi*) must constantly seek to bring itself to be. It seeks to escape from "its factual existence" (its being here and now as such) in a flight "toward an impossible future . . . where the for-itself [the *pour-soi*] would be an in-itself-for-itself [*en-soi-pour-soi*]": the mode of being proper to God, who is, however, banned from the Sartrian universe at the outset.[43] In his place is something akin to the Nietzschean *Supermensch*, who is constantly caught up in the vain attempt at self-coincidence: the attempt to simultaneously occupy the position of object and subject. Such, more specifically, is one who simultaneously is and makes himself to be.[44] Hence, the very "*meaning*" of Sartrian desire "is ultimately the project of being God": of becoming the foundation of one's own existence.[45]

It follows as a simple matter of course for Sartre that "the child does not contain the man [nor the woman, as transactivist Jay Stewart reminds us with

---

myself to be: that my freedom is unfounded except as chosen at each moment by me.

39 Indeed, it is formulated by Sartre within what Philippe Sabot presents as "the historical collapse of a metaphysical model of the subject as assured of itself and of its own identity in its immanent relation to the Absolute" (Sabot, foreword to Butler, *Subjects of Desire*, ix).

40 This intrinsic void is described by Beauvoir as a "formless night" (*Ethics of Ambiguity*, 129) and by Butler as "the existential loneliness of every consciousness, its differentiation from substance, its exile from the real of being" (*Subjects of Desire*, 162).

41 De Beauvoir, *Ethics of Ambiguity*, 44. That is why "meaning," for Sartre, "is nothing other than a fixed movement of transcendence" (*Being and Nothingness*, 452).

42 See Sartre, *Being and Nothingness*, 785.

43 Sartre, *Being and Nothingness*, 472.

44 "To be God would mean, finally," Butler explains of Sartre's position, "to achieve a coincidence of for -itself and in-itself such that human freedom would be at the origin of the in-itself" (Butler, *Subjects of Desire*, 136).

45 Sartre, *Being and Nothingness*, 724.

regard to Beauvoir's most famous dictum[46]] [whom] he [or she] will become."[47] It could hardly be otherwise, for once nature is no longer acknowledged as "the beginning [*entelecheia*] that contains the end [*telos*] within itself," what remains—Robert Spaemann astutely remarks—is "nothing more than a *terminus a quo* for an endless journey into no man's land."[48] Or, as Henri de Lubac aptly argued in the same year in which Beauvoir penned her *Ethics of Ambiguity* in the original French (1947), it is "meaningless" to speak of "becoming" in the absence of nature.[49] It is only "another word for absurdity. If there is 'becoming' there must be fulfilment, and if there must be fulfilment there must have been always something else beside[s] 'becoming.'"[50] That is why—as Sartre perfectly summarizes his own doctrine—"Man is a useless passion."[51]

It is nonetheless not so much *absurdity* as *ambiguity* that characterizes the intrinsically "forlorn" character of man, as Beauvoir interprets Sartrian doctrine.[52] For, although "nothing is *useful*" to man in his "original helplessness," "nothing is *useless*" either, Beauvoir claims. Because, for Sartre, man is the final authority when it comes to making value claims of his own actions, it follows that there is "no outside appeal, no objective necessity" by which to justify his passions or his acts or even his values other than the projects and ends that he chooses for himself.[53] None of these are inflicted from without. They are chosen

---

46 See Jay Stewart, "We Are Living on the Cusp of a Gender Revolution," February 23, 2015, https://www.youtube.com/watch?v=UpQd-VrKgFI. Stewart quotes the famous phrase, "One is not born, but rather becomes a woman" (Simone de Beauvoir, *The Second Sex*, trans. and ed. H. M. Parshley [New York: Vintage Books, 1989], 267).

47 De Beauvoir, *Ethics of Ambiguity*, 43.

48 Robert Spaemann, "A Philosophical Autobiography," in *A Robert Spaemann Reader: Philosophical Essays on Nature, God, and the Human Person*, trans. and ed. D. C. Schindler and Jeanne Hefferman Schindler (Oxford: Oxford University Press, 2015), 17.

49 See Simone De Beauvoir, *Pour une morale de l'ambiguïté* (Paris: Gallimard, 1947). The English translation (*Ethics of Ambiguity*) was published in the following year by Philosophical Library (New York).

50 Henri de Lubac, *Catholicism: Christ and the Common Destiny of Man*, trans. Lancelot C. Sheppard (London: Burns and Oates, 1950), 198–99. The original French was published in 1947.

51 Sartre, *Being and Nothingness*, 784. It merits reading this passage in context: "Every human reality is a passion in that it projects losing itself so as to found being"—that is to say, it founds its own existence in "nothingness" by uprooting human existence from the doctrine of creation—"and by the same stroke to constitute the In-itself [the Sartrian term for objective reality] which escapes contingency by being its own foundation, the *Ens causa sui*, which religions call God. Thus the passion of man is the reverse of that of Christ, for man loses himself as man in order that God may be born. But the idea of God is contradictory and we lose ourselves in vain. Man is a useless passion."

52 Unlike the movement of an atom, which is judged by the famous French feminist as "absurd" because it is not free, the movements that follow upon human freedom (movements based upon a choice) are charged with meaning, Beauvoir explains. See de Beauvoir, *Ethics of Ambiguity*, 25. That is why, "From the very beginning, existentialism defined itself as a philosophy of ambiguity" (8). On the forlorn character of human existence, see Sartre, *Existentialism and Human Emotions*, 22–23, 50–51.

53 De Beauvoir, *Ethics of Ambiguity*, 10 (emphasis added).

instead, and this means that human freedom is the origin of every "passion" or "drive toward being."[54] Clearly, as Andrew Leak sees it, Sartre is on a "crusade . . . to establish desire as a structure of consciousness," as differing from the Aristotelian-Thomistic presentation of desire as serving nature's drive for perfection or fulfillment.[55] Leak's interpretation serves Sartre's claim that the "fundamental project" defining the person is "everywhere in all desires" and that it is "never apprehended except through desires."[56] Or, as Judith Butler perfectly summarizes Sartre's position, "every particular desire indicates an existential choice of how to be," which in turn means that desires "are not contingent features of otherwise self-subsisting subjects." Rather, Sartrian desires are "the modes through which the subject [the *pour-soi*] comes to subsist; they are, to extend the metaphor, the subject's very subsistence. Desire does not indicate a ready-made self, but reveals instead a self having-to-be-formed; indeed, desire is the mode through which the self comes to be, i.e., its mode of realization" out of the nothingness of forlorn freedom.[57]

If, in fact, man "isn't ready made at the start,"[58] he nonetheless realizes and even founds his freedom—indeed, his very existence—in the act of projecting himself beyond himself.[59] We could hardly be further from the Aristotelian-Thomistic presentation of human freedom as being drawn passively in ecstasy (*ex-stasis*) under the attractive influence of the good, the true, and the beautiful.[60]

The Sartrian acknowledgement that "man's destiny is within himself"[61] is thus also to be understood far differently than the Aristotelian-Thomistic presentation of his perfection or end (*telos*) as already contained within his

---

54 De Beauvoir, *Ethics of Ambiguity*, 45.

55 Leak, *The Perverted Consciousness: Sexuality and Sartre* (London: Macmillan, 1989), 58.

56 Sartre, *Being and Nothingness*, 725.

57 Butler, *Subjects of Desire*, 123. In other words, "The implicit dimension of desire is, for Sartre, not the presence of an ontology that explains a pre-established identity, but a certain pre-reflective knowledge that identity is that to be created" (132). "The person is understood as a fundamental desire which is, in turn, the concretization of a choice" (135).

58 Sartre, *Existentialism and Human Emotions*, 43.

59 See Sartre, *Existentialism and Human Emotions*, 50. After all, for Sartre, "man makes himself" (43). See also Butler, *Subjects of Desire*, 139.

60 See Peter A. Kwasniewski, *The Ecstasy of Love in the Thought of St. Thomas Aquinas* (Steubenville, OH: Emmaus Academic, 2021); and Peter A. Kwasniewski, "St. Thomas, *Extasis*, and the Union with the Beloved," *The Thomist* 61, no. 4 (1997): 587–603. For an application, see Michele M. Schumacher, "A Lamentation of *Eros*: Challenging the Sexual Revolution Fifty Years Later" in *Why* Humanae Vitae *is Still Right*, ed. Janet Smith (San Francisco: Ignatius, 2018), 227–46; as well as Michele M. Schumacher, "A Woman in Stone or in the Heart of Man? Navigating between Naturalism and Idealism in the Spirit of Veritatis Splendor," *Nova et Vetera* 11, no. 4 (2013): 1249–86.

61 Sartre, *Existentialism and Human Emotions*, 36.

form, which in turn is the seat of his various powers and passions awaiting actualization. For the French existentialist, the *pour-soi* is "nothing else than his plan" or "the ensemble of his acts."[62] And because the life of the *pour-soi* has "no a priori meaning,"[63] not only his values but also his personal character and even his relation to the objective world in which he finds himself[64] are determined by him "little by little" without being able to foresee their development.[65] Hence, the "drama of original choice," which is at the origin of both values and passions, is such that "it goes on moment by moment for an entire lifetime, that it occurs without reason, before any reason, that freedom is there as if it were present only in the form of contingency," a contingency that "recalls" something of the arbitrary "grace" of a Calvinistic notion of predestination, except that it does not issue "from an external tyranny" but only from the subject's own agency.[66]

Again, such an idea is in stark opposition to the Thomistic presentation of reason as directing appetites, desires, or inclinations in accord with the good befitting the human person: with, that is to say, the plentitude, or perfection, of human nature as discerned by reason. Because the Sartrian man is not given to himself, as the doctrine of creation would have us believe, the original movement of his existence and freedom consists in admitting that there is no preordained being that defines him. Nor is there a "ready-made" world, "chain[ing] up" human freedom, whence—it bears insisting—the intrinsically forlorn character of human existence.[67]

It follows that desire is not given, but is, rather, created and recreated by the *pour-soi* at each moment. Indeed, the denatured Sartrian subject remains radically unaffected by objects, which—as the ancient and medieval tradition would have it—might literally be thrown (*jacere*) in his way (*ob-*), overcoming him by a power before which he remains at least somewhat passive. Such are objects that confront or entice, impel or repel, encourage or dissuade, attract or push away. From Sartre's point of view, there can be no such "bewitching" objects because his consciousness "cannot be *acted upon* by anything outside

62 Sartre, *Existentialism and Human Emotions*, 32.

63 Sartre, *Existentialism and Human Emotions*, 49.

64 "Because the [Sartrian] world cannot be reclaimed as a constitutive aspect of consciousness," as Judith Butler observes in her reading of Sartre, "consciousness must set up another relation to the world; it must interpret the world and imaginatively transfigure the world." Hence, desire is "a way in which we impulsively situate ourselves in the world" (Butler, *Subjects of Desire*, 97). In other words, "Sartre's consciousness instates itself in the world, but never belongs to it" (129).

65 De Beauvoir, *Ethics of Ambiguity*, 34. Or, as Butler puts it, the Sartrian man "labor[s] under impossible goals" (*Subjects of Desire*, 168).

66 De Beauvoir, *Ethics of Ambiguity*, 43–44. In words presumably borrowed from Sartre, she maintains that man is "a being who 'makes himself a lack of being so that there might be being'" (35).

67 De Beauvoir, *Ethics of Ambiguity*, 42.

of itself."[68] In other words, the Sartrian man cannot (except in virtue of "bad faith," which is explained below) be the subject of passions, which—from the Greek *paschō* (πάσχω), meaning "to suffer" or "to be acted on"—are passive faculties. As such, they are moved by ends or goods, which draw their subject to themselves by a force of attraction, a force that may be ascribed even to inanimate objects insofar as they exercise an attractive, even binding, force in virtue of their intrinsic (that is, *created*) goodness. That objects might exert such an impelling force nonetheless entails a complementary force within the subject, whereby he or she is naturally, albeit passively, drawn to a good or repelled by an evil. St. Thomas suggests,

> Love belongs to the appetitive power which is a passive faculty. Wherefore its object stands in relation to it as the cause of its movement or act. Therefore the cause of love must . . . be love's object. Now the proper object of love is the good; because . . . love implies a certain connaturalness or complacency of the lover for the thing beloved [that is to say, a sort of "match" made in heaven by the divine Artist], and to everything, that thing is a good, which is akin and proportionate to it. It follows, therefore, that good is the proper cause of love.[69]

That is why Aquinas teaches that love is "a first cause" and that "love precedes desire."[70] By this, he means that the connatural good incites the appetite to awaken, under the force of its spell, and to respond by seeking union with the beloved thing or person. That is why love of the objective good is considered primary with respect to all other natural inclinations.[71]

As for Sartre, in contrast, he refuses to admit any "host of propensities, inclinations, [or] possibilities" pushing man toward fulfilllment from within. Hence for the existentialist as defined by Sartre, "there is really no love other than one which manifests itself in a person's being in love," that is to say, a love

---

68 Leak, *Perverted Consciousness*, 155.

69 Aquinas, *ST* I–II, q. 27, a. 1. See also, q. 26, a. 2. On the passive nature of all human love, see also the well -developed argument by Josef Pieper in his *On Love*, in *Faith, Hope, Love*, trans. Richard Winston, Clara Winston, and Mary Frances McCarthy (San Francisco: Ignatius, 1997).

70 Aquinas, *ST* I–II, q. 28, a. 6.; q. 25, a. 2. See also q. 28, a. 1.

71 As Servais Pinckaers points out, "Saint Thomas somewhat clarifies the natural foundation of volition by saying that the will spontaneously seeks not only the good in itself, but also all that is appropriate to human nature, including objects proper to all its faculties considered good. We spontaneously will truth, being and life, and all that is necessary to maintain it, and so on. From this derive the various precepts of natural law [cf. *ST* I–II, q. 94, a. 2]. . . . Let us note, however, that from this point of view, desire of the good is primary, with the love of truth and of the conservation of being appearing as kinds of goods, but inseparable from the love of the good" (Pinckaers, "Appendice I," 331).

which is "constructed" by man.[72] It follows as a matter of course that the Sartrian man cannot be overcome by love or be *ecstatically* de-centered from himself (*ex*-) and his own "stability," or "stand" (*stasis*).[73] To be sure, Sartre admits that one might claim to be "victimized by desire, or to be totally enthralled with the object of desire," but this is nothing more than an example of what he calls "bad faith": a failure to live up to one's convictions or a willingness to lie to one's own self. When this occurs—when, for example, consciousness is "clogged" by desire or when man lies to himself or claims to be overtaken by desire—human consciousness is not lost. On the contrary, it might be said, as Judith Butler comments on Sartrian doctrine, to work "its hardest—one arranges for enthrallment, one arranges one's own victimization. In effect, one 'sets it up.'"[74]

From the perspective of the Sartrian universe, which is profoundly "hostile to human desire,"[75] all "tastes" or desires "represent" therefore "a certain appropriative choice of being,"[76] which is to say, a rational decision betraying "the fundamental projects of the person"[77] or the personal determination of his own identity. Because these in turn—the projects or plans projected by man whereby he determines the meaning of his life—are said by Sartre to constitute reality, "empirical desire" is simply "a symbolization of a fundamental concrete desire which is the person himself." Only in this sense is it possible to acknowledge that the "fundamental project," which is the person himself, is "everywhere in all desires" and even that it (the person-project) is "never apprehended except through desires."[78] In short, *to desire*, for Sartre, is *to choose*: to assert oneself or one's "project," which emerges "*ex nihilo* from the for-itself [the *pour-soi*]."[79] A purer form of voluntarism would be difficult to find, except, perhaps—to return to the subject at hand—in Butler's philosophy of "gender," which is nonetheless, as is my purpose to demonstrate, rooted in the Sartrian brand of atheistic existentialism.[80]

---

72 Sartre, *Existentialism and Human Emotions*, 32. This is particularly apparent in the original French, which is more literally translated: "There is no love other than that which is constructed; there is no possibility of love other than that which is manifest in a love." *L'existentialisme est un humanisme*, 56–57: "il n'y a pas d'amour que celui qui se construit, il n'y a pas de possibilité d'amour autre que celle qui se manifeste dans un amour."

73 For an extensive development of this idea, see Schumacher, "Lamentation of *Eros*."

74 Butler, *Subjects of Desire*, 131.

75 Butler, *Subjects of Desire*, 162.

76 Sartre, *Being and Nothingness*, 784.

77 Sartre, *Being and Nothingness*, 783.

78 Sartre, *Being and Nothingness*, 725.

79 Butler, *Subjects of Desire*, 161. Similarly, freedom itself is "an *ex nihilo* creation" (140).

80 Voluntarism is characterized by the primacy of the human will over knowledge and of the assertive character of that will, which decides without being passively influenced by the good.

NOTHINGNESS AS THE FOUNDATION OF SARTRIAN FREEDOM AND DESIRE

To summarize the foregoing, the "lack of being" at the origin of Sartrian desire ought not to be understood with respect to a natural fullness or perfection, as characterizes the Aristotelian-Thomistic perspective.[81] Here there can be no promise of a fruitful or self-transcending encounter, of being led or drawn out of one's own interior depth to encounter another freedom in view of forming an authentic communion of persons. Nor can one (except by "bad faith") be affected—far less perfected—by a good outside of oneself.[82] On the contrary, the Sartrian lack can only be measured against the intrinsic void, or "nothingness," that replaces the category of essence, or nature, as the foundation of human (or more accurately for Sartre, *personal*) freedom. "Freedom is existence," Sartre claims, "and in it existence precedes essence."[83] In other words, it belongs to human freedom to create the essence of each individual human being, and that is why "there can be no question of determining *a priori* and ontologically [nor ethically] what appears in all the unpredictability of a free act."[84] "Reality alone is what counts" for Sartre, and this means that "dreams, expectations, and hopes"—together with passions and inclinations—"warrant no more than to define a man as a disappointed dream, as miscarried hopes, as vain expectations. In other words, to define him negatively [by the ontological void] and not positively [by the personal project of each man for himself]."[85]

Far from "suppress[ing] my instincts, desires, plans, and passions," however, the Sartrian acknowledgement of the radical lack of being (or "nothingness") at the heart of personal existence allows them to be considered as projected by freedom.[86] "Anguish, desire, appeal, laceration"[87]—even

[81] See Sartre, *Existentialism and Human Emotions*, 66.

[82] In the Thomist tradition, for example, as André Malet presents it, "the faculties are never creative of their object, but only able to reach it and marry with it. The good is a value in itself and requires to be desired as such, otherwise it is no longer the good" (*Personne et amour dans la théologie trinitaire de saint Thomas d'Aquin* [Paris: Vrin, 1956], 126). For a personalist perspective of fulfilment through communion from a phenomenological perspective that opposes Sartrian existentialism, see Antonio Malo, *Transcending Gender Ideology: A Philosophy of Sexual Difference*, trans. Alice Pavey (Washington, DC: The Catholic University of America Press, 2020).

[83] Sartre, *Being and Nothingness*, 725. Consequently, it is "impossible to find in every man some universal essence" (Sartre, *Existentialism and Human Emotions*, 38).

[84] Sartre, *Being and Nothingness*, 726.

[85] Sartre, *Existentialism and Human Emotions*, 33. Hence, as Judith Butler reads Sartre, desires seem to be "an assertion of freedom in the face of factic limitations" (Butler, *Subjects of Desire*, 169).

[86] De Beauvoir, *Ethics of Ambiguity*, 13.

[87] De Beauvoir, *Ethics of Ambiguity*, 47.

"nausea"[88]—are all said to reveal the "nothingness" that emerges when man distances himself from the objective world of things. Indeed, Sartrian desire "is identical with lack of being," a lack which is symbolized by the hole: "the empty image of myself" or "a nothingness 'to be filled' with my own flesh."[89] Man's pursuit of himself is thus symbolized by "plugging up holes," "filling empty places," or "*establishing* a plentitude" (as differing from the Aristotelian-Thomistic presentation of desire as *striving for* a normative plenitude). Hence, for example, by putting his fingers in his mouth or by sucking his thumb, a young child is said by Sartre to "wall up the holes in his face." Similarly, the act of eating is perceived by Sartre as an effort to "cement" shut the mouth's opening. And such is also the manner in which, Sartre suggests, we might consider the "obscenity of the feminine sex." Its opening gap is "*an appeal to being* [which herein assumes the form of a penis] as all holes are."[90] It is no wonder that Beauvoir recognizes woman as "the second sex": the one who is "defined and differentiated with reference to man," who alone represents a certain fullness, "and not he with reference to her."[91]

In fact, from the Sartrian perspective, it is the negative (the refusal of a given essence or of an objective existence in which "existential conversion" is said to consist[92]) that provokes the positive (the project that constitutes one's existence and the emergence of an objective world by the conscious act of transcending it[93]), the void that appeals to fullness, the admission of nothingness that triggers the desire for being. It is "desire which creates the desirable, and the project [chosen by each man for himself] which sets up [or determines] the end."[94] We are worlds away from the profoundly positive character of the Aristotelian-Thomistic perspective, which appeals to fullness or perfection as normative with respect to both being (ontology) and acting (ethics) and

88 For Sartre, the term refers to a physical sensation whereby the contingency of the body is revealed to consciousness. See, for example, Sartre, *Being and Nothingness*, 450–51.

89 Sartre, *Being and Nothingness*, 725, 781.

90 Sartre, *Being and Nothingness*, 782. Emphasis added in the first case; given in the second. The hole, Sartre explains, is "an excavation which can be carefully moulded about my flesh in such a manner that by squeezing myself into it and fitting myself tightly inside it, I shall contribute to making a fullness of being exist in the world" (781).

91 De Beauvoir, *Second Sex*, xxii. Hence, to continue, "she is the incidental, the inessential as opposed to the essential. He is the Subject, he is the Absolute—she is the Other."

92 De Beauvoir, *Ethics of Ambiguity*, 13.

93 To be a *pour-soi* "is to surpass the world and to cause there to be a world by surpassing it," Sartre explains (*Being and Nothingness*, 430). In other words, it is in the act of consciousness with respect to an objective world that I transcend it and simultaneously make it to be reality for myself. "If I am in the midst of the world, this is because," Sartre explains, "I have caused the world to-be-there by transcending being toward myself" (429).

94 De Beauvoir, *Ethics of Ambiguity*, 18.

thus also to freedom and desire. For Sartre, only the imaginary realm of art and literature can temporarily relieve consciousness "of its estrangement from plenitude," as Butler acknowledges.[95]

Because, in short, Sartre portrays desires as products of the free will, they remain radically unanchored with respect to anything resembling or connected to human nature, including natural ends such as sexual union and procreation, of course, but also happiness itself, which—as the final end of human nature and thus as the cause of causes (*causa causarum*)—is said by St. Thomas to motivate all authentically human actions and all human desires.[96] That is why the human will must, by necessity, Aquinas teaches, adhere to happiness as its last end.[97] "For our will to be happy does not appertain to free will," the Angelic Doctor explains, "but to natural instinct."[98]

MY BODY, *HIS* DESIRE: OBSTACLES TO SARTRIAN FREEDOM

As for "second-wave" trans-theorist Andrea Long Chu, who obviously follows Sartre over Aquinas, "desire and happiness are independent agents," and that is why "transition doesn't have to make me happy for me to want it."[99] Chu—a natal man who identifies as a trans woman—argues against the assumption that people transition "because they think it will make them feel better." Chu knows from experience that nothing could be further from the truth. "I feel demonstrably worse since I started on hormones," Chu reports. "Her" estrogen pills come with "delayed-release sadness," guaranteeing "a good weep within six to eight hours," and "her" dysphoria—like that of "many" of Chu's trans friends—has "balloon[ed]" since transition began.[100] In other words, Chu is

95 Butler, *Subjects of Desire*, 158.

96 See Aquinas, *ST* I–II, q. 5, a. 2, ad 1; I, q. 60, a. 2.

97 See Aquinas, *ST* I, q. 82, a. 1.

98 Aquinas, *ST* I, q. 19, a. 10.

99 Andrea Long Chu, "My New Vagina Won't Make Me Happy. And It Shouldn't Have To," *New York Times* (November 24, 2018), https://www.nytimes.com/2018/11/24/opinion/sunday/vaginoplasty-transgender-medicine.html. On Chu as a "second-wave" gender theorist, see Sessi Kuwabara Blanchard, "Andrea Long Chu Is the Cult Writer Changing Gender Theory," *Vice* (September 11, 2018), https://www.vice.com/en/article/ev74m7/andrea-long-chu-interview-avital-ronell-gender.

100 "Dysphoria," Chu explains, "is notoriously difficult to describe to those who haven't experienced it, like a flavor. . . . Dysphoria feels like being unable to get warm, no matter how many layers you put on. It feels like hunger without appetite. It feels like getting on an airplane to fly home, only to realize mid-flight that this is it: You're going to spend the rest of your life on an airplane. It feels like grieving. It feels like having nothing to grieve" (Chu, "My New Vagina Won't Make Me Happy").

acutely aware of all that remains of "her" maleness under the new female mask.[101] We are not far from the Sartrian notion of "nausea": the contingency of the body made known to consciousness. Chu cannot be accused of bad faith, however. The young trans-theorist admits of being suicidal, which was not previously the case; and it is with remarkable lucidity that Chu acknowledges: "my new vagina won't make me happy."

> Until the day I die, my body will regard the vagina as a wound; as a result, it will require regular, painful attention to maintain. This is what I want, but there is no guarantee it will make me happier. In fact, I don't expect it to. That shouldn't disqualify me from getting it.[102]

In this way, Chu's plea—this is no apology!—for the right to surgery breaks radically with more traditional arguments in favor of the universal right to basic human goods: goods that are measured by the plenitude of a common human nature. Of course, Chu knows the Hippocratic oath, "Do no harm," as well as Paul McHugh's argument against "cooperating with mental illness," which we considered in chapter 1.[103] Even Chu's own father, a pediatrician, "would no sooner prescribe puberty blockers to a gender dysphoric child than he would give a distemper shot to someone who believed she was a dog." Chu is nonetheless convinced that "the negative passions—grief, self-loathing, shame, regret—are as much a human right as universal health care, or food." Hence, "no amount of pain, anticipated or continuing" justifies withholding transition surgery. In fact, Chu's argument is not about goods at all—"there are no good outcomes in transition," Chu admits, but only desires that are determined by consciousness (as Sartre would have it) and thus "people, begging to be taken seriously." In short, "surgery's only prerequisite should be a simple demonstration of want."[104] This conclusion follows as a logical consequence of the presentation of freedom as the origin of desires, which in turn are tools for constructing the self-made man or the man-made female, whom we will encounter in our next chapter.

It is in this same—profoundly atheistic—spirit that transgender activist Jay Stewart presents human rights as based "upon the idea of pursuing that which we wish to become." Far from limiting ourselves to "biological determinism,"

[101] Chu gives the example of being acutely aware of the size of "her" index finger and of "patronizing" remarks about "her" "beauty."

[102] Chu, "My New Vagina Won't Make Me Happy."

[103] See McHugh, "Surgical Sex: Why We Stopped Doing Sex Change Operations," *First Things* (November 2004), http://www.firstthings.com/article/2004/11/surgical-sex, as referenced by Chu, "My New Vagina Won't Make Me Happy."

[104] Chu, "My New Vagina Won't Make Me Happy."

and thus to the "absurd" notion that one's sex is based "on the visual, physical, sex characteristics" known as "genitalia" (conveniently divorced, we might add, from the consideration of the reproductive sexual powers that will be considered in chapter 5), Stewart suggests that we break out of the "comfort zone of essentialism": the idea that there is something "permanent . . . to what we are as individuals," something based upon a given, or created, nature. It is "absurd" that we should be legally limited to two sex options (male and female) when Facebook offers seventy-two, Stewart argues. After all, it is only by defying nature (or "essentialism") that we might be free, Stewart believes, to pursue "that which we wish to become."[105] Similarly, Martine Rothblatt argues that instead of "impos[ing]" a "male or female label" upon people prior to their choice, "gender exploration should come first," and sex should be freely chosen. Hence, "sex is just the label for one's chosen gender."[106]

Stewart's and Rothblatt's assumption that freedom to self-determination requires "freedom" from nature reads as a paraphrase of a 1992 US Supreme Court decision that almost explicitly defies the doctrine of creation: "At the heart of liberty is the right to define one's own concept of existence, of meaning, of the universe, and of the mystery of human life."[107] Ultimately, in fact and in sum, we are faced with the choice between the wise man (*homo sapiens*), who is called to "direct and regulate his life and actions and . . . make use of his own body" in accord with the Creator's purposes, as inscribed within man's natural inclinations to goodness and truth, and the Sartrian man, who is at the helm of his own destiny and free to make of himself what he will.[108]

Sartre's profoundly uninhibited view of human freedom is nonetheless characterized by a twofold obstacle: the reality of the human body and the givenness of the human "other." Not unlike the Butlerian attempt to theorize the human body as a social construct, Sartre presents one's personal body as necessarily mediated to the conscious subject, or *pour-soi*, by other conscious beings, who perceive him differently than he perceives himself. Hence, for example, "in one sense" my body "is what I am," but "in another sense," Sartre admits, "I am separated from it"—so separated, in fact, that it is revealed

[105] Stewart, "We Are Living on the Cusp of a Gender Revolution."

[106] Rothblatt, *From Transgender to Transhuman: A Manifesto on the Freedom of Form*, ed. Nickolas Mayer (self-pub., 2011), 12.

[107] Planned Parenthood v. Casey, 505 U.S. 833 (1992), available at the Legal Information Institute of Cornell Law School, https://www.law.cornell.edu/supct/html/91-744.ZO.html.

[108] Congregation for the Doctrine of the Faith, introduction to the Instruction on the Respect for Human Life in Its Origin and on the Dignity of Procreation: Replies to Certain Questions of the Day *Donum vitae* (February 22, 1987), no. 3; cited by John Paul II, Encyclical Letter *Veritatis Splendor* (August 6, 1993), §50.

to me by other conscious beings, even in the very act whereby I objectify them.[109] "I never apprehend the Other as body without at the same time in a non-explicit manner apprehending my body as the center of reference indicated by the Other."[110] Or, to put it differently, it is only through the process of objectifying another *pour-soi* that I become conscious of my own self as an objective being (an *en-soi*). Meanwhile, the Other is also apprehending me. He "*looks* at me," thereby rendering me an objective being (an *en-soi*) and simultaneously making me conscious of my own objectivity. In this way he is said by Sartre to hold "the secret of my being, he knows what I *am*."[111] That is to say, he possesses knowledge of me that is beyond my own hold or beyond the realm of my own consciousness. In fact, "to get any truth about myself," the French philosopher recognizes that "I must have contact with another person," who alone can reveal me—as an objective being—to myself.[112] What the Other reveals is, more specifically, "*my being* . . . but at a distance," whence the challenge of "mak[ing] myself be by acquiring the possibility of taking the Other's point of view on myself."[113]

Such is the origin, as Sartre sees it, of the necessarily conflictual mode of existence in a world inhabited by others.[114] Even "love is a conflict" for the famous French existentialist.[115] For although Sartre recognizes personal freedom as unlimited in itself, he nonetheless admits that the *pour-soi* is constantly rubbing up against the freedom of others, by whom he can be seen and even manipulated in virtue of his body. The Other "reveals to me the being which I am without my being able either to appropriate that being or even to conceive it."[116] In fact, the only objective knowledge that I possess of myself is that which is imparted by

---

[109] Sartre, *Being and Nothingness*, 429.

[110] Sartre, *Being and Nothingness*, 451.

[111] Sartre, *Being and Nothingness*, 473 (emphasis original). Hence, as Judith Butler explains, "the agent of desire can make use of the Other's gaze as the instrument of its own self-objectification" (*Subjects of Desire*, 141).

[112] Sartre, *Existentialism and Human Emotions*, 37–38. More explicitly, "If someone looks at me, I am conscious of *being* an object" (*Being and Nothingness*, 363). Sartre goes so far as to claim that "the other is indispensable to my own existence, as well as to my knowledge about myself" (*Existentialism and Human Emotions*, 38). In short, "To be other to oneself—the ideal always aimed at concretely in the form of being *this Other* to oneself—is the primary value of my relations with the Other" (*Being and Nothingness*, 476).

[113] Sartre, *Being and Nothingness*, 475 (emphasis original). In this way, "I identify myself totally with my being-looked-at" (476).

[114] "Conflict is the original meaning of being-for-others" (Sartre, *Being and Nothingness*, 475). In the first instance, this is due to the fact that "from the moment that I exist I establish a factual limit to the Other's freedom. I *am* this limit, and each of my projects traces the outline of this limit around the Other" (530).

[115] See Sartre, *Being and Nothingness*, 477.

[116] Sartre, *Being and Nothingness*, 473.

the Other, Sartre claims. After all, such (objective) knowledge necessarily differs from what is comprehended by way of personal consciousness.

If, then, the Other might be said to "possess" me, this does not mean that he might penetrate or violate my consciousness but only that he has access to my body in a way that I do not. As if to prepare the way for Butler's presentation of the body as "materialized" by social norms, as we saw in chapter 2, Sartre maintains that by his look, or gaze (*son regard*), the Other "fashions my body in its nakedness, causes it to be born, sculptures it, produces it as it *is*, sees it as I shall never see it." He—not I!—is thus the foundation of my *objective* (as differing from my conscious, or subjective) existence, of my "being-for-others." But because my consciousness remains my own, so does my responsibility for my being, which the Other has nonetheless "stolen . . . from me." That is why responsibility for one's own being is experienced as an effort to recuperate it from the Other's grasp: to "*lay claim* to this being which I am" in view of becoming "the foundation of myself."[117]

This, in fact, is the inescapable Sartrian dilemma: although my consciousness renders me a being-for-myself (a *pour-soi*)—a being who is absolutely free to create his own destiny—my corporeality makes me vulnerable, even captive, to other consciousnesses who are constantly making of me a being-for-others: an objective being upon whom others have a hold.[118] Their freedom is such that it "moulds my being and *makes me* be, it confers values upon me and removes them from me."[119] It follows that the Sartrian presentation of desire as a structure of consciousness is nonetheless deviated or perverted by the Other, for whom I am perceived as an incarnate being to be manipulated (an object: *en-soi*).[120] My relations with others are thus entirely governed by my manner of interiorizing what they reveal of my objective being.[121] Because I am, in fact, constantly seeking to recover my being from their objectifying gaze, I become, as Sartre puts it, "the project of the recovery of my being": a project that is achieved by squelching, or "absorbing," the Other's freedom, as he has done to me.[122] That

[117] Sartre, *Being and Nothingness*, 475 (emphasis original).

[118] "My freedom is alienated in the presence of the Other's pure subjectivity which founds," Sartre explains, "my objectivity" (*Being and Nothingness*, 489).

[119] Sartre, *Being and Nothingness*, 433, 477.

[120] "Desire is consciousness since it can *be* only as a non-positional consciousness of itself" (Sartre, *Being and Nothingness*, 502). Hence, desire "does not come *to* consciousness as heat comes *to* the piece of iron which I hold near the flame. Consciousness chooses itself as desire," and that is why "there must be a motive" to desire (508; emphasis original).

[121] See Sartre, *Being and Nothingness*, 473. As for the Other, "he flees me when I seek him and possesses me when I flee him" (529).

[122] "My project of recovering myself is fundamentally a project of absorbing the Other," Sartre explains (*Being and Nothingness*, 475).

is why the *defensive* project of recovering my own being implies the *offensive* "project of assimilating and making an object of the Other."[123] Human relations are thus animal-like—dog-eat-dog—except that they always involve a clever game of freedom lost and freedom regained.[124]

We are far from the "ongoing exodus out of the closed inward-looking self," who finds "liberation through self-giving," as Pope Benedict XVI describes the Christian life.[125] After all, the Sartrian man, who lays down his freedom at another's foot, hardly finds himself thereby. To "respect" another's freedom entails for the French philosopher nothing less than that "I identify myself totally with my being-looked-at," with, that is to say, the Other's lustful or utilitarian conception of me.[126] The manipulated self then manipulates in turn (by the power of seduction) such that—as the trans-theorist Andrea Chu sees it—one's own "vanity" becomes "the expression of someone else's narcissism."[127] As for Sartre, it is not surprising that he recognizes unity with the Other as "unrealizable."[128] For him, a sexual relation is the very epitome of the conflictual mode of being with others. Either I reduce the Other to an object (sadism) or I become an object for him (masochism).[129] In the first case, I seek to take hold of "the Other's free subjectivity through his objectivity-for-me."[130] I "plunge" his "freedom into flesh without ceasing to be the one who *provokes*, who grabs hold, who seizes, etc."[131] In the second case, "I make myself in shame an object of desire."[132] That is, "I make myself flesh so as to fascinate the Other by my nakedness and to provoke in her the desire for my flesh."[133]

In both cases, the *pour-soi* (or the conscious subject) encourages the Other to compromise his personal freedom by succumbing to his own body, or by

---

[123] Sartre, *Being and Nothingness*, 474.

[124] "My project of recovering my being can be realized only if I get hold of this [the Other's] freedom and reduce it to being a freedom subject to my freedom" (Sartre, *Being and Nothingness*, 477). Such is the never-ending "circle" (474): "I can turn back upon the Other so as to make an object out of him in turn since the Other's object-ness destroys my object-ness for him" (473).

[125] Pope Benedict XVI, Encyclical Letter on Christian Love *Deus Caritas Est* (December 25, 2005), §6.

[126] Sartre, *Being and Nothingness*, 476.

[127] Andrea Long Chu, *Females* (New York: Verso, 2019), 27.

[128] Sartre, *Being and Nothingness*, 477.

[129] Hence as Butler summarizes, "sexual exchange is a 'circle' in which the inversion of sadism into masochism, and masochism into sadism, follows according to the ontological necessity that every determinate individual is what he is not, and is not what he is" (*Subjects of Desire*, 139).

[130] Sartre, *Being and Nothingness*, 497. Precisely this attempt is what Sartre calls "sexual desire."

[131] Sartre, *Being and Nothingness*, 519 (emphasis original).

[132] Sartre, *Being and Nothingness*, 492. Masochism, Sartre explains, occurs when "consciousness apprehending itself in its facticity demands to be apprehended and transcended as body-for-the-Other by means of the Other's consciousness" (516).

[133] Sartre, *Being and Nothingness*, 514.

"mentally enchain[ing] him," thanks to "the complicity of his own flesh."[134] One need only recall Sartre's presentation of the "obscenity of the feminine sex" with its gaping hole: a hole that "appeals to a strange flesh" (the penis) in view of plugging or filling it, thereby "transform[ing] her into a fullness of being by penetration" (masochism). But Sartre recognizes that this same hole is also "a mouth and a voracious mouth which devours the penis—a fact which can easily lead to the idea of castration" (sadism).[135] Hence, the one who is desired is not simply an object, for she is capable of using her freedom to trap, by means of seduction—including what Chu calls the "vigorous, compulsive submission to technique"—the very one whose look intends to trap her by reducing her to an object of his pleasure.[136]

In short, for Sartre, sexual relations are highly dangerous to human freedom. "Let any man consult his own experience; he knows how consciousness is clogged, so to speak, by sexual desire." Despite Sartre's strongest conviction that man is nothing more than his freedom and that desire is merely an expression thereof, the famous French philosopher is thus forced to admit that in the experience of sexual desire "one is invaded by facticity, that one ceases to flee." In other words, one "slides toward a *passive* consent to desire": a desire that "*takes hold of you*," that "*overwhelms you*," that even "*paralyzes you*."[137] Such, in fact, is the experience of "the necessity" of one's own "contingency," "the clogging of a consciousness by its facticity," or "the ensnarement of a body by the world."[138]

COMPROMISED FREEDOM AND SECOND-WAVE GENDER THEORY

In this way, Sartre sets a precedent for gender theorists. As if to reverse the Sartrian formula that desires are projections of human consciousness, or freedom, Andrea Chu suggests that consciousness is actually projected by desires: desires not of our own making, however, but those that are forced upon us instead. For Chu, this is what it means to be "female": "to become what someone else wants," and even to be "made into an incubator for an alien force."[139] These

[134] Suzanne Lilar, *A propos de Sartre et de l'amour* (Paris: Gaillimard, 1984), 62.

[135] Sartre, *Being and Nothingness*, 782.

[136] Chu, *Females*, 29–30.

[137] Sartre, *Being and Nothingness*, 504 (emphasis original).

[138] Sartre, *Being and Nothingness*, 505, 509. Consciousness is "ensnared" in the body when it is "no more than consciousness (of) the body and consequently a reflective consciousness *of* corporeality" (515; emphasis original).

[139] Chu, *Females*, 74, 11. Still more straightforwardly, Chu defines as female "any psychic operation in which the self is sacrificed to make room for the desires of another" (11).

statements ought not, however, to be read in line with Beauvoir's treatment of woman as the "second sex." To be sure, Chu does share Beauvoir's conviction that one is not *born* female. "Femaleness is not an anatomical or genetic characteristic of an organism," the controversial trans-theorist maintains, "but a universal existential condition." And this in turn means that it is inescapable. "Everyone is female," Chu writes unabashedly; and what's more, "everyone hates it" (and rightly so: being a female is "always bad for you").[140]

This, of course, is where Chu takes leave of Beauvoir. As the latter observes, "man" is both a generic term for all that is human (so as to include the concept of woman) and a gendered term (specifying the male sex). That is to say, "man" is the universal against whom "woman" is defined as a relative term and consequently a relative being. For Beauvoir,

> A man never begins by presenting himself as an individual of a certain sex; it goes without saying that he is a man. The terms *masculine* and *feminine* are used symmetrically only as a matter of form, as on legal papers. In actuality, the relation of the two sexes is not quite like that of two electrical poles, for man represents both the positive and the neutral, as is indicated by the common use of *man* to designate human beings in general; whereas woman represents only the negative, defined by limiting criteria, without reciprocity. . . . [In short,] there is an absolute human type, the masculine.[141]

Chu, in contrast, explains that the "one and only structure of human consciousness" is the female version, namely, "a universal sex defined by self-negation."[142] Hence, "to be female"—and remember, *everyone* is female—"is to let someone else do your desiring for you, at your own expense."[143] "At bottom" (undoubtedly the pun is intended), "everyone is a sissy."[144]

If Chu departs from Beauvoir, "she" nonetheless encounters Sartre in his doctrine of consciousness (or *freedom*) compromised by sexual desire. It is not, however, in the *sadistic* desire to submit the Other to one's own fantasies that Chu meets Sartre but in the *masochistic* desire to be willingly so submitted: in the desire to freely become, as Sartre would have it, "body-for-the-Other"

140 Chu, *Females*, 11.

141 De Beauvoir, *Second Sex*, xxi.

142 Chu, *Females*, 12.

143 Chu, *Females*, 11.

144 Chu, *Females*, 74.

and to "identify" oneself "totally with my being-looked-at."[145] Or, from Chu's perspective, such is the desire to be reduced to nothing more than a body, like Gigi Gorgeous, who has "sanded her personality down to the bare essentials." In what has become an unending male-to-female transition, Gorgeous is wholly and obediently submitted to technique: "the stroke of a contouring brush, the precise curve of a breast. If it's not perfect, it must be done again." After all—at least as Chu sees it—"gender transition, no matter the direction, is always a process of becoming a canvas for someone else's fantasy. You cannot be gorgeous without someone to be gorgeous *for*." Because Gigi Gorgeous has hollowed out "her" inner self to make room for others' desires, "she is miraculously free of serious opinions. She has become, in the most technical sense of this phrase, a dumb blonde."[146] It is no wonder that Chu, who is no dummy, "env[ies] her tremendously."[147] In fact, Gorgeous probably doesn't even realize that "she" does "not get to consent" to "her" self, even though "she" "might deserve the chance."[148] Gorgeous is one who has, as Sartre would have it, freely and entirely identified with "being-looked-at" or with "being-as-object" so as to be willingly assimilated to "the *other freedom*."[149]

To be sure, this is not an argument—pace Sartre—about forcing anyone "into complicity with his body."[150] Rather, from the viewpoint of "*her*" (Chu's) extremely limited experience of living as a woman[151] and of *his* (likewise Chu's) longer experience of "liking women," indistinguishable from the experience of "wanting to be like them,"[152] Chu seeks to point out what many of us have apparently taken for granted: the "fact" that no one is really looking for the body of his dreams. What we all really want is the body of *someone else's* dreams. And it is this desire, namely the desire *to be desired*, that makes of us—all of us—"female." "To be female," Chu claims, "is, in every case, to become what someone else wants."[153] In point of fact, "if there is any lesson of gender transition—from

[145] Sartre, *Being and Nothingness*, 516, 476.

[146] Chu, *Females*, 30. In this way, "she" incarnates Chu's presentation of what it means to "be" "female." See Chu, 11.

[147] Chu, *Females*, 29.

[148] Chu, *Females*, 38.

[149] Sartre, *Being and Nothingness*, 476.

[150] Leak, *Perverted Consciousness*, 66.

[151] Chu's book was released within months of her vaginoplasty.

[152] Chu claims, "I have never been able to differentiate liking women from wanting to be like them" (Andrea Long Chu, "On Liking Women," *N+1 Magazine* 30 [Winter 2018], https://nplusonemag.com/issue-30/essays/on-liking-women/). The latter, Chu explains, is what Valerie Solanas calls "pussy envy."

[153] Chu, *Females*, 74.

the simplest request regarding pronouns to the most invasive surgeries—it's that gender is something other people have to *give* you."[154]

At this point, Chu's book, which claims to be about something other than gender, shows its true face as a much-developed theory of "gender" (at least as activists interpret the word), a theory that goes beyond the central claim of first-wave theorists, who argue that gender is socially constructed.[155] That position is "wildly incomplete," as Chu sees it; for "what makes gender *gender*—the substance of gender, as it were—is the fact that it expresses, in every case, the desires of another." Hence, to further articulate: "If sexual orientation is basically the social expression of one's own sexuality, then gender is basically a social expression of someone *else's* sexuality. In the former case, one takes an object [what Sartre calls *masochism*]; in the latter case, one *is* an object [what he identifies as *sadism*]. From the perspective of gender, then, we are all dumb blondes."[156] Instead of making men out of women, as Beauvoir recommends that we do in her Sartrian form of feminism, Chu makes women out of men.[157] In so doing, "she" willingly abandons what Butler identifies as the "posture of freedom": the attitude of one constantly seeking to recover his or her freedom from the objectifying regard of the Other.[158] Whether literally or figuratively, Chu would have us believe that we all opt for the opposing attitude of laying our freedom down: not, to be sure, in view of self-transcendence through communion but by folding to the desires of others for the sake of self-affirmation. Far from boosting our self-regard, however, the desire to be desired only empties us of our own desires and sends us to the "simulator" (to borrow from Chu, who borrows from *The Matrix*), whereby we are continuously conformed to stereotypes dictated by foreign desires.[159] For Chu this means—as "she" readily acknowledges—being willfully dependent upon two daily dosages of estrogen.

The performative self is thus swallowed by the script and the Sartrian attempt to safeguard human freedom from the "threat" of natural inclinations backfires, producing a mutiny of desires to which freedom is subjected. As Chu sees it, anyway, we are all controlled by desires: not those that are grounded in

---

[154] Chu, *Females*, 38.

[155] Chu, *Females*, 12: "When I talk about females [which is, of course, the title of Chu's book], . . . I'm not talking about gender."

[156] Chu, *Females*, 35–36.

[157] Admitting that it is woman's "misfortune" to be "biologically destined" (de Beauvoir, *Second Sex*, 64) to transmit life and thus "more enslaved to the species" than is man (255), Beauvoir counsels her to flee the body and its constraints: to rise above the so-called "animal" act of *giving* life and to participate instead in the properly masculine act of *risking* life. See *Second Sex*, 64.

[158] Butler, *Subjects of Desire*, 142.

[159] See Chu, *Females*, 52–55.

the body, but those that ground the body, forcing it to become nothing more than "a grid" for the inscription of these same desires, especially those of others and one's own cooperating desire to be desired.[160] In the powerful words of Angela Franks, "desire becomes the autonomous agent, replacing the personal subject," who is reduced to a simple "by-product."[161] Thus understood, "desire" is no longer akin to the natural impulses originating within the inner depth of the subject and drawing him to objects or persons which/who are *attractive* because they are *good* (and considered as such, because they contribute to personal fulfillment or to a plentitude of being). On the contrary, they operate as forces of constraint, bearing down upon us from without and *impeding our good* by diverting our personal fulfillment—or at least our own self-projects, as Sartre would have it—in favor of the freedom and projects of others. In the end, as Chu puts it in characteristically provocative style, "Isn't that the whole point of gender—letting someone else do your living for you?"[162]

[160] See Angela Franks, "Deleuze, Balthasar, and John Paul II on the Aesthetics of the Body," *Theological Studies* 81, no. 3 (2020): 649–70.

[161] Angela Franks, "Deleuze on Desire," *First Things* 302 (April 2020), https://www.firstthings.com/article/2020/04/deleuze-on-desire.

[162] Chu, *Females*, 55.

CHAPTER 5

Morphology vs. Biology? Conflicting Views of the Body

The Sartrian presentation of freedom as *compromised* by desire is—to summarize the foregoing—a far cry from the Aristotelian-Thomistic conception of freedom as *fostered* by natural desires, which are said to provide order to the natural law precepts. In fact, it is of no little significance to the subject at hand—that of the relation between the human body and human freedom—that the inclination to reproduce and to raise offspring is counted by St. Thomas among these most basic inclinations.[1] So fundamental to nature, and thus to natural law, is in fact the inclination to generate—or, in the case of the human being, to *procreate*[2]—that the word *nature* has, as Marie-Joseph Nicolas observes, "come to designate that which is the very end of generation, that is to say, the essence of the species that is communicated by generation."[3] Indeed, as Aristotle would have it:

1 See Aquinas, *ST* I–II, q. 94, a. 2. This natural inclination to reproduce and to raise offspring is listed as the third of five natural inclinations by St. Thomas, being preceded by (1) the natural yearning for the good and (2) the inclination to preserve one's being and followed by (4) the yearning for truth and (5) the natural inclination to live in society. Pinckaers points out that "Thomas' perspective is already substantially present in Cicero in a text that Thomas seems never to have read (*De officiis* 1.4)" (Servais Pinckaers, *Morality: The Catholic View*, trans. Michael Sherwin [South Bend, IN: St. Augustine's Press, 2001], 98).

2 Marie-Joseph Nicolas has good reason to argue, with reference to Thomas Aquinas, that "the intention of nature in human sexuality is not like that of animal sexuality to safeguard the species: it is to procreate a human person who is significant in him- or herself (*etiam individua sunt de principali intentione naturae*), and consequently to lead him or her to full stature and autonomy by means of education" (Nicolas, "L'idée de nature dans la pensée de saint Thomas d'Aquin," *Revue thomiste* 74, no. 4 [1974]: 571). Cf. Aquinas, *ST* I, q. 98, a. 1. Similarly, Pinckaers argues that sexual inclination in the human being, as differing from that of animals, "is not solely biological, even though this component is a characteristic feature of it. It engages the entire personality through the bonds of affection," whence the distinction between the two ends of marriage: the procreative and the unitive ends of marriage. These Pinckaers recognizes as "naturally aid[ing] each other" (*Morality: The Catholic View*, 103–104).

3 Nicolas, "L'idée de nature," 543; cf. Aquinas, *ST* III, q. 2, a. 1. Similarly, the word gender "binds the resemblance among individuals to their generation [*engenderment*]," as Sylviane Agacinski fittingly points out. "The word *gender* is tied to generation and generality, as words of the same family (generic, genetic,

> The most natural act is the production of another like itself, an animal an animal, a plant a plant, in order that, as far as its nature allows, it may partake in the eternal and divine. That is the goal towards which all things strive, that for the sake of which they do whatsoever their nature renders possible. Since then no living thing is able to partake in what is eternal and divine by uninterrupted continuance (for nothing perishable can forever remain one and the same), it tries to achieve that end in the only way possible to it . . . ; so it remains not indeed as the self-same individual but continues in something like itself—not numerically, but specifically one [i.e., of the same species].[4]

In short, a natural thing is considered "perfect" by the Aristotelian-Thomistic tradition "when it can reproduce its like."[5]

What we might draw from this understanding of perfection for our present study is that the natural inclination to reproduction—not unlike the other natural inclinations—implies a real power that is not reducible to morphology, as the transgender lobby would have us believe. For, by reason of our generation, we are naturally empowered to engender. In virtue of so-called sex-change operations, in contrast, these engendering powers are usurped, and the body is artificially equipped to feign reproductive acts that are necessarily devoid of their life-giving potency.

GENERATIVE POWERS VS. GENERATING POWERS: NATURE VS. ARTIFICE

Such is the distinction between natural generation and human (in this case, surgical) art, which in turn implies the distinction between a living body, replete with its natural powers, and a simple artifact. One need only consider the "artifice of gender" and the "hallmarks of the sexualized performance of femininity," which conveniently hid Caitlyn Jenner's penis during "her" famous coming-out in *Vanity Fair* in 2015: "the constructions, fabrications and deceptions of Jenner's airbrushed and silicone body," including "the state of semi-undress in a satin corset; long, tumbling hair; exposed 'look-at-me'

---

genital, gene, genius, genesis, *gens* and *gent*, genealogy, and let us not forget generosity)." (Agacinski, *Femmes entre sexe et genre* [Paris: Editions du Seuil, 2012], 61).

4 Aristotle, *De Anima*, trans. J. A. Smith, in *The Complete Works of Aristotle: The Revised Oxford Translation*, vol. 1, ed. Jonathan Barnes (Princeton, NJ: Princeton University Press, 1984), 2.4.415a28–415b3 (p. 661) (hereafter, *De An.*). Cf. Aquinas, *ST* I, q. 78, a. 2.

5 Aquinas, *ST* I, q. 5, a. 4.

breasts in a push-up bra; and a cinched waist to give an hour-glass figure," as Heather Brunskell-Evans observes, in words that nearly cost her her university post.[6] It is no wonder that *Vanity Fair* gives credit not only to an author and a photograph but to a "stylist" as well.[7] In question, however, are not the creative powers of "the artists"—the surgeons, the stylists, and the photographers—in their attempts to reproduce a likeness to (or an assimilation of) a natal woman. For behind all that is "made up" is the denial, even refusal, of a *real* power to procreate. As Abigail Favale puts it in very poignant terms, if a surgeon today may be thought to make a vagina "out of a wound," this is the case only "because the vagina is no longer seen as the door to a womb."[8]

The most serious danger of these surgeries is, however, not simply that of feigning the natural, but of profoundly deforming—even sacrificing—it. In the case of Jenner, "her" so-called sexual-reassignment surgery actually obliterated his (pronoun intentional) productive powers. "It's just a penis," Jenner remarks rather flippantly. After all, the famous transgender advocate has already fathered six children with three consecutive wives. "It has no special gifts or use for me other than . . . the ability to take a whiz in the woods."[9] Nonetheless, as Sylviane Agacinski observes with regard to such a controversial operation as Jenner's:

> Medicine does not construct; it reconstructs. Much more, it reconstructs in an approximate manner and, in the end, fabricates only morphological appearances, without functional biological powers. Surgery can suppress the organs of generation, but it does not know how to construct them, nor how to create *their powers*.[10]

These powers can only be transmitted by the act of generation, whose "ultimate term" is, as St. Thomas observes, the soul, wherein these powers reside as in their "subject" or "first act."[11] That is why already at birth—indeed even

6 Heather Brunskell-Evans, *Transgender Body Politics* (North Geelong, Australia: Spinifex, 2020), 3.

7 See Buzz Bissinger, "Caitlyn Jenner: The Full Story," photography by Annie Leibovitz, styled by Jessica Diehl, *Vanity Fair*, June 25, 2015, https://www.vanityfair.com/hollywood/2015/06/caitlyn-jenner-bruce-cover-annie-leibovitz.

8 Abigail Favale, "The Eclipse of Sex by the Rise of Gender," *Church Life Journal*, March 1, 2021, https://churchlifejournal.nd.edu/articles/the-eclipse-of-sex-by-the-rise-of-gender/.

9 Louise Randell, "I'm A Celeb: Star Caitlyn Jenner's Brave Confession about Gender Reassignment Surgery," *Mirror*, November 14, 2019, https://www.mirror.co.uk/3am/celebrity-news/im-celeb-star-caitlyn-jenners-20879863.

10 Agacinski, *Femmes entre sexe et genre*, 131 (emphasis original). See also Walt Heyer, "'Sex Change' Isn't Surgically Possible, My Surgeon Testified in Court," The Stream, February 24, 2020, https://stream.org/sex-change-isnt-surgically-possible-my-surgeon-testified-in-court/.

11 See Aquinas, *ST* I, q. 77, a. 1. To speak of the soul as "first act" means, more specifically, St. Thomas explains, that the soul "as subject of its powers" "is not always actual with respect to its vital operations." It is thus a first act with a "further relation to the second act" (*ST* I, q. 77, a. 1). Similarly, St. Thomas argues, "In

in utero—our bodies are marked with the visible signs of these powers (yet in potency) whereby we might ourselves become generators, likened unto either the mother or father who act together to engender.[12]

Such a likening of the engendered to those who engender is—it bears repeating—of the essence of what it means to be of any given species. For as the scientist, medical doctor, and man of letters Leon Kass remarks, the end, or *telos*, of natural generation is what Aristotle calls "the mature *eidos* (i.e., species or 'looks') of the particular organism in question."[13] If Kass insists upon this philosophical concept and the accompanying English translation, "looks," which admittedly appears odd in the context, his purpose is to emphasize that the species transmitted by natural generation is marked by certain visible characteristics (whence the Latin, *species*, signifying "appearance," "form," or "beauty"), recognizable to even the untrained scientist. These visible traits are not, however, to be misunderstood as *simply* apparent (perceived by sight alone), so as to lack any profundity beyond mere appearance. On the contrary, the word *eidos* is meant to "preserve Aristotle's appreciation" for the fact "that the distinctive look of an animal reveals what it is." In other words, "the 'inside' shines forth and makes itself known in its presentation on and to the 'outside'—in its appearance and in its visible activities. *Eidos* refers both to the *what* of the particular animal, as distinguished from its *hyle*, or material, *out of which* it is composed, and thus also to the *kind* or *species* of animal it is. Each dog," for example, "is what it is because it *is* dog."[14] Hence, the notion of *eidos* (or "look") is "more than shape and more than a mere aggregate of parts. It is a unified whole on display," as might also be expressed by the German word *Gestalt*. It is, "at least in speech, distinct from the materials that carry it, as the representation of a painting is other than the oils and canvas. The looks of animals differ, each more or less after its kind."[15]

To refer to the mature *eidos* as the end, or *telos*, of engenderment is thus to suggest that this end is, as Kass puts it, "a standard as well as a goal." In other words, the end of generation is a being likened unto those from whom it is engendered. The engendering animal is a model, as it were, for the one who is engendered. The former displays certain features that we expect to find in its

all things not generated by chance, the form must be the end of any generation whatsoever" (*ST* I, q. 15, a. 1).

12 As Sylviane Agacinski remarks, "sexual distinction is deduced from the conditions in which individuals are engendered one from another" (*Femmes entre sexe et genre*, 62).

13 Leon Kass, *Toward a More Natural Science: Biology and Human Affairs* (New York: The Free Press, 1985), 254.

14 Kass, *Toward a More Natural Science*, 259, footnote.

15 Kass, *Toward a More Natural Science*, 321.

progeny. And because this unmistakable species-specific "look" is not simply on the level of appearance but points to certain essential, or species-defining, traits that are transmitted from one generation to the next, they are best explained by what Kass calls "internal teleology" or by what Robert Spaemann calls a "'plan of construction,' which is not simply a function of the observer who discovers it or the user who invents it."[16]

REVISITING THE BODY-SOUL UNITY

In this way we are invited to revisit the question of sexual differentiation within the larger context of the study of life (biology), as differing from the physiochemical study of matter (anatomy and physics). Indeed, from a purely biological point of view, any member of a given species "comes to be as the result of numerous biochemical reactions, coded for, specified, regulated, directed, and ordered by the blueprint," for this particular being, a blueprint that really is *in* its DNA, which in turn is contained within the nucleus of the fertilized egg.[17] This "plan of construction," or blueprint, might also refer to what philosophers have traditionally identified as the soul: "the form," or "actuality," as Aristotle defines it, "of a natural body having life potentially within it."[18] As such, it does "not add anything to an existing entity or plurality of entities" but is rather "the structural principle of a living unity."[19]

The soul, in other words, is that which brings order or that which, as Aristotle puts it, renders "account of the thing": account not just of *any*thing—machines, for example, do not have souls, although they too are ordered—but, in the case at hand, that precise thing that is "a *natural* body . . . having *in itself* the power of setting itself in movement" and correlatively of bringing itself to rest.[20] A living body is a *self*-maintaining system, or structure, and not one that is maintained by an outside source, such as a user or an inventor. It is likewise, Kass points out, "self-producing, self-organizing, . . . self-preserving,

---

[16] Kass, *Toward a More Natural Science*, 257; Robert Spaemann, *Persons: The Difference between 'Someone' and 'Something,'* trans. Oliver O'Donovan (Oxford: Oxford University Press, 2012), 156.

[17] Leon Kass, "Teleology and Darwin's *The Origin of Species*: Beyond Chance and Necessity?," in *Organism, Medicine, and Metaphysics: Essays in Honor of Hans Jonas on His 75th Birthday, May 10, 1978*, ed. Stuart F. Spicker (Boston: D. Reidel Publishing Company, 1978), 100.

[18] Aristotle, *De An.* 2.1.412a 20–21 (Barnes, 656); cf. Aquinas, *ST* I, q. 76, a. 8, ad 2: "The soul is the act of an organic body."

[19] Spaemann, *Persons*, 155.

[20] Aristotle, *De An.* 2.1.412b11, 16–17 (Barnes, 657) (emphasis added). From an analytical perspective, see Gertrude Elizabeth M. Anscombe, "Embryos and Final Causes," in *Human Life, Action and Ethics*, ed. Mary Geach and Luke Gormally (Exeter, UK: Imprint Academic, 2005), 45–58.

. . . self-healing," and—it should be recalled—self-directing in view of an end that "is a standard [whence the idea of a 'blueprint'] as well as a goal."[21]

The Aristotelian definition of the soul as "the form of a natural body having life potentially within it" ought not, however, to mislead us into thinking that a soulless body is "potentially capable of living."[22] In other words, the soul cannot simply be *added* to a formless body to give it life. Nor, on the other hand, as St. Thomas points out, can the potentiality for life exclude the soul.[23] It is only the body united to the soul that is capable of life. Such is the meaning of Aristotle's precision that the soul is the *substantial* (as differing from an accidental) form of a natural body.[24] It is therefore "clear"—so says Aristotle—that "the soul is inseparable from its body," allowance being made for the immortality of the specifically human soul.[25] So inseparable is the soul from the body, in fact, that the former is "in the whole body, and in each part thereof," and this in turn explains, Aquinas reasons, why "no part of the body retains its proper action" when the soul withdraws from the body.[26] To ask whether the soul and the living body are one is thus to raise a false question, like asking "whether the wax and its shape are one," or still more generally, Aristotle continues, "[whether] the matter of a thing [say the wood that constitutes a table] and that of which it is the matter [the table itself]" are one.[27]

Of course, wood can exist without being made into a table, and a table can be made of matter other than wood. That is why the form of the table is said to be *accidental* with respect to the wood, but not with respect to the table.[28] In the absence of the form introduced by the intermediary of a carpenter, wood

---

[21] Kass, *Toward a More Natural Science*, 256–57.

[22] See Aristotle, *De An.* 2.1.412b25–27 (Barnes, 657).

[23] See Aquinas, *ST* I, q. 77, a. 1.

[24] See Aristotle, *De An.* 2.1.412a20 (Barnes, 656). An accident may come and go, but a substantial form is "indivisible from the matter it actualizes" (Robert Pasnau, *Thomas Aquinas on Human Nature: A Philosophical Study of* Summa theologiae *Ia 75–89* [Cambridge: Cambridge University Press, 2002], 93). That is why, "when the soul leaves the body there is no longer an eye, [n]or flesh except in name" (Aquinas, *Commentary on Aristotle's* De Anima, Bk II, lect. 2, no. 237, trans. Kenelm Foster and Silvester Humphries [Notre Dame, IN: Dumb Ox Books, 1994]).

[25] Aristotle, *De An.*, 2.1.413a4 (Barnes, 657). However, the functioning of the soul's intellectual operation requires that it be united to the body, and that is why the separated soul retains "an aptitude and a natural inclination to be united to the body," St. Thomas argues (*ST* I, q. 76, a. 1, ad 6). For further explanation, see Joseph Moreau, "L'homme est son âme, selon saint Thomas d'Aquin," *Revue Philosophique de Louvain* 74, no. 21 (1976): 5–29.

[26] Aquinas, *ST* I, q. 76, a. 8. Even within the living body, it is not accurate to speak, for example, of the eye as seeing. Rather, it is the composite substance—the human person, who is an embodied soul—who sees.

[27] Aristotle, *De An.* 2.1.412b6–7 (Barnes, 657).

[28] "A form consisting in composition and order, such as the form of a house, . . . is accidental," St. Thomas explains (*ST* I, q. 76, a. 8).

remains merely shapeless matter. It is the form—in this case, the idea, or intention, of the carpenter—that makes the table to be a table, and it enters into its definition insofar as it denotes its purpose or end. Analogically, it is the soul that makes the living body to be what it is, without, however, the intervention of an exterior agent.[29] Indeed, the body is actually "*caused* by the operation that this soul is capable of performing."[30] "To one asking why there are so many members in a natural body—hands, feet, mouth, and the like," St. Thomas therefore suggests that we respond:

> They are to serve the soul's variety of activities. The soul itself is the cause and principle of these members, and what they are, the soul is virtually. For the body is made for the soul, and not the other way around. From this perspective, the natural body is a certain fullness of the soul; unless the members exist with an integral body, the soul cannot exercise fully its activities.[31]

Such is the meaning of the affirmation that the soul is the substantial form of the human body: it *in-forms* it, literally giving form (shape, order, and purpose) to the whole and to each of the parts from within. As the life principle of the human body, the soul is also, St. Thomas explains, "the primary principle of our nourishment, sensation, and local movement; and likewise of our understanding."[32] Such, moreover, is the case of "all biological activity, even at the molecular level": it can be characterized, as Stephen Talbott has observed in his previous studies of living beings, "as purposive and goal-directed."[33] In fact,

> What distinguishes the language of biology from that of physics is its free and full use of the *because* of reason [which makes sense within a context of meaning, as differing from the *because*

29 See Aquinas, *ST* I, q. 76, a. 1.

30 Dominique Pignat, "Définition de l'âme chez Aristote," *Nova et Vetera* (French) 92, no. 1 (2017): 29. To be sure, this is not to say that the soul is produced before the body. Because "the soul is naturally the form of the body, it was necessarily created, not separately, but in the body," St. Thomas reasons (*ST* I, q. 90, a. 4, ad 1).

31 Aquinas, *Super Epistolam B. Pauli ad Ephesios lectura* 1, lect. 8, no. 71, in *Commentary on the Letters of Saint Paul to the Galatians and Ephesians*, vol. 39 of the Latin/English ed. of the *Works of St. Thomas Aquinas*, trans. Fabien R. Larcher and Matthew L. Lamb, ed. John Mortensen and Enrique Alarcón (Lander, WY: The Aquinas Institute for the Study of Sacred Doctrine, 2012).

32 Aquinas, *ST* I, q. 76, a. 1.

33 Talbott, "Evolution and the Purposes of Life. On Biology's Unasked Questions about the Goal-Directed Activities of Organisms," *The New Atlantis* 51 (Winter 2017), https://www.thenewatlantis.com/publications/evolution-and-the-purposes-of-life.

> of physical law, which passes by necessity[34]]. Where the inanimate world lends itself in some regards to application of a "deadened," skeletal language—a language that perhaps too easily invites us to think in terms of mechanisms—the organism requires us to recognize a full and rich drama of meaning.[35]

Talbott nonetheless suggests that we ought to "reject conscious human performance as a model for organic activity . . . , not because it reads too much wisdom and effective striving into the organism, but rather because it reads far too little."[36]

Despite possible appearances to the contrary, these metaphysical and biological descriptions of the body-soul relation hardly provide evidence for the idea of transgender "theorists" that the human body might be altered at will to "fit" an interior vision of oneself: to mutilate the masculine body to match a female perception of oneself, for example, or to maim the female body to suit a male conception of oneself. Far less does it point to the possibility of the mind assuming a "form"[37] beyond the body, in a manner likened to the way in which it is said to choose a gender.[38] As the transhuman theorist Martine Rothblatt explains:

> Freedom of form arises because twenty-first-century software makes it *technologically* possible to separate our minds [a concept that is already a reduction of the metaphysical understanding of the human soul] from our biological bodies [considered here as nothing more than external appearances]. This can be accomplished by downloading enough of our neural connection contents

---

[34] One need only think of the law of gravity, whereby heavy objects necessarily fall to the ground. As Talbott clarifies, "the *because* of physical law applies to things that do have more or less precisely defined and delimited relationships, which therefore lack a meaning-driven character. We need not appeal to 'what makes sense' in a larger, more richly expressive context, because a proposed physical law is either 'obeyed' or not, despite any look of the eyes or gesture of the hand. A thrown ball respects the law of gravity even if a strong wind is blowing it this way or that" (Talbott, "What Do Organisms Mean? How Life Speaks at Every Level," *The New Atlantis* 30 [Winter 2011], https://www.thenewatlantis.com/publications/what-do-organisms-mean).

[35] Talbott, "What Do Organisms Mean?"

[36] Talbott, "Evolution and the Purposes of Life."

[37] In this case, the word does not refer—as it does in the Aristotelian-Thomistic tradition—to that which makes a thing to be what it is: its internal ordering principle. Instead, it denotes its accidental, outer packaging, as it were.

[38] In the words of Martine Rothblatt, "One's gender is merely an important subset of choosing one's form. By 'form' I mean that which encloses our beingness—flesh for the life we are accustomed to, plastic for the robots of science fiction, mere data for the avatars taking over our computer screens" (Rothblatt, "Mind Is Deeper Than Matter: Transgenderism, Transhumanism, and the Freedom of Form" in *The Transhumanist Reader: Classical and Contemporary Essays on the Science, Technology, and Philosophy of the Human Future*, ed. Max More and Natasha Vita-More [West Sussex: Wiley & Sons, 2013], 317).

> and patterns into a sufficiently advanced computer, and merging the resultant "mindfile" with sufficiently advanced software—call it "mindware" [the mind "embodied" by a disk, as it were[39]]. Once such a download and merger is complete, we would have chosen a new form—software—although we would be the same person. It would be quite like changing gender from male to female, or female to male. Transsexuals choose a new form [that is, a new outer appearance and not a new soul] although they are still the same person.[40]

To adhere, on the other hand, to what Rothblatt acknowledges as the "common public view" that "God or Nature endowed only humans with a [human] soul, and [that] consciousness is its earthly manifestation" entails—at least in its metaphysical version described above—that the order and purpose of the whole body-soul being is caused by an operation of the soul, which is its life principle.[41] Consequently, the organs of the human body—and of course it is the reproductive organs that most particularly concern us here—"are not tools 'screwed on' from the outside on an already existing soul." Rather, "it is the soul itself," as the Swiss philosopher Pierre-Marie Emonet explains of the Aristotelian tradition, "that makes them 'grow into a body' to attain its end."[42] Hence, for example, the soul "arranges material structures as organs so that they might fittingly serve as means through which the soul's various powers can operate effectively," as John Finley explains.[43] It "not only unifies the parts into a whole but also brings about the very being of those parts," forming, for example, the lungs, heart, kidney, and reproductive organs.[44]

It bears insisting that this is hardly an outdated metaphysical perspective with no scientific underpinnings. Talbott points, for example, to the development of the human embryo as a sort of "gesturing into existence" of the

---

39 Elsewhere, Rothblatt explains that the term ("mindware") refers to a sort of digital cloning of the human mind: a replica of "how you think, feel, and react based on a huge digital database of your thoughts, feelings and reactions" (*From Transgender to Transhuman: A Manifesto on the Freedom of Form*, ed. Nickolas Mayer [self-pub., 2011], 13). See also Lisa Miller, "The Trans-Everything CEO," *New York Magazine*, September 7, 2014, https://nymag.com/news/features/martine-rothblatt-transgender-ceo/.

40 Rothblatt, *From Transgender to Transhuman*, 13 (emphasis original). For more explication of how we "can replicate life without DNA," see Rothblatt, "Are We Transbemans Yet?," *Journal of Evolution & Technology* 18, no. 1 (May 2008): 94–107.

41 Rothblatt, "Mind Is Deeper Than Matter," 321.

42 Pierre-Marie Emonet, *The Greatest Marvel of Nature: An Introduction to the Philosophy of the Human Person*, trans. Robert Barr (New York: Crossroads Publishing, 2000), 11–12.

43 Finley, "The Metaphysics of Gender: A Metaphysical Analysis," *The Thomist* 79 (2015): 597.

44 Timothy Fortin, "Finding Form: Defining Human Sexual Difference," *Nova et Vetera* 15, no. 2 (2017): 423.

specific structures of its body, such that "fixed form not only shapes movement, but is first of all the result of movement."[45] The embryotic body "does not behave like a plumber, first connecting the water pipes in a house and then turning the water on." On the contrary, "first blood-like liquid . . . simply trickles through gaps in the tissues," as Talbott points out in words borrowed from the evolutionary biologist Wolfgang Schad. "Preferred channels develop only very gradually as blood cells are deposited along the edges and eventually merge into the beginnings of vessel walls."[46] Similarly, "the respiratory movements by which air is drawn in through the trachea are sequels of activities [of the thorax and diaphragm] preregulated long before birth in the most complicated fashion." That is why, "strictly speaking, it is incorrect," as anatomy professor Erich Blechschmidt points out, "to call the inspiration occurring after birth the 'first' breath."[47]

It is thus evident that the relationship between part and whole is not the same for a human being (or any living being, for that matter) as it is for a machine. It is the whole (the organism) that determines the parts (cells, organs, members) and not the parts that determine the whole. For unlike mechanical parts that are simply assembled in a particular way, the parts of a living organism "*grow* within an integral unity from the very start."[48] Therefore, rather than seeking to explain a phenomenon by an underlying mechanism (a Darwinian survival strategy or a hormonal or genetic mechanism, for example, which tend to lead us *away* from the phenomenon itself), the Nature Institute's director, Craig Holdrege, suggests that we adopt a Goethean approach to science: one in which the phenomenon is regarded "as a kind of surface that is pregnant with a depth we may be able to plumb"[49] and in which each natural being is

[45] Stephen L. Talbott, "The Embryo's Eloquent Form," The Nature Institute, Biology Worthy of Life, May 22, 2008, updated March 18, 2013, https://bwo.life/mqual/embryo.htm.

[46] Wolfgang Schad, "A Dynamic Morphology of the Cardiovascular System," in *The Dynamic Heart and Circulation*, ed. Craig Holdrege, trans. Katherine Creeger (Fair Oakes, CA: AWSNA Publications, 2002), 80; cited by Talbott in "Embryo's Eloquent Form."

[47] Erich Blechschmidt, *The Beginnings of Human Life*, trans. Transematics, Inc. (New York: Springer-Verlag, 1977), 78–79; cited by Talbott in "Embryo's Eloquent Form."

[48] Stephen L. Talbott, "The Unbearable Wholeness of Beings: Why the Organism Is Not a Machine," *New Atlantis* 29 (Fall 2010), https://www.thenewatlantis.com/publications/the-unbearable-wholeness-of-beings. "The two ways of looking at the matter couldn't be more profoundly different," Talbott explains elsewhere. "It's the difference between starting with the whole or with the part—between imagining we can understand the organism as a collection of given bits and pieces simply by tracing their individual impacts upon one another, or else realizing that we always rely in one way or another upon our recognition of a unity preceding and giving direction to every fragmentary movement" (Talbott, "Embryo's Eloquent Form").

[49] Craig Holdrege, "Delicate Empiricism: Practicing a Goethean Approach to Science," in Holdrege and Steve Talbott, *Beyond Biotechnology: The Barren Promise of* Genetic *Engineering* (Lexington, KY: The University Press of Kentucky, 2008), 208. In this way, he suggests that we might avoid the danger typifying

encountered as "a whole, unique world that's just waiting to be disclosed."[50] Or, to describe this scientific outlook in the words of Johann Wolfgang von Goethe himself, the famous German poet and lesser-known scientist whom Craig Holdrege presents as particularly sensitive to "the human propensity to substitute abstractions for reports of experience":[51]

> If I look at the created object, inquire into its creation, and follow this process back as far as I can, I will find a series of steps. Since these are not actually seen together before me, I must visualize them in my memory so that they form a certain ideal whole. At first I will tend to think in terms of steps, but nature leaves no gaps, and thus, in the end, I will have to see this progression of uninterrupted activity as a whole. I can do so by dissolving the particular without destroying the impression.[52]

As if to stress this same primacy of the whole with regard to the parts, Leon Kass highlights the correlation between "internal structure and outward appearance" in living bodies. Hence, for example, from a purely biological perspective, "an increased power to see" among higher mammals "is paralleled by an increased complexity and subtlety of what is to be seen."[53]

As for the human body,

> [It] shows all the marks of, and creates all the conditions for, our rationality and our special way of being-in-the world. Our bodies demonstrate, albeit silently, that we are more than just a complex version of our animal ancestors, and, conversely, that we are also more than an enlarged brain, a consciousness somehow grafted onto or trapped within a blind mechanism that knows only survival. The body-form *as a whole* impresses on us its inner powers of thought and action. Mind and hand, gait and gaze, breath and tongue, foot and mouth—all are part of a single package, suffused

---

a positivist approach to science—namely, that of "seeing everywhere embodiments of our models and theories rather than the things themselves. We see a moving survival strategy rather than a fleeing prairie dog; we see a genetic defect rather than a person" (226).

50 Holdrege, "Delicate Empiricism," 222.

51 Holdrege, "Delicate Empiricism," 226.

52 Johann Wolfgang von Goethe, *Goethe, Collected Works*, vol. 12, *Scientific Studies*, ed. Douglas Miller (Princeton: Princeton University Press, 1995), 64; cited and translated by Craig Holdrege in his "Delicate Empiricism," 213.

53 Kass, *Toward a More Natural Science*, 328.

> with the presence of intelligence. We are *rational* (i.e., *thinking*) animals, down to and up from the very tips of our toes.[54]

In short, no body other than the specifically human body, in all of its intricate complexities, could live up to the needs and demands of the spiritual soul. One need only think of the human mouth that does not simply serve to chew, taste, and swallow but also to express emotions and to articulate sounds that allow for communication by speaking; the human hand with its opposable thumb that enables us to accomplish intricate work such as sewing and writing; or our upright posture, allowing for free motion, complex tasks, perception from a distance, and face-to-face encounters.[55] We might thus conclude that it is the immaterial form (the soul) that accounts for the physical form, the invisible that provides explanation of the visible. Or, in the words of St. Thomas, "the form is not for the matter, but rather the matter for the form,"[56] whence the fact that our bodies are naturally designed—designed by nature or more properly by its Author—to suit our souls. In the case of the organs, their presence "indicates a particular configuration of matter for the sake of one of the soul's powers [again, that of reproduction in the case at hand], which in turn flows from the essence of the soul," as Finley clarifies;[57] whence the validity of Aquinas's claim: "nature always operates by a form."[58]

It follows that the form, whereby the human being, like all other creatures, "is determined to a species,"[59] is likewise that *in virtue of which* the male procreates by begetting or the female by conceiving, since the soul is the seat of our procreative powers, as is true of all the soul's powers. Of course, it goes without saying that no individual human being can be "the cause of human nature absolutely," for this would entail being, as Sartre would have it, the cause of oneself.[60] Nor, for the same reason, can one be the cause of the form (the soul) that is transmitted, for the soul of the progenitor is "essentially the same" as that of one's descendants.[61] So too, parents are not the cause of the being *as such* nor of being *tout court* of their children. They may, however, be rightfully considered

[54] Kass, *Toward a More Natural Science*, 289.

[55] See Kass, *Toward a More Natural Science*, 285–89.

[56] Aquinas, *ST* I, q. 76, a. 5. See also I–II, q. 2, a. 5.

[57] Finley, "Metaphysics of Gender," 596. Cf. Aquinas, *ST* I, q. 77, aa. 6–7; a. 7, ad 1.

[58] Aquinas, *SCG* IV, c. 81, 5.

[59] Aquinas, *ST* I, q. 45, a. 7.

[60] Aquinas, *ST* I, q. 45, a. 5, ad 1. See also Aquinas, *De Ver.* q. 4, a. 4.

[61] Aquinas, *ST* I, q. 104, a. 1.

"the cause of human nature being *in* the man begotten."[62] Their causal action is, moreover, necessarily shared: it is only and always *together* that they generate.

Of course, this does not mean, Sylviane Agacinski explains, "that one [sex] disposes of a power lacking to the other (according to androcentric or phallocentric logic)." Rather, "the power that they have in common—that of engendering—is shared between them" and the power of each "is not the same [as the other]."[63] The generative powers of the human race are thus, strictly speaking, "cogenerative,"[64] and that is why, as Aristotle explains, "by a male animal we mean that which generates in another, and by a female that which generates in itself."[65] Or, from the perspective of modern science:

> Human reproductive power reveals not just distinct organs, but also distinct activities and proximate objects: testes produce sperm while ovaries produce eggs; the male organs are capable of cogenerating an indefinite number of offspring within a nine-month period, while within the same time a woman's organs can cogenerate—but also sustain and nourish—at most a small number of offspring. The same analysis reveals distinct reproductive powers even within one gender, most clearly in the case of woman, who possesses powers for both reproduction and sustenance of offspring. Because the cogenerative powers share the same ultimate object, namely reproduction of another human, they can be grouped under one type of power, analogous to the way in which the five senses can be grouped under one type of power. Yet because the cogenerative powers do not share the same proximate object, as their organs and activities manifest, they remain distinct powers as co-contributors to human generation.[66]

BEGOTTEN, NOT MADE

When sexual differentiation is thus understood in terms of a complementary differentiation of biological powers, it is evident that sexual inclination, and thus sexual attraction, cannot be considered an end in itself. On the contrary,

---

[62] Aquinas, *ST* I, q. 45, a. 5, ad 1; emphasis mine.

[63] Agacinski, *Femmes entre sexe et genre*, 153. It is thus "difference (*altérité*) that creates the dynamic," and this difference affects every sexed being, who is "always *the other of the other*" (108).

[64] See Finley, "The Metaphysics of Gender," 597.

[65] Aristotle, *GA* 1.2.716a14–15 (Barnes, 1112).

[66] Finley, "Metaphysics of Gender," 603.

both sexual inclinations and sexual powers are specified by the natural end of procreation, which in turn entails admitting to the "difference between true *generation*, whereby one precedes from another as a son, and *making*," as St. Thomas observes in his explanation of the begetting of the eternal Son of God from the Father.[67] In metaphysical terms, Son and Father necessarily share a same nature, replete with nature's powers. For as Robert Spaemann does well to point out, unlike all that is created and which, as such, is "*qualitatively* inferior to the creator," the Son is of equal dignity and power to the Father. Such is the implication of the credal statement that he is "begotten and not made" (*gentium, non factum*): "The Son, the *Logos*, does not owe his existence to the Father's will, but to the common divine nature."[68]

The same cannot be said of art that issues from the artist. Although the artist and his art may be said to share a common form, the latter nonetheless exists differently in each one: the form conceived in the artist's mind takes on a visual "form" in his art by way of his effort and will.

> We do not say that the form of the man who generates is the idea or exemplar of the man who is generated; but we use these terms only when an agent acting for an end has determined the end himself—whether the form imitated be within him or outside of him. For we say that the form of art in the artist is the plan or idea of the artistic product, and we also say that a form outside the artist is a plan if he imitates it when he makes a thing. This, therefore, seems to constitute the character of an idea: It must be a form which something imitates because of the intention of an agent who antecedently determines the end himself.[69]

In the case of an artifact, this form may even provide a secondary (external) source of movement and operation, but it is a "source" in only an analogical sense because it lacks the internal (or self) directedness proper to a living being. That is why, in fact, it is only with caution that we might compare the unity whereby "a lock and its key are one mechanism" or "a violin and a bow are

---

67 Aquinas, *ST* I, q. 41, a. 3 (emphasis added).

68 Robert Spaemann, "*Vivere viventibus est esse.* Procréation, naissance, mort" (an unedited conference delivered by Spaemann in Louvain, March 2002, my translation) in Spaemann, *Chasser le naturel?*, trans. Stéphane Robilliard (Paris: Les Presses universitaires de l'IPC, 2015), 131 (emphasis original). Cf. Aquinas, *Super Evangelium S. Ioannis lectura* 3, lect. 6, no. 545, in *Commentary on the Gospel of John*, trans. Fabian R. Larcher, ed. Aquinas Institute, vol. 35 of the Latin/English ed. of the *Works of St. Thomas Aquinas, Biblical Commentaries* (Lander, WY: The Aquinas Institute for the Study of Sacred Doctrine, 2013) (hereafter, *Super Ioan.*); cf. *Super Ioan.* 1, lect. 1, no. 41; 5, lect. 3, no. 753; *ST* I, q. 32, a. 1, ad 3; and q. 41, a. 2.

69 Aquinas, *De Ver.* q. 3, a. 1. See also *ST* I, q. 15, a. 1.

one musical instrument" to the unity of man and woman, whom C. S. Lewis appropriately designates "a single organism."[70]

Despite, however, the obvious limitations of the analogy of the machine—so vivid in Rothblatt's transhumanist example of a "mindfile"—Leon Kass suggests that it provides still another means by which to consider the nature-art analogy that has accompanied us throughout these pages. In virtue of its functionality and thus also its directedness toward predefined goals, a machine bears an unmistakable likeness to the obstinate tendencies of living organisms. For these are naturally inclined to predetermined (species-defined) ends in virtue of which they are perfected: the ends of, for example, generation, nourishment, growth, development, sensation, motricity, knowledge, and the maintenance of inner unity or organization. Far from being compromised by the analogy of technology, the notion of orientation (or teleology), which characterizes life to the point of being indispensable to its understanding, is likewise considered by Kass as "indispensable" to the formulation of a mechanistic inquiry and even to the intelligibility of its findings.[71] Just as living organisms are organic, or articulated, wholes—so as to be more appropriately considered as structures than as aggregates, or piles of unordered mass—so too machines can only really be understood as more than the mere sum of their parts. In both cases, the whole is adequately described only in terms of *its purpose*, which is "not a material or a mechanism," but a *meaningful end*.[72] After all, apart from the chance discovery, a machine is made in such a way that its parts are chosen and systematically coordinated in view of a specific operation.

When it comes to *understanding* a machine, therefore, one usually asks—Kass observes—the practical question, "'*how* does it work' only after one knows the 'what' and the 'what for' [the purpose] of the 'it.'"[73] The American bioethicist concludes that teleological analysis is used not only to identify the end of a technological product but also "to evaluate how well or badly it is achieved."[74] That is why, to return to a timeless analogy, the truly competent builder does not refer to a house merely in terms of its material components—"stones, bricks, and timbers"—but also in terms of the "form in that material with that purpose

70 C. S. Lewis, *Mere Christianity* (New York: Fount Paperbacks, 1977), 93. See also Alexander R. Pruss, "Not Out of Lust but in Accordance with Truth: Theological and Philosophical Reflections on Sexuality and Reality," *Logos* 6, no. 4 (Fall 2003): 51–80.

71 Kass, *Toward a More Natural Science*, 258.

72 David S. Crawford, "Public Reason and the Anthropology of Orientation: How the Debate over 'Gay Marriage' Has Been Shaped by Some Ubiquitous but Unexamined Presuppositions," *Communio* 43, no. 2 (Summer 2016): 255.

73 Kass, *Toward a More Natural Science*, 255.

74 Kass, *Toward a More Natural Science*, 257.

or end" that is proper to a house, namely, providing "shelter against destruction by wind, rains, and heat."[75]

As these words occur in Aristotle's treatise "On the Soul" (*De Anima*) for the purpose of explaining what a soul *is* by what it *does*, we are reminded once again of the simple reason why so-called "sex-change" (or "sexual-reassignment") operations can suppress reproductive organs and "artistically" assimilate certain physical features typical of a given sex (namely, secondary sexual characteristics) but they cannot create the generating powers that nature so effortlessly bequeaths upon members of the human race when they are engendered (that is to say, as a consequence thereof). Because, as St. Thomas puts it in an insight that is assuredly Aristotelian, "the form of the generator"—the human soul, in the case at hand—"is the end of the generating action," it is in virtue of this same action of engendering that the engendered being is equipped with the power to become, in turn, a generating principle.[76] That is why, as Aristotle puts it humorously, "man is born from man, but not bed from bed."[77] Or, in the more serious terms of St. Thomas, "An animal receives from the generating agent, at the time of its generation . . . the generative power" in virtue of which it is likened to its generator, "not only in its species, but also in this characteristic of being the cause of others."[78]

Assuredly, this is not to deny that there are a non-negligible number of persons who are infertile at birth. We cannot conclude therefrom, however, that the power to procreate is not normally (that is, *normatively*) transmitted from progenitors to their offspring along with the human soul, wherein those powers are seated. No surgical intervention, in contrast, can reach the depth that marks the origin and seat of the powers to engender: the human soul. Nor can sociocultural forces do so, regardless of the extent of their influence. Although social organization can, for example, compose certain human relationships on the basis of biological organization, it cannot create the specific organization that makes life possible "any more than formal logic can construct the schema of generation," as Sylviane Agacinski astutely remarks.[79] Neither desire nor appetite can be understood in terms of their object unless one takes

---

[75] Aristotle, *De An.* 1.1.403b4–6 (Barnes, 643).

[76] Aquinas, *SCG* III, c. 19, 2: "forma generantis est finis generationis"; cf. Aristotle, *Phys.* 2.7.198b2 (Barnes, 339): "for this [the form] is the end or that for the sake of which."

[77] Aristotle, *Phys.* 2.2.193b9 (Barnes, 330).

[78] Aquinas, *SCG* III, c. 21, 5.

[79] Agacinski, *Femmes entre sexe et genre*, 68.

into account "the 'forces' that animate bodies,"[80] forces that are intelligible in light of their acts: of what they are capable of accomplishing.[81]

Because, on the other hand, human nature is also characterized by intellect and will, it might be admitted that man is "by nature an animal that lives by art" and "by convention": by his own ingenuity. Consequently, his specific *eidos*, or "look," is "partly of his own making."[82] After all, as St. Thomas famously points out, although nature did not provide man with weapons and clothing, as it did the other animals, it provided him instead with "reason and hands," whereby "he is able to get these things for himself."[83] We should not be surprised, then, that some of the greatest works of art in the ancient world are those used to decorate the human body and to protect it: jewelry, weapons, clothing, and hairpieces. As for the particular "look" of the human species, it is, as Kass describes it, that of "looking good": making oneself corporeally attractive to the human eye, of course, but also living up to social standards and gaining public approval. If, in fact, as the maxim goes, it is clothes that make the man, this is because they are indicative of our social status and likewise because they provide means to public approval and social ranking. They are, therefore, one of the most basic examples of the fact that "our being to ourselves is inextricably interwoven with our being to others."[84]

The fact that clothing serves a *practical*, as well as a conventional, purpose—that of protecting us by means of our own creativity not only from inappropriate regards but also from the elements, as do feathers for birds and fur for various animals—nonetheless serves to highlight the fact that the specifically "human look" of man is only "*partly* of his own making."[85] Like all species naturally endowed with bodies, the human species is, to put it more straightforwardly, also marked by necessity—that of our own nature—and this is what Kass identifies as "a mark of our lowliness." The act of "recognizing and owning up to our relation to necessity," on the other hand, is an unmistakable "mark of our dignity."[86] Only the human being, among all earthly species, is capable of reflecting upon himself so as to recognize his own natural and personal limitations. That is why natural necessities are lived differently by human

80 Agacinski, *Femmes entre sexe et genre*, 152–53.

81 See Finley, "Metaphysics of Gender," 603.

82 Kass, *Toward a More Natural Science*, 338: "The *human*-look of the human animal depends upon art and convention."

83 Aquinas, *ST* I–II, q. 5, a. 5, ad 1; cf. I, q. 76, a. 5, ad 4.

84 Kass, *Toward a More Natural Science*, 343.

85 Kass, *Toward a More Natural Science*, 338 (emphasis added).

86 Kass, *Toward a More Natural Science*, 292.

beings than they are by other animals. Our bodies require nourishment, as do the bodies of other animals, but we alone are capable of refusing food when we are hungry or of continuing to eat when our bodies are already adequately nourished.[87] We alone can *voluntarily* fast and *willingly* feast, and both fasts and feasts are signs of our rational nature: a nature that allows us to transcend natural necessities by reason and thus to transgress nature's laws, although not without repercussions.

One need only consider, as proof of the seriousness of this statement, the example of Martine Rothblatt's proposition that we "break with the DNA-based definition of *homo sapiens*," which "no longer dictates all aspects of our individual survival," including—the trans theorist suggests—"our ability to pass on our genes," thanks to in vitro fertilization (IVF). Furthermore, Rothblatt daringly suggests that the phenomenon of transgenderism provides "sociobiologists with evidence of a new species."

> An important part of most species' signature [presumably the term is akin to Kass's "look" or Aristotle's "*eidos*" clarified above] is the characteristically gender dimorphic behaviors of their members. However, thanks to culture and technology, humans are leaving those gender dimorphic behaviors behind as they come to appreciate the limitless uniqueness of their sexual identities. As our creativity has blossomed, we have matured from *homo sapiens* into *persona creatus* [a term that is meant to refer to both humans and transhumans].[88]

Ultimately, Rothblatt imagines that "sexual identity will be liberated not only from genitals, but [even] from flesh itself." In other words, beyond the manner in which gender is "free to flow beyond the confines of one's flesh genital," transhuman minds, formed by the transfer of consciousness to software, will be literally free of "the obstacle of a penis screaming 'but you're a man.'"[89] After all, as Rothblatt imagines it, human "reproduction will no longer necessarily occur . . . via joined DNA. Instead, people of flesh will upload into software the contents and processes of their minds" to be combined with the "mindware"

[87] Of course, this is not to deny the phenomenon of "hyperphagia," whereby certain species eat and drink as much as possible so as to gain weight for their long winter hibernation. For more on the special circumstances under which some wild animals may eat more than strictly needed, see Rory Boothe, "Do Wild Animals Ever Overeat?," Indiana Public Media, A Moment of Science, October 28, 2021, https://indianapublicmedia.org/amomentofscience/do-wild-animals-ever-overeat.php.

[88] Rothblatt, "Mind Is Deeper Than Matter," 318. On the meaning of *persona creatus*, see Rothblatt, *From Transgender to Transhuman*, 13.

[89] Rothblatt, "Mind Is Deeper Than Matter," 322, 321.

of their partners to produce "fertile offspring" of the new "species *persona creatus*."[90] Lest there be any confusion, however, it is important to admit that this "species" is not of Adam's stock. It is an invention of human technicians and not a work of the divine Artist.

The fact that we are able to defy our own nature in such imaginative ways—despite the highly questionable success of the attempt and the obviously dangerous consequences thereof—makes of us, as the American essayist Wendell Berry observes, the "most dangerous of animals" to both ourselves and our fellows. Although other animals "are usually restrained by the limits of physical appetites, humans have mental appetites that can be far more gross and capacious than physical ones."[91] Hence, for example, only man is capable of "'freeing' natural pleasure from natural consequence" and thus of treating his own body as "a pleasure machine" devoid of any connection to the spirit or the soul.[92] We should perhaps not be surprised, then, that although we still commonly recognize our lungs as serving the end of respiration and our stomachs as serving digestion, our sexual organs—or at least our genitalia—are generally regarded as serving no other purpose than that of our own pleasure.[93] The human being is in fact free to ignore what he alone is capable of consciously acknowledging: his natural dependency upon and his responsibility toward both nature and other human persons, a dependency and a responsibility that are, as it were, inscribed within his own body.

THE "TRANS-ING" OF REPRODUCTIVE TECHNOLOGIES

If, in fact, one's ancestors are "inscribed" within the navel of the human body and our descendants in our genitalia, then the human body itself stands as a reminder that nature has bound us tightly to one another in community, and it has done so precisely in and through the human body.[94] The navel witnesses to our having been engendered by others, while the genitalia point to our

---

[90] Rothblatt, *From Transgender to Transhuman*, 13.

[91] Berry, "Getting Along with Nature" (1982), in *The World Ending Fire* (New York: Penguin Books, 2018), 168.

[92] Berry, "Feminism, the Body, and the Machine," in *What Are People For?* (Berkeley: Counterpoint, 2010), 191. Such is what Berry (in the same work) calls "industrial sex": sex that has been reordered by the human will to reflect human desires.

[93] Again, one need only think of Jenner's statement that his penis served no other purpose than that of taking "a whiz in the woods."

[94] See Kass, *Toward a More Natural Science*, 293.

dependency in the shared act of engendering.[95] That is why the attempts of gay and lesbian couples to have children using artificial reproductive technologies is "parasitic on the irreducible originality of the masculine and feminine polarity."[96] On the other hand, man's characteristic defiance of his own nature has recently opened up an entirely new frontier in the domain of artificial reproductive technologies. As Stanford University professor Henry Greely sees it, at any rate, sex as a means of procreation will become obsolete within the next twenty to forty years.[97]

Such is an example of what Hans Jonas identified, already in 1966, as "the almost irresistible tendency in the human mind to interpret human functions in terms of the artifacts that take their place, and artifacts in terms of the replaced human functions."[98] As a case in point, reproductive technologies have become a sort of springboard for the so-called *trans-ing* of human biology. "Transbiology," as Sarah Franklin coined the term, is "a biology that is not only born and bred, or born and made, but *made and born*."[99] Coming to us "via the cyborg embryo, and in particular via assisted conception," it has begun to redefine the traditional boundaries marking life at its origin. In fact, although IVF gained popularity with its promise of "greater conformity to traditional family values" by promoting the "normative" quality of "'biological' parenting," it has since "undermined the very basis" of this norm, Franklin observes, "by introducing a seemingly endless, and inevitably somewhat parodic, *sequelae* of quasi-, semi- or pseudo-biological forms of parenting."[100]

We should not be surprised, then, that the "*trans*-work of embryo transfer"[101] and other means or forms of artificial reproduction "naturally" lend themselves to alliance with gender theorists by offering the means to—or at least the promise of—surpassing the final frontier delineating between bodily appearance and

---

95 It is worth pointing out that for St. Thomas such full development of the child implies that he or she be educated, whence the importance of both sexes. It is "abundantly evident," St. Thomas maintains, "that the female in the human species is not at all able to take care of the upbringing of offspring by herself, since the needs of human life demand many things which cannot be provided by one person alone. Therefore, it is appropriate to human nature that a man remain together with a woman after the generative act," and this for "no short period of time" (Aquinas, *SCG* III, c. 122, 6, 8).

96 David S. Crawford, "Liberal Androgyny: 'Gay Marriage' and the Meaning of Sexuality in Our Time," *Communio* 33, no. 2 (2006): 262.

97 See Henry T. Greely, *The End of Sex and the Future of Human Reproduction* (Cambridge MA: Harvard University Press, 2016).

98 Hans Jonas, *The Phenomenon of Life: Toward a Philosophical Biology* (New York: Harper & Row, 1966), 110.

99 Sarah Franklin, "The Cyborg Embryo: Our Path to Transbiology," *Theory, Culture & Society* 23, 7–8 (2006): 171 (emphasis original). It is thus a "remaking of biological functions" (174).

100 Franklin, "Cyborg Embryo," 177.

101 Franklin, "Cyborg Embryo," 171.

organic functioning, between physiology and biology, between artifact and nature.[102] A greater disanalogy between nature and art would, in fact, be difficult to find. Although, for example, they initially "seemed to be 'just imitating' the biological facts of sexual reproduction," these technologies have since proven "to be so radically disruptive to this equation," Franklin observes, "that it is no longer possible to refer to the so-called facts of life with anything like biological certainty at all anymore."[103]

Hence, for example, the first so-called "test-tube babies" were, as Franklin accurately portrays them, "miraculous because they were 'impossible,' and especially miraculous because they were normal."[104] We are a far step from the clarity of Georges Cottier's distinction between *biological powers* that are operative in the human act of procreation and the *mechanical powers* that are operative in technical interventions that characterize the art of fabrication instead.

> The transmission of life is an activity that is attributed to subjects who are progenitors. I mean to say that in any activity of a living being, which is achieved organically, it is the subject himself who acts through his organs. If I insist on this point, it is because the logic inherent to the practices of artificial reproduction is one implying a mechanistic conception of the human body, whose functions could, by means of technical intervention be exercised in an autonomous manner, *independently of the agent, who possesses those functions*. The activity of the living agent has its source in the soul. It is the latter which, thanks to the sexual organs, is, in the subject, the principle of generation. By the joint action of two subjects, the father and the mother, the process of generation ultimately results in a new individual of the same species.[105]

Because it is, in fact, achieved organically, a procreative act need not even be reflected upon at all. In no way does it "require a higher lucidity of attention," as do artistic activities, "but quite the opposite: the individualizing consciousness surrenders at the moment of conception into," as Robert Spaemann puts it, "the non-individualized stream of life."[106]

---

[102] See Michael Hanby, "When Art Replaces Nature," *Humanum: Issues in Family, Culture & Science* 2, no. 2 (2014): 22–25, http://humanumreview.com/articles/when-art-replaces-nature.

[103] Franklin, "Cyborg Embryo," 178. See the example of Laura Mamo, *Queering Reproduction: Achieving Pregnancy in the Age of Technoscience* (Durham, NC: Duke University Press, 2007).

[104] Franklin, "Cyborg Embryo," 177.

[105] Georges Cottier, "Questions sur l'embryon humain et l'âme spirituelle," in *Défis éthiques* (Saint Maurice, Switzerland: Editions Saint-Augustin, 1996), 184–85 (my translation, emphasis added).

[106] Spaemann, "*Vivere viventibus est esse*," 131.

With, however, the muddying of the distinctions between a natural, organic operation and a technical one, it has become increasingly difficult to distinguish between therapeutic interventions, which repair, restore, or heal natural functions—in this case natural fertility—and those which actually "dominate the processes of procreation."[107] Hence, just as "consensus" has become the new "purpose of medicine," as Ryan Anderson observes in the case of gender dysphoria and the demand for sexual-reassignment therapies, so also in the field of reproductive technologies.[108] We are, in fact, witnessing a "shift away from a medical model of trying to treat, heal, and restore natural fertility" and one "toward the manufacturing of babies."[109] And this, in turn, is achieved by trans-ing nature: "the coupling of nature with the 'helping hands' of techno-science in the context of IVF."[110] Hence, within thirty years' time, Greely predicts:

> Instead of being conceived in a bed, in the backseat of a car, or under a "Keep off the Grass" sign, children will be conceived in clinics. Eggs and sperm will be united through in vitro fertilization (IVF). The DNA of the resulting embryos will then be sequenced and carefully analyzed before decisions are made (passive voice intentional) about which embryo or embryos to transfer to a womb for possible development into one or more living, breathing babies.[111]

Of course, Greely does not deny that human reproduction "can only start off with the basic materials (for example, the utilization of somatic cells for cloning) consequent upon and containing the continuing life energy of the sexual union of man and woman, materials which," as David Crawford points out, "can be manipulated, but which cannot themselves be manufactured in the laboratory."[112] Nonetheless, the scientific vision of the world behind many of these reproductive innovations seems eerily close to what Pope Benedict XVI

---

[107] Pope John Paul II, cited by the Congregation for the Doctrine of the Faith, Instruction on the Respect for Human Life in Its Origin and on the Dignity of Procreation: Replies to Certain Questions of the Day *Donum vitae* (February 22, 1987), no. 1. Such, John Paul II adds, is "the temptation to go beyond the limits of a reasonable dominion over nature."

[108] Ryan T. Anderson, *When Harry Became Sally: Responding to the Transgender Moment* (New York: Encounter Books, 2018), 112. This new "purpose" entails an abolishing or denial of the norms upon which the medical science is founded. "The distinction between ordered and disordered development is based on an understanding of purpose and function in the systems of an organism," Anderson explains. "To abolish the concept of the normal in human development is to erode the foundations of medical science" (91–92).

[109] See Jennifer Lahl, "Modern Families and the Messes We Make," Public Discourse, November 1, 2013, https://www.thepublicdiscourse.com/2013/11/11111/.

[110] Franklin, "Cyborg Embryo," 174.

[111] Greely, *End of Sex*, 1–2.

[112] Crawford, "Liberal Androgyny," 262.

describes as that of a windowless "concrete bunker," in which "we ourselves provide lighting and atmospheric conditions," since we refuse to "obtain either from God's wide world."[113]

This is not to say that reproductive technologies should be shunned because they are artificial. After all, it is precisely as such that they "bear witness to the possibilities of the art of medicine," as the Congregation for the Doctrine of the Faith judges important to point out.[114] Hence, for example, the restoration of sight to the blind and of hearing to the deaf by means of surgical intervention might be counted among the wonders that nature has provided to the human race through the ingenuity of human reason. Such is also the case of the installation of pacemakers and the transplanting of organs, among which we might mention the recent advancement in the area of womb transplants. At the time of this writing, at least twenty-one children have been born in the United States alone of previously womb-less mothers, subsequently endowed with donor wombs.[115] Many of these scientific advances are to be applauded.[116]

The same scientific innovation of womb transplants is now being considered, however—and this is where science ventures beyond the therapeutic realm, which suits the traditional aim of medicine—to serve a goal that is arguably opposed to nature's own purpose: that of permitting a man identifying as trans to have "her" "own" uterus.[117] Of course, the presumption is made that so-called transwomen will also become mothers: progenitors who act by nature rather than by art. If they do in fact become "mothers," however, it is obviously not in virtue of ova produced by their own ovaries; nor in virtue of their own natural hormones providing the adequate body temperatures to sustain life; nor

[113] Pope Benedict XVI, "The Listening Heart: Reflections on the Foundations of Law," Address to the Bundestag (Berlin, September 22, 2011), https://w2.vatican.va/content/benedict-xvi/en/speeches/2011/september/documents/hf_ben-xvi_spe_20110922_reichstag-berlin.html.

[114] Congregation for the Doctrine of the Faith, *Donum vitae*, no. 3.

[115] Denis Mann, "Good Outcomes From First Five Years of Uterus Transplants But Concerns Remain," *US News*, July 7, 2022: https://www.usnews.com/news/health-news/articles/2022-07-07/good-outcomes-from-first-5-years-of-uterus-transplants-but-concerns-remain.

[116] In its present state, uterus transplants pose ethical concerns, because all uterus transplant recipients must also undergo in vitro fertilization to retrieve and then fertilize their eggs. (ibid.)

[117] See Sanchez Manning and Stephen Adams, "Wombs for Men: Astonishing Prospect as Fertility Doctors Back Operations on NHS So Transgender Women Born as Boys Can Have Babies," *Daily Mail*, July 1, 2017, https://www.dailymail.co.uk/news/article-4657830/transgender-women-born-boys-babies-NHS-doctors.html; Lisa Kaplan Gordon, "Surgery Could Give Men Wombs of Their Own within Five Years," *Yahoo Lifestyle*, November 18, 2015, https://www.yahoo.com/lifestyle/surgery-could-give-men-wombs-130236009954514 2.html; Federica Umani Ronchi and Gabriele Napoletano, "Uterus Transplantation and the Redefinition of Core Bioethics Precepts," *Acta Bio Medica* 92, no. 5 (November 3, 2021): 1–2, https://mattioli1885journals.com/index.php/actabiomedica/article/view/12257/10234; and Wesley J. Smith, "Do Transgender Women Have a 'Right to Gestate'?," *National Review*, November 8, 2021, https://www.nationalreview.com/corner/do-transgender-women-have-a-right-to-gestate/.

in virtue of so many other natural traits relative to the female body—that is to say, primary sex characteristics—whereby women are naturally suited to sustain and nourish a developing embryo within their wombs, bring a child to birth, and nourish it with milk produced by their own bodies. Instead, it is simply assumed that human ingenuity can provide externally and artificially for what nature provides internally and naturally, even when that entails experimenting with human life and destroying human embryos.[118]

To be sure, these daring predictions are not altogether unlikely. Journalist Lisa Kaplan Gordon reported in 2015 that medical advances, already current at the time, allow natal men identifying as transwomen to "adjust their biochemistry to suppress male and introduce female hormones, have breasts that can lactate, and obtain surgically constructed vaginas that include a 'neoclitoris,' which allows sensation."[119] As for natal women identifying as transmen, they might follow the lead of the world's first "pregnant man," Thomas Beatie, who forthright admits, "I used my female reproductive organs to become a father."[120] It was not without donor sperm, however, which is now increasingly available and even publicly subsidized, that "he" achieved this feat.[121] However, unlike other legal but non-natal males, who have temporarily put off phalloplasty

---

[118] A survey conducted by the Rand Corporation revealed that there were at least 396,526 embryos in storage in the United States alone as of April 2002, a figure which is likely to have significantly multiplied in subsequent years given the increased use of reproductive technology and the wide resistance among fertility patients, reported by Jacqueline Pfeffer Merrill, to thaw and discard their embryos, to donate them for research, or even to offer them for adoption by infertile couples. See David I. Hoffman et al., "How Many Frozen Human Embryos Are Available for Research?," *Rand Research Brief* (2003), https://www.rand.org/pubs/research_briefs/RB9038.html; and Jacqueline Pfeffer Merrill, "Embryos in Limbo," *The New Atlantis* (Spring 2009): 18–28. More recently, it has been reported that in the meantime, "hundreds of thousands" of frozen embryos have been abandoned by former patients of the more than five hundred fertility clinics in the United States alone who are no longer willing to pay the annual storage fee of $500 to $1000 to keep those embryos alive. See Mary Pflum, "Nation's Fertility Clinics Struggle with a Growing Number of Abandoned Embryos," NBC News, August 12, 2019, https://www.nbcnews.com/health/features/nation-s-fertility-clinics-struggle-growing-number-abandoned-embryos-n1040806. Moreover, hundreds of embryos have been "damaged" or destroyed by maintenance problems affecting the freezer tanks where they were stored. See Brie Zeltner, "University Hospital Notifies 700 Fertility Patients of Freezer 'Fluctuation' and Potential Damage to Stored Eggs and Embryos," Cleveland.Com, March 8, 2018, updated January 30, 2019, https://www.cleveland.com/healthfit/2018/03/university_hospitals_notifies.html; and Susannah Cullinane, "Second US Fertility Clinic Reports Egg Storage Tank Malfunction," CNN, April 5, 2018, https://edition.cnn.com/2018/03/12/health/frozen-eggs-second-clinic-malfunction/index.html.

[119] Gordon, "Surgery Could Give Men Wombs."

[120] Cited by R. J. Wilson, "'The First Pregnant Man,' Ten Years Later: Thomas Beatie Reflects on a Difficult Decade," Urbo, July 12, 2018, https://www.urbo.com/content/the-first-pregnant-man-10-years-later-thomas-beatie-reflects-on-a-difficult-decade/.

[121] The United Kingdom's Department of Health, for example, has used public funding to launch a national sperm bank. See Sanchez Manning, "NHS to Fund Sperm Bank for Lesbians: New Generation of Fatherless Families Paid for by YOU," *Daily Mail*, August 2, 2014, https://www.dailymail.co.uk/news/article-2714321/NHS-fund-sperm-bank-lesbians-New-generation-fatherless-families-paid-YOU.html.

("bottom" surgery to remove female organs and to create an artificial penis) for the express purpose of becoming "fathers,"[122] Beatie has no intention of transitioning beyond "his" mastectomy and hormonal treatments. "Probably the biggest misconception [that people have in my regard] is that I went back to being a woman to get pregnant," "he" explains. "For me, this is the furthest thing from the truth. I was a fully legal man and husband before I got pregnant, while I was pregnant, and right now. I never vacillated. I got pregnant and delivered my three children to be a father."[123] Beatie feels no need to remove "his" female reproductive organs, claiming that to do so would not make "him" "any more of a man or any less of a woman." Nor did the experience of pregnancy make Beatie feel more feminine. "I did not feel maternal or motherly or womanly and pregnant," Beatie claims. "I felt like Nancy's husband, and I felt like the father of my child."[124] "Throughout my pregnancies, I maintained a very solid male gender identity. I was simply a pregnant husband; something I would hope any man would do for his family, if his wife were unable to do so."[125]

Despite these allusions to "husband" and "child"—concepts which by definition imply interdependence, responsibility, and the anchoring of the person within a family history—the spirit of autonomy and androgyny that this story conveys is striking. After all, while claiming to be a "father" (presumably in a psychological sense), from a purely biological standpoint, Beatie remains a mother. As for Freddie McConnell, the subject of the 2019 BBC documentary *The Seahorse*,[126] it took "him" "a long time to separate identity from biology."[127] But McConnell has now come to terms with it, explaining, "I'm just using my hardware [uterus, ovum, hormones] to do a thing [gestate new human life]. It's pragmatic." Hayden Cross—who was acclaimed Britain's "first pregnant man" until Scott Parker stole the title by proving that "he" had given birth some months previously—admits some regret over "his" own pregnancy, especially

---

[122] See Amanda Devlin and Richard Wheatstone, "UK's First Pregnant Man: Who Is Hayden Cross, How Can a Man Fall Pregnant, and How Did He Give Birth to Daughter Trinity Leigh?," *The Sun*, January 9, 2019, https://www.thesun.co.uk/news/2567386/hayden-cross-pregnant-man-first-uk-trinity-leigh/; AFP, "Transgender Man Gives Birth in Finland First," *The Express Tribune*, April 4, 2018, https://tribune.com.pk/story/1677448/3-transgender-man-gives-birth-finland-first/.

[123] Cited by R. J. Wilson, "'The First Pregnant Man,' Ten Years Later."

[124] Cited by Alan B. Goldberg and Katie N. Thomson, "Exclusive: 'Pregnant Man' Gives Birth to Second Child," ABC News, June 9, 2009, https://abcnews.go.com/2020/story?id=7795344&page.

[125] Cited by R. J. Wilson, "'The First Pregnant Man,' Ten Years Later."

[126] Simon Hattenstone, "The Dad Who Gave Birth: 'Being Pregnant Doesn't Change Me Being a Trans Man,'" *The Guardian*, April 20, 2019, https://www.theguardian.com/society/2019/apr/20/the-dad-who-gave-birth-pregnant-trans-freddy-mcconnell.

[127] See *The Seahorse: The Dad Who Gave Birth*, directed by Janie Finlay, produced by Grain Media in association with Glimmer Films and *The Guardian* (2019), https://seahorsefilm.com/.

with respect to "his" public persona, claiming that "it's a very female thing to carry a baby and it goes against everything I feel in my body."[128] In fact, "Trans guys are notorious for avoiding PAP smears or anything else that involves the 'down-there' bits," Cross admits. "I had no idea how I could possibly open up to let out a baby, given my intense discomfort with my own bottom half."[129]

It is no wonder that the Midwives Alliance of North America (MANA) points out, "Pregnancy, birth and breastfeeding are times when biologic changes and social expectations can affect our perception of gender." That is why, in fact, they are "committed to promoting the additive use of gender-neutral language in traditionally woman-centric movements (birth and reproductive justice)."[130] But, as Andrea Chu puts it with an unusual attentiveness to the real that must be unsettling for many transactivists, "In childbirth, there is too much blood, too much meat, too much of the thinginess of the thing for politics. Remember: pregnancy is a form of body modification so extreme that its result is another person. In this, it resembles nothing—except, perhaps, sex change."[131]

Thanks to continuous scientific innovations, however, it might not be long—such is the claim of certain members of the scientific community—before natal women identifying as men will no longer have to decide between a complete phalloplasty and the possibility of being a biological parent. Of course, they have long had the possibility of freezing their eggs before undergoing hormonal therapy and surgery: an option that allows them to choose among a number of scientific procedures now available to lesbians couples wishing to share motherhood, including a recent technique "producing" "three-parent" embryos using DNA from two women and one man.[132] Presumably still more

---

[128] Kate O'Malley, "Two British Men Become First to Give Birth after Postponing Gender Reassignment Surgeries," *Elle*, November 7, 2017, https://www.elle.com/uk/life-and-culture/culture/news/a36967/british-men-become-first-to-give-birth/. Simone Hattenstone reports that Hayden's title was removed when Scott Parker came out as having given birth a few months earlier. See Hattenstone, "The Dad Who Gave Birth." See also Rebekah Scanlan, "Man Who Gave Birth Opens Up about Pregnancy Regrets," Kidspot, January 10, 2019, https://www.kidspot.com.au/parenting/real-life/in-the-news/man-who-gave-birth-opens-up-about-pregnancy-regrets/news-story/3b831b09b10e1eeb1996abd74b44ee43.

[129] Cited by Kidspot, "Meet Hayden, The First British Man Set to Give Birth," January 8, 2017, https://www.kidspot.com.au/parenting/real-life/in-the-news/meet-hayden-the-first-british-man-set-to-give-birth/news-story/a47bd06d1a189b1822c63efe13d82549.

[130] Midwives Alliance of North America (MANA), "Position Statement on Gender Inclusive Language," September 9, 2015, https://mana.org/healthcare-policy/position-statement-on-gender-inclusive-language. Hence, rather than address a "pregnant woman," the statement suggests that we speak of a "pregnant individual." On "pregnant men," see Heather Brunskell-Evans, *Transgender Body Politics*, 25–27.

[131] Chu, "All Reproduction Is Assisted," *Boston Review*, August 14, 2018, https://bostonreview.net/forum/all-reproduction-assisted/andrea-long-chu-extreme-pregnancy.

[132] See Ian Sample, "UK Doctors Select First Women to Have 'Three-Person Babies,'" *The Guardian*, February 1, 2018, https://www.theguardian.com/science/2018/feb/01/permission-given-to-create-britains-first-three-person-babies; and Associated Press, "Designer Baby Warning as Embryos Are Made Using TWO

attractive to many natal women identifying as men, scientists are now said to be "a step closer to mimicking [the] way [the] human"—dare we say, *male*?—"body creates sperm," and some believe they will one day be capable of manufacturing both sperm cells and ova from adult stem cells.[133] This might well serve as an eerie foreboding of what Greely calls "uniparents": those who, by way of scientific invention, are the biological mother *and* the biological father of their children.[134] For those taking science as their creed, the only limit in sight is that sperm cells produced from the skin cells of women can "produce" only female embryos, since they necessarily lack a Y chromosome.[135]

Given, moreover, the nonnegotiable number of lesbian and so-called transgender men who are likely to have recourse to this technology, it is not difficult to imagine the long-term effect that it might have on the proportional balance between the sexes: causing a sort of reversal of what has occurred in, for example, modern-day China, where men outnumber women by more than thirty-three million, due largely to sex-selection abortions under its only recently revoked one-child policy.[136] Nor are any other number of physical, psychological, social, familial, and even species-related consequences hard to imagine, when it is no longer necessary nor socially advisable, let alone medically affordable, to procreate in the "old-fashioned" manner.[137] Think, for

Women and One Man by Oregon Scientists," *Daily Mail*, October 22, 2012, https://www.dailymail.co.uk/news/article-2222622/Oregon-Health--Sciences-University-Scientists-swap-embryos-DNA-using-women-man.html. See also Sonia Azad, "Same-Sex Couple Carries Same 'Miracle' Baby in What May Be Fertility World First," *USA Today*, October 29, 2018, https://eu.usatoday.com/story/news/nation-now/2018/10/29/same-sex-couple-carries-same-baby-ivf-fertility-treatment-first/1804554002/.

133 Hannah Devlin, "Scientists a Step Closer to Mimicking Way Human Body Creates Sperm," *The Guardian*, January 1, 2018, https://www.theguardian.com/science/2018/jan/01/scientists-a-step-closer-to-mimicking-way-human-body-creates-sperm. See also Debora L. Spar, "Opinion: The Poly-Parent Households Are Coming," *New York Times*, August 12, 2020, https://www.nytimes.com/2020/08/12/opinion/ivg-reproductive-technology.html; and Greely, *End of Sex*, 131–36.

134 See Greely, *The End of Sex*, 136.

135 See Tamar Lewin, "Babies from Skin Cells? Prospect Is Unsettling to Some Experts," *The New York Times*, May 16, 2017, https://www.nytimes.com/2017/05/16/health/ivg-reproductive-technology.html. Henry Greely does not rule this out, however. "Making sperm from women seems more complicated" than making eggs from men, "particularly making sperm that will yield boys, but it is not clearly impossible," he explains (Greely, *End of Sex*, 135).

136 See Council on Foreign Relations, "China's Baby Blues: When Better Policies for Women Backfire," July 5, 2018, https://www.cfr.org/blog/chinas-baby-blues-when-better-policies-women-backfire; Phoebe Zhang, "China's Gender Equality Falls and Falls," Inkstone, December 20, 2018, https://www.inkstonenews.com/society/china-falls-103-2018-global-gender-gap-report/article/2178898; and Mara Hvistendahl, *Unnatural Selection: Choosing Boys over Girls, and the Consequences of a World Full of Men* (New York: Public Affairs, 2011).

137 With regard to species-related consequences, one reader of Greely's prediction comments: "We must be on guard against culturally evolving our species down a blind alley, one where humanity is eventually left unable to procreate without the assistance of technology—or even *at all*. For example, the female pelvis widens substantially at puberty (relative to boys) and narrows with menopause, when that additional

example, of the compulsory screening of embryos against hereditary or genetic diseases that insurance companies are likely to require of new parents, given the possibility. Imagine the pressure experienced by parents who are forced to choose one embryo among all the others—Greely suggests at least one hundred[138]—knowing that they will be subsequently condemned to destruction or to an indefinite "life span" within a freezer storage unit.[139] Consider the emotional and even legal consequences of embryos that are abandoned, lost, damaged, or accidently discarded.[140] Envision, if you will, the challenges to marital relationships or partnerships when they are caught in "negotiations" over which embryo to adopt.[141] Consider—even despite the rhetoric of "quality assurance" and "the idiom of improvement"[142]—the still unknown, but nonetheless imaginable, health risks to both child and mother.[143] Ponder what

---

width carries no benefit. But if children no longer gestate in the womb, this evolutionary adaptation would no longer be selected for" (NJ_citizen, commenting on Shehab Khan, "Within Thirty Years We Will No Longer Use Sex to Procreate, Says Stanford Professor," *Independent*, July 4, 2017, https://www.independent.co.uk/news/science/sex-procreation-hank-greely-stanford-professor-prediction-humans-no-longer-reproduce-a7821676.html).

138 "Prospective parents will be told as much as they want to know about the DNA of, say, 100 embryos and the implications of that DNA for the diseases, looks, behaviors, and other traits of the child each of those embryos might become. Then they will be asked to pick one or two to be transferred into a womb for possible gestation and birth. And it will all be safe, legal, and, to the prospective parents, free" (Greely, *End of Sex*, 2).

139 See Pfeffer Merrill, "Embryos in Limbo"; and Stacy A. Trasancos, "The Death of Embryos and 'The Conception Problem,'" *The Catholic World Report*, May 2, 2018, https://www.catholicworldreport.com/2018/05/02/the-death-of-embryos-and-the-conception-problem/.

140 See Gerard Letterie and Dov Fox, "Lawsuit Frequency and Claims Basis over Lost, Damaged, and Destroyed Embryos over A 10-Year Period," *Fertility & Sterility* 1, no. 2 (September 2020): 78–82; and Katherine Rosman, "The Lost Embryos," *The New York Times*, April 16, 2021, https://www.nytimes.com/2021/04/16/style/freezing-eggs-and-embryos.html.

141 As Greely himself puts it, "I think one of the hardest things about this will be all the divorces that come about when she wants embryo number 15 and he wants embryo number 64. . . . I think the decision making will be a real challenge for people. How do you weigh a slightly higher chance of diabetes with slightly lower risk of schizophrenia against better musical ability and a much lower risk of colon cancer? Good luck" (The Tribune News Desk, "Stanford Professor Believes in the Future We Won't Have Sex to Procreate," *The Tribune*, July 2, 2017, https://tribune.com.pk/story/1448660/stanford-professor-believes-future-wont-sex-procreate/).

142 Franklin, "Cyborg Embryo," 178.

143 To be sure, some research has already pointed to negative consequences in this domain. See, for example, Barbara Luke et al., "Assessment of Birth Defects and Cancer Risk in Children Conceived Via In Vitro Fertilization in the United States," *Jama Open Network* 3, no. 10 (October 29, 2020, corrected on December 3, 2020): 1–10, https://jamanetwork.com/journals/jamanetworkopen/fullarticle/2772342; Barbara Luke et al., "Risk of Prematurity and Infant Morbidity and Mortality by Maternal Fertility Status and Plurality," *Journal of Assisted Reproduction and* Genetics 36, no. 1 (January 2019): 121–38; Charlotte Dupont and Christophe Sifer, "A Review of Outcome Data Concerning Children Born Following Assisted Reproductive Technologies," *International Scholarly Research Network Obstetrics and Gynecology* (July 17, 2012): 1–5, https://www.ncbi.nlm.nih.gov/pmc/articles/PMC3385632/; Vic Larcher, "The Health of Children Conceived by Assisted Reproductive Technologies," *Achieves of Disease in Childhood* 92, no. 8 (August

it must mean for a child to acknowledge that he or she was "swapped" as an embryo in exchange for another[144] or that his or her father is a sperm donor.[145] Reflect upon what it must be like to consider oneself a "lab specimen" chosen from a batch of embryos, conjured up in a laboratory, most of whom have met an unhappy fate.[146] Consider, finally, the eugenic possibilities that these technologies put within the hands of parents themselves.[147] As the author of an impeccably researched book on the subject put it, "we have not relinquished the notion that reproduction should be controlled; instead, we have shifted it to our own families. In China and California alike, mothers have become their own eugenicists."[148] Ominously real are the words of C. S. Lewis, written just at the end of the Second World War: "the power of Man to make himself what he pleases means the power of some men to make other men what *they* please."[149]

2007): 668–69; "IVF Babies May Face Later Cardiac Risks," Health.am, April 20, 2012, http://www.health.am/ab/more/ivf-babies-may-face-later-cardiac-risks/; Jennifer Lahl, "Does IVF Cause More Cancer in Children or Not?," Center for Bioethics and Culture, October 7, 2013, http://www.cbc-network.org/2013/10/does-ivf-cause-more-cancer-in-children-or-not/.

[144] See Leah McDonald, "'Looking to Transfer Before Christmas': Brooklyn Actress, 37, Posts Online Appeal Asking Women to Swap One of Their Male Embryos for Her Female One, Because She Wants Another Son," *Daily Mail*, November 3, 2018, https://www.dailymail.co.uk/news/article-6350193/Actress-37-New-York-appeals-offers-trade-female-embryo-male-one.html.

[145] See the numerous testimonials on the websites Them before Us: Children's Rights before Adult Desires, https://thembeforeus.com/; Anonymous Us, https://anonymousus.org/; and My Daddy's Name Is Donor (Institute For American Values), https://www.wearedonorconceived.com/uncategorized/my-daddys-name-is-donor/.

[146] See Alana S. Newman, "Life as a Lab Specimen," *Humanum: Issues in Family, Culture and Science* 2 (2014): 2, https://humanumreview.com/articles/life-as-a-lab-specimen; and Alana S. Newman, "Children's Rights, or Rights to Children?," Public Discourse, November 10, 2014, https://www.thepublicdiscourse.com/2014/11/13993/.

[147] See, for example, Samantha Pearson, "Demand for American Sperm Is Skyrocketing in Brazil," *The Wall Street Journal*, March 22, 2018, https://www.wsj.com/articles/in-mixed-race-brazil-sperm-imports-from-u-s-whites-are-booming-1521711000; and David Plotz, *The Genius Factory: The Curious History of the Nobel Prize Sperm Bank* (New York: Random House, 2006).

[148] Hvistendahl, *Unnatural Selection*, 258.

[149] Lewis, *Abolition of Man*, 72.

CHAPTER 6

Consequences of Inverting the Nature-Art Analogy

Although it is not difficult to imagine the possible negative repercussions of the new reproductive technologies that we cited at the conclusion of our previous chapter—many of which we have in fact already witnessed since the birth of Louise Joy Brown, the first test-tube baby, in 1978—much still remains unknown to us. Such, moreover, is also the case of the possible negative consequences of the surgical and chemical manipulation of various secondary—and even primary—sex characteristics. The long-term consequences can, in fact, hardly be otherwise than unknown, not only because we do not have the same foresight as our Creator but also because modern science has reversed the order between theoretical and practical knowledge.

Traditionally, the former (the *art* of any given science accumulated throughout the centuries and passed from one generation to the next) preceded the latter (its application to any given case or situation) on the basis of the principle that we should think before we act. It was, therefore, simply taken for granted that the human will follows the human intellect in the order of operation.[1] Presently, however, many of our contemporaries—aligned, at least indirectly, with the philosophy of Sartre, Beauvoir, and Butler—no longer recognize the will as limited by anything other than human desire. As for human knowledge, it has been reduced to the practical realm, according to the Hobbesian principle that to know something is "to know what we can do with it when we have it."[2] Instead of taking the often-painstaking effort and time to pursue the theoretical question *What is this or that thing?* and to search the answer through careful observation of its natural operations, modern science almost immediately pursues the practical question *How can we employ this thing?*

[1] In the Thomistic tradition, see Michael S. Sherwin, *By Knowledge and by Love: Charity and Knowledge in the Moral Theology of St. Thomas Aquinas* (Washington, DC: The Catholic University of America Press, 2005).

[2] Thomas Hobbes, *Leviathan*, ed. Richard Tuck (Cambridge: Cambridge University Press, 1991), chap. 3, no. 9 (p. 21). See also Michael Allen Gillespie, *The Theological Origins of Modernity* (Chicago: University of Chicago Press, 2008), 37–43, 230–31.

REPLACING CREATED *MEANING* WITH MAN-MADE *UTILITY*

Ultimately, in fact, we are confronted with two very different scientific and world views, which in turn are based on two contrasting, even opposed, understandings of truth, meaning, and knowledge: one in which the aforementioned are understood objectively, so as *to be discovered* by the human being, and one in which they are understood subjectively, so as *to be accorded* by the human being instead.

In the first sense—proper to a traditional metaphysical and realist worldview—the things of this world are considered as *meaningful in themselves* independently of any humanly assigned purpose. Indeed, it is the very meaningfulness of things—their purposeful orientations or inclinations to determined ends—that makes them knowable to us. Hence, for example, the specific, or characteristic, operations and behaviors of an animal traditionally served to define it. "Its activities, taken together, are," as Kass points out, "most of all what the animal *is* and what the animal *is for*."[3] Hence, to define a thing, from this same realist perspective, is to categorize it according to its genius and species. This is a process that takes for granted an ordered universe in which things are really (and not just nominally) oriented to ends, or goods, which characterize each nature or species as such. This orientation occurs in virtue of specific (that is to say, species-specified or natural) inclinations, powers, and potencies. To speak of ends or goods, in turn, is necessarily to address the actions or operations proper to each being as perfective of its essence. Hence, as we saw in chapter 3, for example, the end of a natural appetite is not so much the attractive object that compels or incites in virtue of its intrinsic goodness but that which contributes to the perfection of the natural being who is attracted: "not knowledge, but being knowledgeable; not the good, but being good."[4]

When, therefore, St. Thomas teaches that "everything is on account of its operation," he means to emphasize the fact that created things are naturally ordered *from within*—in virtue of their specific forms—to goods that actualize or perfect them as such.[5] "Each thing is perfect," Aquinas reasons, "insofar as it is actual": insofar as it has accomplished its highest operation, realized its

---

[3] Leon Kass, *Toward a More Natural Science: Biology and Human Affairs* (New York: The Free Press, 1985), 256 (emphasis original).

[4] Jean-Hervé Nicolas, footnote to *ST* I, q. 5, a. 5, in Thomas d'Aquin, *Somme théologique*, vol. I (Paris: Cerf, 1984), 187.

[5] Aquinas, *ST* III, q. 9, a. 1.

powers, or actualized its potencies so as to perfect, or fulfill, its being.[6] Hence, although the specific form (which makes a thing to be what it is in accord with its species) might be considered the end of generation, "it is not the end of the engendered being."[7] That end, as Jean-Marie Henri-Rousseau explains, is the operation whereby the creature is fully actualized.[8] For "nature always operates by a form."[9]

When, on the other hand, we raise the question at the heart of empirical science, including the new "science" of transgenderism—"how does this thing work?" in view of knowing "what can we do with it?"—there is no attempt to understand, define, or classify things according to their species and thus to acknowledge them as having meaning or purpose independently of the meaning assigned to them by the human mind. Instead, in accord with the maxim made popular by Francis Bacon, knowledge is power (*scientia potentia est*), knowledge is viewed as an assertive act: an act *assigning meaning*, or purpose, to otherwise meaningless matter. We are obviously not far from the philosophy of Jean-Paul Sartre.

Nor are we far from the reasoning of the biological evolutionist Richard Dawkins, who assigns to the human mind the "purpose" that is often and "falsely" attributed to natural beings:

> We humans have purpose on the brain. We find it difficult to look at anything without wondering what it is "for," what the motive for it or the purpose behind it might be. The desire to see purpose everywhere is a natural one in an animal that lives surrounded by machines, works of art, tools and other designed artifacts—an animal, moreover, whose waking thoughts are dominated by its own goals and aims. [However] . . . the mere fact that it is possible to frame a question does not make it legitimate or sensible to do so.[10]

---

6 Aquinas, *ST* I–II, q. 3, a. 2.

7 "The species of anything is derived from its form" (Aquinas, *ST* I, q. 76, a. 1). Similarly, to acknowledge that the soul is a substantial form "is to imply that it is of the essence and 'whatness' of the body it animates," St. Thomas explains. "For this form is essential to the thing, and is denoted by the definition of what the thing is" (Aquinas, *Commentary on Aristotle's* De Anima, trans. Kenelm Foster and Silvester Humphries [Notre Dame, IN: Dumb Ox Books, 1994], bk. II, lect. 2, no. 236).

8 Jean-Marie Henri-Rousseau, "L'être et l'agir," *Revue Thomiste* 54, no. 2 (1954): 270–71. Cf. Aquinas, *ST* I, q. 5, a. 5; I–II, q. 49, a. 3.

9 Aquinas, *SCG* IV, c. 81, 5.

10 Richard Dawkins, "God's Utility Function," *Scientific American* (November 1995): 85. Instead, Dawkins suggests that the "true process that has endowed wings, eyes, beaks, nesting instincts and everything else about life with the strong illusion of purposeful design" can be reduced to Darwinian natural selection. "Darwin realized that the organisms alive today exist because their ancestors had traits allowing them

That is why, as Joseph Ratzinger summarizes the position of the Italian philosopher Giambattista Vico, "all that we can truly know is what we have made ourselves" (*verum quia factum*).[11]

From this utilitarian perspective, the domination of nature, including that of the human body, by technology becomes the end of all scientific knowledge, as Descartes foretold,[12] with primacy being awarded to *praxis* and thus also to utilitarianism and pragmatism.[13] As for the idea of nature espoused by this method, it is nothing more than "an aggregate of objective data linked together in terms of cause and effect," as the early Hans Kelsen would have it.[14] There need be no objection, therefore, to its manipulation, to the perversion of its natural inclinations, powers, and ends in view of another, humanly determined purpose. After all, once nature is no longer viewed as "the expression of a creating reason," it can no longer serve as the foundation of moral principles; for nothing can be inscribed within being, as Ratzinger acknowledges, if being itself is merely the "product of evolution."[15] Or, to borrow from Nietzsche, as does Judith Butler, "there is no 'being' behind doing, effecting, becoming; 'the doer' is merely a fiction added to the deed—the deed is everything."[16]

It is not difficult to recognize how this second utilitarian view of nature and of the modern scientific method is operative not only in the philosophy of Sartre but also in the surgeon who reasons—to again cite Paul McHugh—"if you can do it and he wants it, why not do it?"[17] So too is it at work in the science of artificial reproductive technologies, which would have us believe that the difference between a child and an experiment lies in the purpose that technical engineers

---

and their progeny to flourish, whereas less fit individuals perished with few or no offspring" (81). See also Janet Radcliffe Richards, *Human Nature after Darwin* (London: Routledge, 2000), 257.

11 Joseph Ratzinger, *Introduction to Christianity*, trans. J. R. Foster (San Francisco: Ignatius, 1990), 31.

12 In fact, we are not far from Descartes's famous axiom that science has as its primary aim that of rendering us "masters and possessors of nature" (René Descartes, *Discourse on Method* [1637], trans. Elizabeth S. Haldane, in *Discourse on the Method; and Mediations on First Philosophy*, ed. David Weissman [New Haven: Yale University Press, 1996], 38); cf. *Discours sur la méthode* (1637), part 6, presented by Laurence Renault (Paris: GF Flammorion, 2009): "nous rendre comme maîtres et possesseurs de la nature."

13 See Georges Cottier, *Humaine raison. Contribution à une éthique du savoir* (Paris: Lethielleux, Groupe Parole et Silence, 2010), 245 (my translation).

14 Cited by Pope Benedict XVI in "The Listening Heart: Reflections on the Foundations of Law," Address to the Bundestag (Berlin, 22 September 2011), https://w2.vatican.va/content/benedict-xvi/en/speeches/2011/september/documents/hf_ben-xvi_spe_20110922_reichstag-berlin.html.

15 Joseph Ratzinger, "The Renewal of Moral Theology: Perspectives of Vatican II and *Veritatis splendor*," *Communio* 32 (Summer 2005): 363. This text was delivered orally, recorded, and elaborated in its present form by Livio Melina.

16 Friedrich Nietzsche, *On the Genealogy of Morals*, trans. Walter Kaufmann (New York: Vintage, 1969), 45; cited by Judith Butler in *Gender Trouble: Feminism and the Subversion of Identity* (New York: Routledge, 1990), 25.

17 McHugh, "Psychiatric Misadventures," *The American Scholar* 61, no. 4 (Autumn 1992): 503.

have in mind. A laboratory-fabricated specimen that is successfully implanted in a woman's uterus with the purpose of being carried to term is defined as "a child." The same specimen that is willfully destroyed is nothing more than "a collection of cells." Human life is thus "disposable when unwanted, purchasable when desired."[18] After all, as one lucky survivor of the embryo selection process puts it, "if it's okay to force a child into existence because it's so *wanted* then why is it not okay to force a child out of existence because it is *unwanted*?"[19]

It would also seem that we are not far from the "ideal" called for by Shulamith Firestone in her 1970 manifesto: the rejection of nature as a "human value," the elimination of "sex *distinction* itself"—at least in the sense that "genital differences between human beings . . . no longer matter culturally"—and the end of "the tyranny of the biological family." This will come about, Firestone claims, when the "reproduction of the species by one sex for the benefit of both" is finally "replaced by (at least the option of) artificial reproduction," with children being "born to both sexes equally, or independently of either, however one chooses to look at it."[20] At any rate, it would be difficult to find a better example of the spirit of autonomy, as well as the spirit of androgyny, which "embodies" it so well, than that of trans-identifying women and men seeking to become "fathers" and "mothers" by means of artificial reproductive technologies, as we saw in our previous chapter. This unmistakable move away from the (natural) normative mode of *co*-generation toward the (artificial) ideal of *autonomous* (or even asexual) generation might well represent the "ultimate" frontier toward the fully independent self-made man or woman, who is also the cultural ideal of Western society in general and of gender ideology in particular.

Ironically, however, such a groundless and sporadically directed freedom is only an illusion because instead of relying upon their own natural—and thus intrinsic—generative powers, these seemingly autonomous individuals have freely and very radically surrendered both themselves and their natural generative powers into the hands of doctors, scientists, surgeons, and fertility experts to do with as they can and will. The subject of science has thus been "perfectly

[18] Rickard Newman, "Journey to Baby Gammy: How We Justify a Market in Children," Public Discourse, August 18, 2014, https://www.thepublicdiscourse.com/2014/08/13701/.

[19] Alana S. Newman, "Life as a Lab Specimen," *Humanum: Issues in Family, Culture and Science* 2 (2014): 2, https://humanumreview.com/articles/life-as-a-lab-specimen.

[20] Shulamith Firestone, *The Dialectic of Sex: The Case for Feminist Revolution* (New York: William Morrow, 1970), 11–12. Firestone's thesis has been recently revived by Sophie Lewis in her book *Full Surrogacy Now: Feminism against Family* (New York: Verso, 2019). See also Marie Solis, "We Can't Have a Feminist Future without Abolishing the Family: The Feminist Thinker Sophie Lewis Has a Radical Proposal for What Comes Next," *Vice*, February 21, 2020, https://www.vice.com/en_us/article/qjdzwb/sophie-lewis-feminist-abolishing-the-family-full-surrogacy-now.

reconstructed as an object of science."[21] There is in fact ample evidence to support Heather Brunskell-Evans's thesis that "the 'transgender child' presumed by medicine and law is not a naturally occurring category of person external to medical diagnosis and legal protection."[22] On the contrary, the social theorist and philosopher convincingly argues that, far from existing independently of medico-legal discourse, this child is "constructed" by it. Evidently forgotten, neglected, or denied is the recognition of Josef Pieper that there is "no conceivable human act analogous to the act of Creation."[23]

It is due, in fact, to the unsurpassable character of the divine analogue of creation that the correlation of any particular thing to the human mind is ultimately—again from the realist, metaphysical position—because of "its primary correlation to God's mind."[24] And that is why human reason (*ratio*) serves *to discover*, rather than to accord, meaning to things on the basis of their own internal *ratio* (or *logos*)—that is to say, on the basis "eternal reasons" accounting for things or the "immanent reason" in each thing, which is its "proper intelligibility" or "essence."[25] After all, "whatever is according to nature is ordered by the Divine Reason, which," St. Thomas explains, "human reason ought to imitate."[26]

Hence, as Joseph Ratzinger summarizes:

> For the ancient world and the Middle Ages, being itself is true, in other words, apprehensible, because God, pure intellect, made it, and he made it by thinking it. To the creative original spirit, the Creator Spiritus, thinking and making are one and the same thing. His thinking is a creative process. Things are, because they are thought. In the ancient and medieval view all being is therefore what has been thought, the thought of the absolute spirit. Conversely, this means that since all being is thought, all being is meaningful, "*logos*," truth. It follows from this traditional view that human thinking is the re-thinking of being itself, re-thinking of

21 Robert Spaemann, "A Philosophical Autobiography," in *A Robert Spaemann Reader: Philosophical Essays on Nature, God, and the Human Person*, trans. and ed. D. C. Schindler and Jeanne Hefferman Schindler (Oxford: Oxford University Press, 2015), 19.

22 Heather Brunskell-Evans, "The Medico-Legal 'Making' of 'The Transgender Child,'" *Medical Law Review* 27, no. 4 (June 25, 2019): 640.

23 Josef Pieper, *Problems of Modern Faith: Essays and Addresses*, trans. Jan van Heurck (Chicago: Franciscan Herald Press, 1985), 281.

24 Josef Pieper, *The Truth of All Things: An Inquiry into the Anthropology of the High Middle Ages*, trans. Lothar Krauth, in *Living the Truth* (San Francisco: Ignatius, 1989), 52.

25 Marie-Joseph Nicolas, "Vocabulaire de la Somme théologique" in Thomas d'Aquin, *Somme théologique*, vol. 1, trans. Albert Raulin (Paris: Cerf, 1984), 115. Hence, as St. Thomas points out, "among the Greeks, 'word' [*verbum*] and 'reason' [*ratio*] are called *logos*" (Aquinas, *SCG* IV, c. 42, 2).

26 Aquinas, *ST* II–II, q. 130, a. 1.

> the thought which is being itself. Man can re-think the *logos*, the meaning of being, because his own *logos*, his own reason, is *logos* of the one *logos*, thought of the original thought, of the creative spirit that permeates and governs his being.[27]

In the final analysis, then, the reasons that we give for justifying our thoughts are themselves "the very reasons that things have for being that which they are."[28]

Here—in the optic of traditional metaphysics—we have a plea for a realist reversal of the Sartrian appropriation of the Cartesian *cogito ergo sum*, such that each thing's relation to the divine mind assumes priority over its relation to the human mind. After all, divine knowledge is, as Pieper explains, "creative in an absolute sense." To be known by God or not to be known by him means, quite simply, "to be or not to be."[29] That is why, in fact, the actual realm of really existing things (things that are really empowered by the forms with which they are endowed by the Author of nature) has priority over the realm of the possible: things and forms that are products of the human imagination.

THE INVERSION OF THEORETICAL AND PRACTICAL KNOWLEDGE: DIVINE TRUTH AND HUMAN IMAGINATION

For Aristotle, as Robert Spaemann explains, "it was self-evidently true that the actual was prior to the possible. Possibility was understood as the range of activity that opens up with each real being. Possibility meant 'to be able.' Only something real 'can.'" For Sartre, Beauvoir, and Butler, in contrast, it is the "sphere of consciousness [that] is understood as the sphere of possibility, from which reality proceeds."[30] Hence, for example, Sartrian existentialism takes as its starting point the assumption that "existence really does precede essence," and this in turn means that it is "impossible for man to transcend

27 Ratzinger, *Introduction to Christianity*, 31–32. Similarly, Pieper recognizes that "the interior word -character of things by which we are cognitively oriented to them simultaneously points to the creative aboriginal Word [*Ur-Wort*] of God himself" (Pieper, *The Concept of Sin*, trans. Edward T. Oakes [South Bend, IN: St. Augustine's Press, 2001], 46).

28 Marie-Joseph Nicolas, "Vocabulaire de la Somme théologique," 115. That is why, as Robert Spaemann explains, "Rationality would be a meaningless notion if nature did not turn a legible face to us" (Spaemann, *Essays in Anthropology: Variations on a Theme*, trans. Guido de Graaf and James Mumford [Eugen, OR: Cascade Books, 2010], xxiv).

29 Pieper, *Truth of All Things*, 55.

30 Robert Spaemann, "A Philosophical Autobiography," 19. This affirmation is made of modernity in general and not with specific regard for Sartre, Beauvoir, and Butler. It is I who make the application to their thought.

human subjectivity."[31] As for Butler, she suggests that we rethink "gender categories outside of the metaphysics of substance" so as to assign them to the "performative" realm instead.[32] It is therefore "real only to the extent that it is performed."[33] So much for practice makes perfect. For Butler, practice makes "to be," tout court.

To be sure, the performative realm is not lacking to the metaphysical tradition, which makes room for it within the classic distinction between theoretical and practical knowledge, which is explained by St. Thomas in terms of the analogy between human art and divine art. The "craftsman [or artist] first intends his end, then thinks out the form of his product, and finally brings it into existence."[34] In this way, the practical intellect of the craftsman or artist is responsible for the original form of the crafted object, which in turn is said to be "in-formed" by the application of his art.[35] Because, in other words, the practical intellect "'pre-forms' within itself the form" of the artifact to be created,[36] it measures that which it causes: for "all works of art find their origin in the intellect of an artist,"[37] and—we might add with respect to the "art" of "gender"—all surgical transformations originate in the mind of the surgeon and all "gender" performances, such as those of the drag queen, originate in the mind of whomever is said, in the Butlerian sense, to "do" "gender." From this (artistic or even technical) perspective, the human mind produces, by way of the practical intellect, the form of the things it creates. "This prescriptive, creative knowledge makes the knowing mind—or rather the paradigmatic form produced in the mind—the 'measure' [or standard[38]] of reality." That is why, as Josef Pieper points out, we know nothing "so thoroughly as the creation of our own mind and our own hands—provided it is truly our own creation."[39]

The speculative intellect, in contrast, is receptive with regard to created things, which means that the relation between forming and being informed

---

[31] Jean-Paul Sartre, *Existentialism and Human Emotions*, trans. Bernard Frechtman and Hazel E. Barnes (New York: Philosophical Library, 1957), 16–17.

[32] Butler, *Gender Trouble*, 25.

[33] Butler, "Performative Acts and Gender Constitution: An Essay in Phenomenology and Feminist Theory," *Theatre Journal* 40, no. 4 (December 1988): 527.

[34] Aquinas, *De Ver.* q. 4, a. 1.

[35] See Pieper, *Truth of All Things*, 39.

[36] Pieper, *Reality and the Good*, in *Living the Truth*, trans. Stella Lange (San Francisco: Ignatius, 1989), 122.

[37] Aquinas, *De Ver.* q. 1, a. 2.

[38] See Pieper, *Reality and the Good*, 121.

[39] Pieper, *Truth of All Things*, 40. This is not to admit, however, the maxim of Vico cited in our previous section, "*verum quia factum*": "all that we can truly know is what we have made ourselves." Cited by Ratzinger, *Introduction to Christianity*, 31.

is reversed.[40] The human mind is like "a writing-[tablet] on which as yet nothing actually stands written," Aristotle explains;[41] and that is why it is potentially "all things,"[42] being "naturally adapted" to spiritually possess the forms of other beings.[43] Hence to acknowledge, as does St. Thomas, that "the idea of the thing known is in the knower"—"not materially," of course, "but immaterially"[44]—is equivalent to saying "that the form of the knowing subject [the human soul in the case at hand] expands" in virtue of "the form of the object known."[45] In this way, it approaches a likeness to the divine intellect, which contains within itself the form and measure of all things.[46] Because, on the other hand, the likeness of things in the human intellect is but a copy of the original image existing in natural things,[47] human knowledge is the inverse of divine knowledge in which "all things pre-exist."[48] Because, in other words, all natural things owe both their existence and their essences (and thus also their forms) to the divine intelligence, truth is found in the human intellect only to the extent of its "conformity with the things whose notions it has."[49] Similarly, because to know means to have the form of that which is known, the knower who is not the thing's creator must be con-formed to its form. Only as such can he or she grasp the true meaning of that thing: God's creative intentions for it.

---

40 See Aquinas, *De Ver.* q. 1, a. 2.

41 Aristotle, *De An.* 3.4.430a1 (Barnes, 683); *ST* I, q. 79, a. 2.

42 See Aquinas, *ST* I, q. 79, a. 2 (with reference to Aristotle, *De An.* 3.4); and *ST* III, q. 9, a. 1 (with reference to *De An.* 3.18).

43 Aquinas, *ST* I, q. 14, a. 1. This is what it means, St. Thomas explains, to acknowledge that "the idea of the thing known" is said to be "in the knower." See also Aristotle, *De An.* 3.4.429a16 (Barnes, 682).

44 Aquinas, *ST* I, q. 14, a. 1; q. 84, a. 2. Aristotle insists that "it is not the stone which is present in the soul [that knows it] but its form" (Aristotle, *De An.* 3.8.431b30 [Barnes, 686]). After all, "A thing is knowable," as St. Thomas explains, "in so far as it is separated from matter" (*De Ver.* q. 2, a. 2). An object understood by us "does not exist in our intellect according to its own nature," therefore. Rather, "it is necessary that its species be in our intellect, and through this species the intellect comes to be in act. Once in act through this species as through its own form, the intellect knows the thing itself" (*SCG* I, c. 53, 2). In short, "the known must be in the knower after the manner of the knower" (*De Ver.* q. 1, a. 2).

45 Etienne Gilson, *Le Thomisme: Introduction à la philosophie de Saint Thomas d'Aquin*, 6th ed. (Paris: Vrin, 1986), 283.

46 See Aquinas, *De Ver.* q. 1, a. 8.

47 See Pieper, *Reality and the Good*, 123. In other words, the real things of this world are "the preforms and models" of what we come to know. Or, to return to our original analogy, just as a "work of art, insofar as it has really 'emerged' into visible reality, is essentially identical with its original model in the mind of the artist," so also "the 'what' of our knowledge, insofar as it is true, is identical with the original 'what' of real objects, which are the measure of knowledge" (124).

48 Aquinas, *ST* I, q. 80, a. 1.

49 Aquinas, *De Ver.* q. 1, a. 8. Similarly, truth is presented by Aquinas as "a conformity of the thing [known] and the intellect [which knows]" (q. 1, a. 1); and "truth in the intellect is measured by things themselves" (q. 1, a. 5).

Or, to express this same insight from the analogy of art, the human intellect is to intelligible objects as clay is to the mold whereby it is fitted by the artist.[50] It is "in-formed" by the "original form" provided by the real things of this world.[51] The object of human knowledge is thus the thing itself that is known; but it is known "by mode of species": by the causal action that it exerts upon the knowing subject.[52] After all, human knowledge is realized by the intermediary of the senses from which the intellect abstracts the in-*form*-ation it needs to form, in its turn, a mental image (or phantasm) of the object known.[53] Human knowledge is thus characterized by both an active and a passive dimension, with the latter consisting in the reception and apprehension of the essential form of the object that is known. As for the active dimension of knowing, it consists in the extraction of the intelligible core of a thing from its matter.[54] Hence, to know a thing in this manner—the manner proper to one who is *not* the thing's creator—means to *first of all receive* its interior essential form by mediation of the senses and only after a certain reasoning process (*ratiocinari*) that follows upon this reception to eventually seize, perceive, or *understand* this same form.

Providing the "link between [the human] intellect and reality" are thus the forms (or species) of real beings, whereby the human mind has access to their "rational core," or intelligibility.[55] After all, it is the form, as it corresponds to a precise idea of a creature within the mind of the divine Artist, that makes a thing intelligible or meaningful. Because it determines what a thing is or makes it to be what it is, it simultaneously distinguishes that thing from other species of beings. Hence, for example, to know Lassie is to know that Lassie is a dog. Because the form is also—indeed foremost—that whereby a thing is "proportioned," or adjusted, "to the divine intellect as a product of art is to art," it thus serves as the mediator between the thing and

---

50 See Aquinas, *ST* I, q. 14, a. 2, ad 3.

51 See Pieper, *Truth of All Things*, 39.

52 See Gilson, *Le Thomisme*, 285. This fact is necessary, Gilson observes, if we wish to maintain the objectivity of human knowledge: it is not the species of the object that is present in our thought but rather the object itself by way of its species. Hence, the latter is "not an added intermediary, or a distinct substitute, which is introduced into our thought in place of the thing [known]." Rather, it is "the sensible species of the thing itself, rendered intelligible by the agent intellect, which becomes the form of our possible intellect" (285–86). On the objectivity of knowledge, see also Pieper, *Reality and the Good*, 135–37.

53 See, for example, Aquinas, *SCG* IV, c. 11, 14.

54 See Pieper, *Reality and the Good*, 133–34.

55 Louis Dupré, *Passage to Modernity: An Essay in the Hermeneutics of Nature and Culture* (New Haven: Yale University Press, 1993), 39. Given this link, Dupré argues that "nowhere does the distance between mind and reality appear more clearly than in the nominalist rejection [shared, at least implicitly, by Sartre and Butler] of the so-called impressed *species*."

the human knower. In the words of St. Thomas, "its likeness being received into the [human] soul, causes the thing itself to be known."[56]

Hence, the analogy between the divine and human intellect entails not only a likeness but also a still greater difference. After all, the human intellect—like all created things—is itself measured according to a divine idea existing in the divine intellect, "as a material house is in the architect's mind."[57] Therefore, just as the creative intellect of the human artist "'pre-forms' within itself the form" of what he subsequently creates, the "creative intellect of God . . . 'pre-forms' within itself the form or nature" of all reality.[58] That is why the divine intellect is also the "rule and measure"—the standard by which to judge the truth, integrity, rectitude, or fittingness—of all created things, including not only the human intelligence but also the bodied person with his or her sex.[59]

Because, in other words, things are true when they correspond to the intellect that created them, "artificial things are said to be true as being related to our [the human] intellect," whereas "natural things are said to be true insofar as they express the likeness of the species [or ideas] that are in the divine mind."[60] It follows for the Angelic Doctor, in the wake of Aristotle, that the natural things from which we obtain scientific knowledge "measure our intellect," while "these [natural] things are themselves measured by the divine intellect, in which are all created things."[61] Because, in fact, their interior forms exist in the divine intellect before they actually exist within the things themselves, they are "measured" accordingly, just as a house is measured by the architect's blueprint. That is why, in the final analysis, our "submission to the real is by definition submission of the created intelligence to God, the Creator of this reality."[62]

---

[56] Aquinas, *De Ver.* q. 1, a. 5, ad 2; cf. *ST* I, q. 85, a. 2, ad 1.

[57] Aquinas, *ST* I, q. 44, a. 3, ad 1.

[58] Pieper, *Reality and the Good*, 121. Similarly, St. Thomas teaches that "originally and virtually, all being [as distinct from every nature] pre-exists" in God "as in its first cause" (*ST* I, q. 79, a. 2).

[59] "Now the mind, that is the cause of the thing, is related to it as its rule and measure" (Aquinas, *ST* I, q. 21, a. 2).

[60] Aquinas, *ST* I, q. 16, a. 1. In the first case—that of artificial things—St. Thomas gives the example of a house, which is true to the extent that it corresponds to the image in the architect's mind. In the second case—that of natural things—he gives the example of a stone, which is true insofar as it "possesses the nature proper to a stone, according to the preconception in the divine intellect." See also *ST* I, q. 21, a. 2.

[61] Aquinas, *De Ver.* q. 1, a. 2. See also *ST* I, q. 21, a. 2. Cf. Aristotle, *Metaphysics*, in *The Complete Works of Aristotle: The Revised Oxford Translation*, ed. Jonathan Barnes, trans. J. A. Smith, vol. 2 (Princeton, NJ: Princeton University Press, 1984), X, 1, 1053a31–33 (p. 1664); X, 6, 1057a10–12 (pp. 1669–70).

[62] Comité d'études sociales et doctrinales, *Connaître le communisme* (Paris: Haumont, 1946), 10; cited by Henri de Lubac, *The Drama of Atheist Humanism*, trans. Anne Englund Nash (San Francisco: Ignatius, 1995), 412.

THE INVERSION OF WORD AND CONCEPT: LANGUAGE AS TRUTH OR WORDS OF DESTRUCTION

This conformity of knowledge to reality is of central importance for language, which is likewise true to the extent that it is in conformity with the reality that it serves to express and communicate. "A person who says what is true utters certain signs which are in conformity with things," St. Thomas explains; and "according as a thing is, or is not, our thoughts or our words about it are true or false."[63] Or, as Pieper explains more specifically, because "real objects are the preforms and models of that which our mind cognitively forms," it is necessarily with reference to these same objects that our words are formed and that language is measured or judged to be true.[64] "Any discourse detached from the norms of reality is," Pieper reasons, "mere monologue;" for "to be true means to be determined in speech and thought by what is real."[65]

It can hardly be otherwise, since the spoken word is always the expression of a mental, or "interior," word (*verbum interius*), which is to the understanding mind what color is to the seeing eye: "that which the one understanding forms when understanding," namely, "a notion [*ratio*] and likeness [*similitudo*] of the thing understood."[66] As "conceptions of the intellect,"[67] words signify what is understood, and that is why the interior word is, as St. Thomas teaches, "naturally prior, being the efficient and final cause of the exterior," or spoken, word, which subsequently "manifest[s] the interior."[68] Hence, "word" signifies "first and chiefly," the Angelic Doctor continues, the "interior concept of the mind" and only "secondarily, the vocal sound itself, signifying the interior concept."[69]

This interior word implies, in turn, a conceptualization, or categorization, of the object understood on the basis of its own inner form, or species. And it is this form, or species, that constitutes its defining characteristic: that which makes any given thing to be *what* it is: a tree, a flower, or a person, for example. Because, in fact, we cannot know "without a phantasm"—that is to say, without

---

[63] Aquinas, *ST* II–II, q. 109, a. 1, ad 3; *ST* I, q. 21, a. 2.

[64] Pieper, *Reality and the Good*, 123.

[65] Josef Pieper, *Abuse of Language, Abuse of Power*, trans. Lothar Krauth (San Francisco: Ignatius, 1992), 17.

[66] Aquinas, *Super Ioan.* I, lect. 1, no. 25. Hence, for example, "the intellect's words of the stone is the stone understood" (*SCG* IV, c. 11, 9).

[67] Aquinas, *ST* I, q. 85, a. 5.

[68] Aquinas, *De Ver.* I, q. 4, a. 1. Similarly, "the word conceived in the mind is representative of everything that is actually understood" (*ST* I, q. 34, a. 3). See also *ST* I, q. 85, a. 2; and *SCG* IV, c. 11, 6.

[69] Aquinas, *ST* I, q. 34, a. 1.

a sensory representation or an image of the object known.[70] It is on this same basis (the form of that which is known, first sensually and then intellectually) that we create the concepts (intelligible forms) expressing the content of our knowledge, which in turn are at the origin of our words. "For by the fact that the intelligible species, which is the form of the intellect and the principle of understanding, is the likeness of the external thing, it follows that the intellect forms an intention like that thing," Aquinas teaches, and "by forming such an intention, [it] knows that thing."[71] Hence, the same concept whereby we know is that whereby we speak, since both derive from the real form of the object known. In fact, to name a thing is to define it on the basis of its form, or species, for this is what serves to categorize it: likening and distinguishing it from other things as a particular (Lassie, for example) belonging to a universal (dog) in virtue of a common form (the likeness, or species—*eidos*—of a dog).

It is precisely this order between the object that is known and the concept whereby it is known and named that is challenged by Judith Butler's attempt to redefine the parameters between the particular (any given object) and the universal (expressed as a concept). Hence, for example, in response to the question of whether lesbians might be considered women, Butler argues:

> I certainly have no qualms about using such terms [those of "lesbians" and "women"] and will reflect . . . on how one might continue *at the same time* to interrogate [in other words, to call into question the concepts themselves] and to use the terms of universality. If the notion of the subject, for instance, is no longer given, no longer presumed, that does not mean that it has no meaning for us, that it ought no longer to be uttered. On the contrary, it means only that the term ["women" or "lesbian"] is not simply a building block on which we rely, an uninterrogated premise for political argument.[72]

Such is still another example of the inversion by gender theorists in the wake of Sartre and Beauvoir of the central analogy that we have been drawing upon in this volume: that of the form existing in the artist's mind to explain the manner in which the world itself and each of its members exists in the mind of God.

---

[70] Cf. Aquinas, *SCG* IV, c. 11, 5. It is the phantasm that provides the raw data for the formation of the concepts that are expressed in thought. For more explanation, see Robert Pasnau, *Thomas Aquinas on Human Nature: A Philosophical Study of* Summa theologiae *Ia 75–89* (Cambridge: Cambridge University Press, 2002), 278; and *ST* I, q. 84, a. 6; a. 7, ad 2; q. 85, a. 1; and q. 85, a. 1, ad 3, ad 5.

[71] Aquinas, *SCG* I, c. 53, 4. See also *ST* I, q. 16, a. 2; and q. 14, a. 2.

[72] Butler, *Undoing Gender* (New York: Routledge, 2004), 179. She concludes by acknowledging, "I suppose that this places me on the divide of the modern/postmodern in which such terms remain in play, but no longer in a foundational mode."

To borrow again from St. Thomas:

> Just as there preexists in the mind of a craftsman a certain image of his external work, so also does there pre-exist in the mind of one who pronounces an exterior [or spoken] word a certain archetype of it. Consequently, just as we consider three things in the case of a craftsman, namely, the purpose of his work, its model, and the work now produced, so also do we find a threefold word in the one who is speaking. There is the word conceived by the intellect, which, in turn, is signified by an exterior vocal word. The former is called *the word of the heart* [or the concept[73]], uttered but not vocalized. Then there is that upon which the exterior world is modeled; and this is called *the interior word* which has an image of the vocal word. Finally, there is the word expressed exteriorly, and this is called *the vocal word.* Now, just as a craftsman first intends his end, then thinks out the form of his product, and finally brings it into existence, so also, in one who is speaking, the word of the heart comes first, then the word which has an image of the oral word, and, finally, he utters the vocal world.[74]

Because, moreover, the art of the human craftsman (like that of the surgeon or the scientist working in reproductive technologies) is always limited both by his own art—the knowledge characterizing his discipline and his own appropriation thereof—and by nature, since he always makes use of things that are in this world, the analogy implies that our words will be limited in the same way. To be still more specific, because human knowledge, like human art, is necessarily limited by the real—by, that is to say, the divine art that both precedes and measures it—our words will also be limited by the real that they serve to convey. Words, after all, express understanding, which in turn requires that the intellect be in act. As differing from the divine intellect, moreover, which as "pure act"[75]

[73] "Whenever we understand, by the very fact of understanding, there proceeds something within us, which is a conception of the object understood, a conception issuing from the intellectual power and proceeding from our knowledge of the object. It is this conception which the spoken word signifies; and it is called the word of the heart signified by the word of the voice" (Aquinas, *ST* I, q. 27, a. 1).

[74] Aquinas, *De Ver.* I, q. 4, a. 1. As this passage explicates, that which is understood as "a terminus of intelligible operation" is, as St. Thomas explains, "distinct from the intelligible species that actualizes the intellect, and that we must consider the principle of intellectual operation though both are a likeness of the thing understood" (Aquinas, *SCG* I, c. 53, 4). Or, as Gilles Emery makes still more explicit, "The word is not that *through which* the mind knows (which is the *species*) but is, rather, the *fruit* of an internal making or conceiving, the expression of the reality known within our mind" (Emery, *The Trinitarian Theology of St. Thomas Aquinas*, trans. Francesca Aran Murphy [Oxford: Oxford University Press, 2007], 184).

[75] Aquinas, *ST* I, q. 14, a. 1, ad 1; q. 79, a. 2.

is "always actually understanding,"[76] the human intellect is "first of all in potency and then in act"[77] or "formable before being formed."[78] It must, in other words, be in-formed by the created things of this world, which are "nothing but a certain real expression and representation of the things comprehended in the conception of the divine Word."[79]

Unlike God, who "understands himself and all things in one act, his single Word," human knowledge thus implies that there be "many words" within our minds "according to the many things that we understand."[80] Moreover, rather than understand things immediately, we require an effort to synthesize our scattered thoughts or to assemble them into a single coherent expression: a mental word that is the "*expression* of the thing known in the mind of the knower."[81] This word thus depends upon a discursive noetic process that St. Thomas compares to understanding "as movement is to rest, or acquisition to possession."[82] Only through such a process of reasoning that begins and ends with the real things of this world—by way, namely, of the phantasms that represent them—do we therefore come to an understanding of these same things.[83] The "word interiorly conceived" is thus "a kind of account and likeness of the thing understood," and to the extent that this interior word is accurate—to the extent that it accords with reality—it is true.[84] Truth, in other words, implies that the intellect "has the likeness of the thing known" or that the thing itself "corresponds to the form which it [the intellect] apprehends about that thing."[85] "For the thought formed from that thing which we know is the word which we speak in our heart," St. Augustine explains in an insight that is assuredly foundational for St. Thomas's own teaching; and "the words themselves in our speech are signs of the things of which we are thinking."[86]

---

[76] Aquinas, *SCG* I, c. 55, 9. See also IV, c. 11, 13.

[77] Aquinas, *Opuscule* XIII: "*De Differentia Divini Verbi, et Humani*," in *Opuscules de Saint Thomas d'Aquin*, III (Paris: Vrin, 1984), 139.

[78] Aquinas, *Super Ioan.* I, lect. 1, no. 26. See also Aquinas, *SCG* IV, c. 11, 10.

[79] Aquinas, *SCG* IV, c. 42, 3.

[80] Aquinas, *ST* I, q. 34, a. 3. See also Aquinas, *Super Ioan.* I, lect. 1, no. 27.

[81] Emery, *Trinitarian Theology of St. Thomas Aquinas*, 182. Cf. Aquinas, *ST* I, q. 79, a. 8. See also *ST* I, q. 85, a. 1; and *De Ver.* I, q. 4, a. 1.

[82] Aquinas, *ST* I, q. 79, a. 8. See also *ST* I, q. 85, a. 1; and *De Ver.* IV, 1. "Knowledge as an accomplished fact is not an 'activity' of the intellect," Pieper explains, "but its realization" (*Living the Truth*, 134).

[83] See Pasnau, *Thomas Aquinas on Human Nature*, 278–95.

[84] Aquinas, *SCG* IV, c. 11, 14; see *ST* I, q. 21, a. 2: "According as a thing is, or is not, our thoughts or our words about it are true or false."

[85] Aquinas, *ST* I, q. 16, a. 2. God, in contrast, "does not direct His act of knowing toward things one by one" (*De Ver.* I, q. 1, a. 5).

[86] St. Augustine of Hippo, *De Trinitate*, trans. Stephen McKenna, *The Trinity* (Washington, DC: The Catholic

Human words, to summarize the foregoing, differ from the divine Word in much the same way as our knowledge differs from divine knowledge, as the creature differs from the Creator. "As a human vocal sound is to a human word conceived in the mind, so is the creature to the divine Word," St. Thomas explains in an insight borrowed from Origen; "for as our vocal sound is the effect of the word conceived in our mind, so the creature is the effect of the Word conceived in the divine mind. *For he spoke, and they were created* (Ps 148:5)."[87] Human words—to insist upon the point—are not creative in this same (absolute) sense. Instead, they are radically dependent upon the created world, which they serve to express. Undoubtedly, there are many things that exist in human thought that do not correspond to the real world. We can imagine pink elephants, polka dotted unicorns, and ten-headed monsters, but all of these thoughts have their origin in things that we really have encountered: gray elephants and pink flowers, dotted dresses and horned animals, and monstrous-looking animals; these are things whose forms have been recomposed within our imaginations. Moreover, even if one day we somehow manage to introduce these imaginative beings into the animal kingdom by way of biological engineering, for example, we will do so only by starting with real animals, whose cells provide the real corporeal material necessary for launching the scientific process, just as their forms are necessary for launching the imaginative process that is still more primary. Similarly, the imaginative process at the origin of both the "art" of "sexual reassignment" and the "art" of artificial reproductive technologies presupposes the real world of sexual beings with real reproductive powers. They are not created out of nothing nor out of imaginative schemas that exist only in the human mind independently of real, bodied persons.

In short, human words are expressions of what is understood, either because the thing understood has been created by us—so as also to be fittingly named by us, such as "iPad," "email," "microwave," and "solar panel," or because we have been in-formed by their natural forms—forms that have been seized by our senses and captured by our intellects. That is why, as St. Thomas puts it, "the Word is specified by the object which it names, and not by him who names it."[88] It is thus not surprising that C. S. Lewis has observed in his study of words from various languages that "similar or even identical semantic operations" are "performed quite independently" in different languages; and this in turns leads him to conclude that there is "something, either in the structure of the mind or

University of America Press, 1963), XV, 10, 19 (p. 476).

[87] Aquinas, *Super Ioan.*, I, lect. 5, no. 135.

[88] Aquinas, *Opusculum* XIV: "*De Natura Verbi Intellectus*" in *Opuscules de Saint Thomas d'Aquin*, III, 142.

in the things it thinks about, which can produce the same results under very different conditions."[89] As for Pieper, he is convinced that "we are just as little capable of fashioning language as we are of fashioning the [human] hand," and he distrusts any so-called "original" definition that would delineate itself "too far apart from ordinary language use."[90]

Of course, this is not to deny that language naturally evolves. It does so, however, not so much in the manner of "an insect undergoing metamorphoses" as instead, Lewis explains, in the manner of "a tree throwing out new branches."[91] As for those words (or more properly those "terms"[92]) that come about in virtue of our own inventions or discoveries—such as "iPad" or "penicillin"—we can have recourse to them, Pieper suggests, only thanks to a living—that is, natural—language: "only on the basis of a non-terminological, that is, a linguistic, agreement, just as we can only 'hand-le' an axe [a man-made tool] with the help of the [natural human] hand."[93]

Again, we could hardly be further from Judith Butler's proposition for a discourse that has the authority to bring about what it names. Such is a proposition for the disjunction of nature's order from that of culture and convention, a disjunction that impoverishes language by its assumption that the *logos* resides "exclusively in the human subject," thereby "depriving all other being of its inherent meaning," as Louis Dupré diagnoses the "art" of sophism.[94] To lose sight of the real that exists independently of our sensory and mental perceptions, so as to resist us, to stand in our way, or to literally be thrown against (*ob-iectum*) us—as is implied in the word *object*—is to risk reversing the traditional order of reference: "to envision reality itself through the prism of language," or to think that things are real because they are thought, known, and/or spoken *by us*.[95] Such, for example, is Butler's attempt "to pillage the Logos for its useful remains,"[96] thereby creating a parallel world of what Pieper calls "nonbinding utterances, with the certain

---

89 C. S. Lewis, *Studies in Words* (New York: Cambridge University Press, 1967), 5–6.

90 Josef Pieper, "Language and the Philosophizing Person: Aperçus of an Aquinas Reader," in Pieper, *For the Love of Wisdom: Essays on the Nature of Philosophy*, ed. Berthold Wald, trans. Roger Wasserman (San Francisco: Ignatius, 2006), 201, 197.

91 Lewis, *Studies in Words*, 8.

92 "Term and terminology are 'made,' artificial, and, by virtue of a convention, restricted and affixed to specific meanings; by contrast, language and word have evolved historically, naturally, and cannot be tied to an unequivocal sense," Pieper explains ("Language and the Philosophizing Person," 200–201).

93 Pieper, "Language and the Philosophizing Person," 201.

94 Dupré, *Passage to Modernity*, 25.

95 Louis Dupré, *Metaphysics and Culture*, The Aquinas Lecture, 1994 (Milwaukee, WI: Marquette University Press, 1994), 7.

96 Butler, *Bodies That Matter*, ix.

ground of reality swept from under one's feet."[97] This, moreover, is no small matter, for "word and language form the medium that sustains the common existence of the human spirit as such," thereby providing the sustenance of every human society and culture.[98] To abuse the word by "verbal artistry" that is detached from the norms of reality is thus to threaten the very tissue of human existence as social and communal.[99]

From this perspective, we might well imagine what Pieper would say of the UK's Health and Safety Executive (HSE)'s decision to replace the word "women" on their website with "people with a cervix"[100] or of the suggestion of Brighton's University Hospital to replace "breastfeeding" with "chestfeeding."[101] So too might we form an idea of Pieper's resistance to the Human Rights Campaign with its recommendation that we reserve the term "vagina" for natal men identifying as trans who have undergone bottom surgery and that we use the term "front hole" for the internal genitals of biological females.[102] As for the Midwives Alliance of North America, they recommend that we substitute "pregnant individual" for "pregnant woman." After all, it is reasoned, "'Woman' refers to gender and is not the same as 'female.'"[103] Tell that to Andrea Chu, who maintains that "while all women are females, not all females are women."[104] Remember, for Chu, "you are female, even—especially—if you are *not a woman*."[105] Of course, one ought not to "assume that every person you meet—trans or otherwise—will use or understand these terms." Nonetheless, the Human Rights Campaign Foundation urges us to keep in mind that "our bodies are

---

97 Pieper, "Language and the Philosophizing Person," 197.

98 Pieper, *Abuse of Language, Abuse of Power*, 15. It is the "reality of the word" that "in eminent ways makes existential interaction happen," Pieper explains.

99 Pieper, *Abuse of Language, Abuse of Power*, 18.

100 See "What Cervical Screening Is," Health and Safety Executive (HSE) website, December 30, 2019, https://www2.hse.ie/screening-and-vaccinations/cervical-screening/what-cervical-screening-is.html. See also Niamh Ui Bhriaian, "Hey Women! We've Been Downgraded to 'Anyone with a Cervix' by the HSE," GRIP, September 19, 2020, https://gript.ie/hey-women-weve-been-downgraded-to-anyone-with-a-cervix-by-the-hse/.

101 Rosie Taylor and Katie Gibbons, "Breastfeeding Is Now Chestfeeding, Brighton's Trans-friendly Midwives Are Told," *The Times*, February 9, 2021, https://www.thetimes.co.uk/article/breastfeeding-is-now-chestfeeding-brightons-trans-friendly-midwives-are-told-pwlvmcnc7.

102 Human Rights Campaign Foundation, "Safer Sex for Trans Bodies" (Whitman-Walker Health, 2020), accessed on January 29, 2021, https://assets2.hrc.org/files/assets/resources/Trans_Safer_Sex_Guide_FINAL.pdf.

103 Midwives Alliance of North America, "Position Statement on Gender Inclusive Language." The statement continues: "Cis-gendered women are females who identify with the qualities generally associated with women. But not all females identify as woman, nor do all females share the same physiology or phenotype."

104 Chu, *Females* (New York: Verso, 2019), 12.

105 Chu, *Females*, 2 (emphasis added).

our own to name and use."[106] Such, after all, as gender theorists would have us believe, is the very "stuff" of which both art and the self are now made.

One can only hope that despite transgender efforts to dismiss the word *woman* as merely a sociocultural category, it will continue to live on in our lexicon, as Alex Byrne predicts that it will:

> There is no reason to think that the utility of a word for the category *adult human female* will markedly decline in the foreseeable future. Unlike scullery maids, cigarette girls and switchboard operators, the mature females of our species will continue to be an important topic of thought and talk. So even if "woman" could somehow be coaxed to change semantically, a new word for the category (a snappier version of "natal woman" or "bio woman," already in occasional use) would very likely fill the lexical vacuum. Ambitious ameliorative projects for "woman" should therefore be viewed with some skepticism.[107]

Presumably Judith Butler would agree. After all, she acknowledges:

> For many . . . the structuring reality of sexual difference is not one that one can wish away or argue against, or even make claims about in any reasonable way. It is more like a necessary background to the possibility of thinking, of language, or being a body in the world. And those who seek to take issue with it are arguing with the very structure that makes their argument possible.[108]

Hence, the very desire to do away with sexual difference "is only further evidence of its enduring force and efficacy."[109] On the other hand, her willingness to use words whose meanings she contests points to her purpose of challenging the traditional meaning and purpose of language itself. Butler argues, more specifically, that we ought not to understand language as based on truth in the classic sense of the term: "a conformity of the thing [known] and the intellect [which knows]," as Aquinas would have it.[110] Instead, as we have seen, language becomes a tool for redefining reality according to a form invented by the human intellect—a technical or artistic form—in view of changing sociocultural norms by political means.

---

[106] Human Rights Campaign Foundation, "Safer Sex for Trans Bodies."

[107] Alex Byrne, "Are Women Adult Human Females?" *Philosophical Studies* 177 (2020): 3800–3801.

[108] Butler, *Undoing Gender*, 176.

[109] Butler, *Undoing Gender*, 177.

[110] Aquinas, *De Ver.* q. 1, a. 3. See also *ST* I, q. 16, a. 1.

Such is also the tactic of Andrea Chu who—despite "her" fidelity to mainstream trans-theory by setting mind over matter, consciousness over desire, and desire over sex—nonetheless insists upon adopting the traditional categories of sex in discourse. In fact, Chu has become a controversial figure for her objection to the policing of expressions like "sex-change surgery." "I'm supposed to write *gender confirmation surgery*, as if all the doctors did was to throw your inner woman a big thumbs-up."[111] Whether against trans-theorists who argue for the strict separation of sex and gender or the "b----" who objects, "Oh, since you were always a woman, you shouldn't have to—," Chu daringly insists that "*change*" is "*the whole point*" of bottom surgery. "That means there has to be a before. Even if that before is uncomfortable."[112] Moreover, as if to challenge those who claim that they "always" knew that they were in the "wrong" body, Chu admits that it took "years" to come to the realization "that I might be a woman." She "hated being a man," but it seemed obvious enough that "being a man was my punishment for being a man. Anything else was greed."[113]

Of course, Chu is pointing thereby to corporeal (if not biological) changes:[114] "her" vaginoplasty entailed a prior act of castration. Nonetheless, let the reader beware! Chu is hardly suggesting a return to essentialism in what Stephen Adubato suggests is a "postmodern-to-premodern turn."[115] On the contrary, in her outrageous book *Females*, Chu offers a satire of *both* premodern essentialism and the postmodern dissolution thereof. As if to poke fun at us all, the young gender theorist and self-proclaimed feminist changes the direction of the standard account of the social construction of gender by directing us away from the self-made man of modernity, along with his "essentially non-referential" desires: his "self-begotten and self-propelled" motives requiring, as Zygmunt Bauman points out, "no other justification or 'cause'" than themselves.[116] Instead, Chu attempts to defend what "she" admits is an

[111] Andrea Long Chu, "All Reproduction Is Assisted," *Boston Review*, August 14, 2018, https://bostonreview.net/forum/all-reproduction-assisted/andrea-long-chu-extreme-pregnancy.

[112] Sessi Kuwabara Blanchard, "Andrea Long Chu Is the Cult Writer Changing Gender Theory," *Vice*, September 11, 2018, https://www.vice.com/en/article/ev74m7/andrealong-chu-interview-avital-ronell-gender (emphasis original).

[113] Chu, *Females*, 51.

[114] See (once again) our treatment in chapter 5 of this volume for a thorough distinction between the two.

[115] Stephen G. Adubato, "Andrea Long Chu's *Females* subverts subversiveness," *The Catholic World Report*, September 16, 2020, https://www.catholicworldreport.com/2020/09/16/andrea-long-chus-females-subverts-subversiveness/.

[116] Zygmunt Bauman, *Liquid Modernity* (Cambridge, UK: Polity, 2000), 74. Desire, from the modern perspective, Bauman explains, "has itself for its constant object, and for that reason is bound to remain insatiable" (75).

"indefensible claim," namely that "femaleness is less a biological state and more a fatal existential condition that afflicts the entire human race—men, women, and everyone else. Or maybe she's just projecting."[117]

"Projecting" is arguably what Chu does best, and "she" does it in the Sartrian sense of forging one's own version of freedom. For although Chu claims that her bottom surgery is an attempt to change herself and not the world, her cleverly crafted book is far more than a simple apology for the raid upon her ("formerly" masculine) body.[118] More properly, it is an offensive attack upon the reader's mind. In fact, it is as if Chu seeks to do *to us* what she claims that sissy porn did to "her" (or rather to *him*): it "forced feminization."[119] Like sissy porn, which "directly addresses its viewers and presumes to inform them of their own desires" in view of transforming them "into females themselves," Chu seeks to convince us that we are all—every one of us—"female": at least in the new sense that Chu assigns to the term, namely, as we saw in chapter 5, the "psychic operation in which the self is sacrificed to make room for the desires of another."[120] In the shadow of her heroine, Valerie Solanas, founder of the Society for Cutting Up Men (SCUM), who "would make statements not because they were accurate or provable, but simply because she *wanted* to," Chu confronts her reader with "desire, not truth."[121] Such, after all, is arguably the purpose of Chu's book: to point out that language is merely a tool of art which, in turn, is "coterminous with life itself." "True art"—not unlike nature or being from Sartre's point of view—could, Chu claims, just as well be "nothing at all."[122]

THE GENDER REGIME: TOLERANCE FOR FEELINGS AND DESIRES, INTOLERANCE FOR TRUTH

Because, to summarize our plea in the foregoing, truth implies (at least by those

---

[117] Chu, *Females*, description from the integrated book cover flap.

[118] "Faced with the decision to change the world or to change yourself, you've [Chu is speaking personally] decided to change yourself" (Blanchard, "Andrea Long Chu Is the Cult Writer Changing Gender Theory").

[119] Chu, *Females*, 76. "Sissy porn," Chu explains, is pornography in which "the women it depicts (some cis, some trans, mostly but not always white) are in fact former men who have been feminized ('sissified') by being forced to wear makeup, wear lingerie, and perform acts of sexual submission. This is executed through the unique form of second-person address in which captions are typically written: sissy porn directly addresses its viewers and presumes to inform them of their own desires: 'You love to be f----- in the a--,' for instance" (75).

[120] Chu, *Females*, 76, 11.

[121] Chu, *Females*, 19.

[122] Chu, *Females*, 86.

who hold to it) the determination of speech and thought by an objective—or *real*—world beyond human consciousness, it is the "reality of the word" that makes authentic human communication possible. For, as Pieper remarks, "we can talk only about reality, nothing else."[123] Of course, this does not mean that we cannot speak of pink elephants, pregnant men, or women with penises. When we do, however, we must be mindful that these concepts are mental ones: they do not reflect an objective world of God's making. Rather, they refer to either an imaginative world or—far more dangerously—to an ideological one of human invention (artifice).[124] In the former case—that of an imaginative world—artistic expression serves to invent a world (such as Lewis's *Narnia*) in view of entertainment, diversion, or even instruction. In an ideological world, in contrast, thoughts, intentions, desires, or goals are imposed upon the real world *in view of its transformation*, as gender theorists know only too well. Because, in fact, sexual identity is detached by gender theory from the objective reality of biological sex (as corporeal, hormonal, genetic, and potentially reproductive), this objective reality has effectively been usurped by subjective desires and personal choices, which in turn have been condoned by our sociopolitical system and even written into law.[125] Such is the origin of the "lie" that sex can be linguistically, hormonally, surgically, genetically, psychologically, and/or socially-culturally altered at will.[126]

Arguing at least two decades before the emergence of virtual reality as we know it, Pieper referred to such an altered world as a "*pseudoreality*" resulting from the "abuse of language" by its detachment from truth and reality.[127] In fact, "the most miserable decay of human interaction" is correlated by the famous German philosopher, who witnessed Hitler's rise to power, "in direct proportion to the most devastating breakdown in orientation toward reality."[128] To speak the truth, in contrast—even at the cost of ruffling the cherished feathers of

[123] Pieper, *Abuse of Language, Abuse of Power*, 15–16.

[124] Or, as Margaret McCarthy points out with respect to the particular "art" of transgenderism, it is actually an "*anti*-artifact because it exists to *hide* (not adorn) and, even worse, 'trouble' [to borrow from Butler]—and ultimately unmake—the boy it hides" ("The Emperor's [New] New Clothes: The Logic of the New 'Gender Ideology,'" *Communio* 46, no. 4 [2019]: 621).

[125] See, for example, Helen Alvaré, "Religious Freedom versus Sexual Expression: A Guide," *Journal of Law and Religion* 30, no. 3 (2015): 475–95.

[126] See Walt Heyer, "'Sex Change' Isn't Surgically Possible, My Surgeon Testified in Court," The Stream, February 24, 2020, https://stream.org/sex-change-isntsurgically-possible-my-surgeon-testified-in-court/; and Michael W. Chapman, "Johns Hopkins Psychiatrist: Transgender Is 'Mental Disorder'; Sex Change 'Biologically Impossible,'" CNS News, June 2, 2015, http://cnsnews.com/news/article/michael-w-chapman/johns-hopkins-psychiatrist-transgender-mental-disorder-sex-change.

[127] Pieper, *Abuse of Language, Abuse of Power*, 34.

[128] Pieper, *Abuse of Language, Abuse of Power*, 33. Similarly, "Public discourse itself, separated from the standard of truth, creates on its part . . . the reign of the tyrant" (31).

subjective convictions, autonomous desires, or sacrosanct personal choices—is to guard our natural homeland of the real against pseudo-realities that are as dangerous as they are deceptive.

As a case in point, one might consider a recent US Supreme Court decision that imposes, as David Crawford and Michael Hanby observe, an essentially "'trans' paradigm" upon Americans,[129] requiring that we interpret "sex" as an umbrella term that is no longer understood as binary (male and female) but henceforth includes sexual identity (transgenderism) and sexual orientation (homosexuality).[130] Or, to better explain the Court's reasoning, which has rightfully been denounced as "sophistry":[131] because the discrimination suffered by a trans individual can be considered "sex discrimination" *only if* the sexes (male and female) are regarded as indistinguishable or interchangeable, such is necessarily the case.[132] Or to put it still more straightforwardly, the Court did not simply evacuate the meaning of the term *sex*; it also informed us—as Margot Cleveland puts it with no bones—that we must "consider men women and women men in the workplace."[133] There could hardly be a better example of the conviction that "gender theory outlaws reality."[134]

From the standpoint of the "interchangeability" of the sexes, however, the Court's argument defeats its own purpose. After all, as Abigail Shrier has pointed out in her attempt to explain why so many transactivists insist

---

[129] Crawford and Hanby, "The Abolition of Man and Woman," *The Wall Street Journal*, June 24, 2020, https://www.wsj.com/articles/the-abolition-of-man-and-woman-11593017500.

[130] The ruling reads: "It is impossible to discriminate against a person for being homosexual or transgender without discriminating against that individual based on sex" (Bostock v. Clayton County, 140 S. Ct. 1731, https://www.supremecourt.gov/opinions/19pdf/17-1618_hfci.pdf). (The phrase in question appears on p. 9.)

[131] See Roger Riska, "US Supreme Court Stuns with Activist Ruling on Anti-Discrimination," Christian Concern, June 22, 2020, https://christianconcern.com/comment/us-supreme-court-stuns-with-activist-ruling-on-anti-discrimination/; and Russell R. Reno, "A Striking Display of Sophistry," *First Things*, June 16, 2020, https://www.firstthings.com/web-exclusives/2020/06/a-striking-display-of-sophistry.

[132] David Crawford has good reason to note, however, that "Whether there really are such things as men and women is not a 'policy preference'" ("The Metaphysics of Bostock," *First Things*, July 2, 2020, https://www.firstthings.com/web-exclusives/2020/07/the-metaphysics-of-bostock).

[133] Margot Cleveland, "Supreme Court: Treat Men and Women as Interchangeable, Or Get Sued into Oblivion," The Federalist, June 18, 2020, https://thefederalist.com/2020/06/18/supreme-court-treat-men-and-women-as-interchangeable-or-get-sued-into-oblivion/. Or, as the Women's Liberation Front put it in their Twitter discussion of the case, "The Court ruled it's discriminatory not to treat a man as a woman under sex-based policies if he 'identifies as transgender'" (Women's Liberation Front [WoLF] on Twitter: "Why the Harris Supreme Court Decision Is Not a Win for Women, Nor Is It Narrow," @WomensLibFront, June 19, 2020, https://twitter.com/WomensLibFront/status/1274096937822834690).

[134] Rod Dreher, "Gender Theory Outlaws Reality," The American Conservative, October 9, 2019, https://www.theamericanconservative.com/dreher/gender-theory-outlaws-reality. See also Rod Dreher, "Totalitarian Wars on Reality," The American Conservative, December 19, 2019, https://www.theamericanconservative.com/dreher/maya-forstater-totalitarian-transgenderism/.

upon the innate character of gender, equal protection is granted to sex under the Fourteenth Amendment precisely because—like race, but unlike hair color, for example—it is considered "immutable."[135] Quite clearly it is not possible to have one's cake and eat it too. So-called "trans" persons might well be entitled to protection under the Equal Rights Amendment, but one would be hard pressed to find a place for this protection under the category of sex. As for the rest of us, at stake in this ruling (*Bostock v. Clayton County, Georgia*) is, as Margaret McCarthy fittingly portrays the situation, the question of whether one's "pre-ideological innate knowledge of oneself as a boy or girl, imbibed quite literally at the maternal breast, will be for all practical and public purposes officially overruled as false, a 'stereotype.'"[136] That is to say, "the cloak of 'gender' . . . render[s] invisible all the naked evidence."[137] Or to follow this intuition still further: even worse than requiring that we live as if this primal knowledge of natal sex is merely a stereotype, the ruling requires us to live as if what we "know to be false [that sex can be changed to match feelings, desires, or states of consciousness] were officially true." In the words of Crawford and Hanby:

> Ironically, what is now "true" is nothing but stereotypes, that bundle of mannerisms, dress, makeup and hairstyles by which one imagines what it feels like to be a woman or a man. Worse still, it [the Supreme Court ruling] prefers them [gender stereotypes], especially when they are at odds with one's actual sex. The war on pronouns, an assault upon the language by which we recognize a world in common, follows of necessity. What we are dealing with is nothing less than a war on reality itself. And everyone has just been pressed into service.[138]

When, however, the language in which human rights has been traditionally framed is called into question—such as, for example, the language we use to protect women from unjust discrimination in the workplace, from domestic

[135] See Abigail Shrier, *Irreversible Damage: The Transgender Craze Seducing Our Daughters* (Washington, DC: Regnery, 2020), 134–35.

[136] Margaret Harper McCarthy, "Overruling the Visible: The Emperor's New Gender," Public Discourse, October 6, 2019, https://www.thepublicdiscourse.com/2019/10/57542/. Similarly, the Women's Liberation Front argues, "Only by preserving the 'woman' stereotype can men claim to 'live as women' or 'identify as transgender.' If sex stereotypes did not exist, Stephens would have no grounds on which to 'identify as' a woman" (WoLF, "Why the Harris Supreme Court Decision Is Not a Win").

[137] McCarthy, "Emperor's (New) New Clothes," 621.

[138] Crawford and Hanby, "The Abolition of Man and Woman."

violence, and from male predators,[139] or to ensure their specialized health care[140] or an equal playing field in women's sports[141]—then we must not only fight against the tyrannical abuse of language and claims of "wrongthink."[142] We must also fight against sacrificing human rights to ideological claims, with "trans" rights trumping women's rights and girls' rights, as Brunskell-Evans and Shrier argue at length.[143] Or, as J. K. Rowling reasons, "If sex isn't real, there's no same-sex attraction. If sex isn't real, the lived reality of women globally is erased. . . . [And] erasing the concept of sex removes the ability of many to meaningfully discuss their lives. It isn't hate to speak the truth."[144]

Assuredly, there is no less likely a candidate for attesting to the truth of these claims than Andrea Chu, with "her" thesis that "femaleness is a universal sex defined by self-negation."[145] Yet, it is precisely Chu who acknowledges with clearheaded tact and sobering honesty what few gender theorists are willing to admit:

---

[139] As Brunskell-Evans points out, in 2017, there were no transgender persons murdered in the UK, but there were 138 women killed by men (*Transgender Body Politics* [North Geelong, Australia: Spinifex, 2020], 145). Meanwhile, "an average of one trans person is murdered each year in the UK," which is "lower than the UK average." Georgia Lee, "Fact Check: How Many Trans People Are Murdered in the UK?," November 23, 2018, https://www.channel4.com/news/factcheck/factcheck-how-many-trans-people-murdered-uk. On the massive "gender-related killings" of women and girls worldwide, see United Nations Office on Drugs and Crime, *Global Study on Homicide: Gender Related Killings of Women and Girls* (Vienna, 2018), https://www.unodc.org/documents/data-and-analysis/GSH2018/GSH18_Gender-related_killing_of_women_and_girls.pdf.

[140] J. K. Rowling gives the example of multiple sclerosis, "a disease that behaves very differently in men and women" ("J. K. Rowling Writes about Her Reasons for Speaking Out on Sex and Gender Issues," June 10, 2020, https://www.jkrowling.com/opinions/j-k-rowling-writes-about-her-reasons-for-speaking-out-on-sex-and-gender-issues/).

[141] A 2020 study discovered that the "15–31% athletic advantage that transwomen displayed over their female counterparts prior to starting gender affirming hormones declined with feminising therapy. However, transwomen still had a 9% faster mean run speed after the 1 year period of testosterone suppression that is recommended by World Athletics for inclusion in women's events." See Timothy A. Roberts et al., "Effect of Gender Affirming Hormones on Athletic Performance in Transwomen and Transmen: Implications for Sporting Organisations and Legislators," *British Journal of Sports Medicine* (December 7, 2020): 1. As for the controversy surrounding this problem, it suffices to consider the case of parents who dare question "how the law, women's rights and Title IX might be handled" in the case of women with an average testosterone threshold of .5 to 2.4 nmols/L competing against transgender "women" who are allowed a testosterone threshold of 10 nmols/L by the NCAA. To this very question, one Ivy League parent was told that "the words biological and genetic had no business being in a discussion about sex and gender" (Swimming World Editorial Staff, "Ivy League Parent Opens Up about Pain and Shock Met during Lia Thompson Controversy," *Swimming World*, March 1, 2020, https://www.swimmingworldmagazine.com/news/ivy-league-parent-i-want-people-to-wake-up-to-the-world-we-are-creating-for-women/). See also Shrier, *Irreversible Damage*, 151–52.

[142] Rowling, "J. K. Rowling Writes about Her Reasons."

[143] See Brunskell-Evans, *Transgender Body Politics*; and Shrier, *Irreversible Damage*.

[144] J. K. Rowling, Tweet of June 7, 2020; @jk_rowling; https://twitter.com/jk_rowling/status/1269389298664701952.

[145] Chu, *Females*, 11.

> Gender transition begins . . . from the understanding that how you identity yourself subjectively—as precious and important as this identification may be—is nevertheless on its own basically worthless. If identity were all there were to gender, transition would be as easy as thinking it—a light bulb, suddenly switched on. Your gender identity would simply exist, in mute abstraction, and no one, least of all yourself, would care.[146]

Chu concludes with words that merit repetition: "If there is any lesson of gender transition—from the simplest request regarding pronouns to the most invasive surgeries—it's that gender is something other people have to *give you*."[147]

In this way, Chu suggests that even if gender is chosen, it must nonetheless be confirmed *from without*: by the pronouncement of those who *speak* of what they have *seen and touched*, of what they hold by knowledge or judgment to be *true*. In this sense, gender bears objective weight and not merely subjective cunning; and it is as such—as objective—that it is affirmed (again, *from without*) as true or valid. We are not far, once allowance is granted for the absence of truth claims, from Sartre's "problem" of "mak[ing] myself be by acquiring the possibility of taking the Other's point of view on myself."[148] As for Chu, "she" is not seeking to be "patronize[d]" or affirmed by gratuitous words motivated by pity. "She" "know[s] what beautiful looks like."[149] What "she" really longs for are words of conviction with regard to "her" chosen gender; words that are inspired by knowledge of the truth; words that are true because they signify the real, the given: *natum est*. After all, "What I want isn't surgery," Chu admits; "what I want is never to have needed surgery to begin with. I will never be natural, but I will die trying."[150]

It is this yearning for the natural, for the real, for the natal body—for what is normative in the natural world—that Chu calls "the Elephant in the Room," presumably because a gender theorist should not speak of such a beast.[151] In fact, Chu dares to say what few trans activists are willing to hear:

[146] Chu, *Females*, 38.

[147] Chu, *Females*, 38.

[148] Sartre, *Being and Nothingness: A Phenomenological Essay on Ontology*, trans. Hazel E. Barnes (New York: Washington Square Press, 1984), 476.

[149] "When she [Chu's girlfriend] tells me I'm beautiful, I resent it. I've been outside. I know what beautiful looks like. Don't patronize me" (Chu, "My New Vagina Won't Make Me Happy").

[150] Chu, "All Reproduction Is Assisted," *Boston Review*, August 14, 2018, https://bostonreview.net/forum/all-reproduction-assisted/andrea-long-chu-extreme-pregnancy.

[151] Chu, "All Reproduction Is Assisted."

"When people today say that a given gender identity is 'valid,' this is true, but only tautologically so. At best it is a moral demand for possibility, but it does not, in itself, constitute the realization of this possibility. The truth is, you are not the central transit hub for meaning about yourself, and you probably don't even have a right to be."[152]

In a similar manner, Daisy Chadra presents her own "trans" experience in a YouTube testimonial during "detransition":

> I didn't have physical dysphoria. What I was told to describe was social dysphoria. It was about being able to control how other people perceive me. I didn't want to be a guy. I wanted to *be seen* by others as a guy. I wanted to express my felt masculinity to the extremest extent that I could. . . . I realize now that I was trying to control the way other people saw me. It was mostly about having control over how people perceive me. . . . I thought I had a male soul. . . . That was the narrative. It was from a place of envy. Vanity was also involved. . . . It's exactly the antithesis of the philosophy of gender fluidity. I didn't understand: why do trans people talk about blurring the lines between genders? I wanted them to be fixed so that I can put myself in a box and be intelligible to people. I couldn't relate to the idea of blurring the lines.[153]

Because, as these examples serve to illustrate, subjective desires, feelings, and inner convictions are the very "stuff" wherein identity (whether personal or sexual) and even personal freedom are thought to dwell within our contemporary, Western, and largely postmodern culture, any form of linguistic expression that calls them into question threatens the most "sacred" of human values. That is why, as Carl Trueman explains, oppression is no longer measured—as it was for our ancestors—principally in terms of distributive justice: by access to or denial of employment, health care, or education, for example. Today, in contrast, it is considered as mostly "linguistic in character":

> Words become all-important because words are speech-acts by which we acknowledge or deny the identity of another. . . . Words are, to use the hyperbolic jargon of our cultural moment, instruments of violence because injury is conceptualized in psychological terms. This is why speech codes are now so important.

---

[152] Chu, *Females*, 38.

[153] Chadra, "I'm Detransitioning," *YouTube*, October 27, 2020, https: / /www.youtube.com / watch?v=R_KD46_Ophg.

> Even the accidental use of an inappropriate pronoun can be seen as an assault on someone's person because it is seen as a denial of their identity.[154]

One need only consider what Jonathan Garcia and Richard Crosby describe as "coded discrimination" consisting of "in-direct, 'in-between the lines,' micro-aggressions that were more difficult to confront than blatant transphobia." Such coded discrimination occurs when "a person doesn't necessarily know that what they are doing is discrimination" but their words or behavior are experienced as aggression. As a case in point, they refer to the specifically "trans" experience of "transphobic things . . . like misgendering in the streets," which is presented as "death by a thousand cuts, wearing you down and invalidating you."[155] To be sure, there can be no question of the very real suffering of one who so deeply longs to be affirmed and for whom *personal* affirmation is equated with *gender* affirmation. Nor should we make light of any habitual inattentiveness or aloofness—far less any aggression—toward so-called "trans" persons who are always (regardless of their own perceptions) far more than their "gender." We cannot assume, however, that every act or word that is subjectively experienced as discrimination should be objectively judged as such. In fact, much of the challenge in our postmodern world is trying to get a handle on what it means to be fair, equal, just, or even objective.

Until recently—to explain by way of contrast—there were not only objective norms for determining justice or injustice but also cultural norms of social conduct that were transmitted from one generation to the next. Because these norms were both built into the culture and sustained by what was acknowledged as a common human nature—whence the notions of common decency, humane actions, and moral virtue, for example—they were more or less imbibed, to return to McCarthy's image, with our mother's milk. In other words, for those of us who grew up in a pre-postmodern society, we knew these standards almost by instinct, and we likewise knew when we were breaking them. With, however, the "queering" of culture—and thus also of law, politics, science, education, and even family—under the influence of what Heather Brunskell-Evans presents as "an extremely small constituency . . . who have secured a monopoly," these norms of conduct have been

[154] Trueman, "The Impact of Psychological Man—and How to Respond," Public Discourse, November 10, 2020, https://www.thepublicdiscourse.com/2020/11/72190/. See also part 1: Trueman, "The Rise of 'Psychological Man,'" Public Discourse, November 9, 2020, https://www.thepublicdiscourse.com/2020/11/72156/.

[155] Garcia and Crosby, "Social Determinants of Discrimination and Access to Health Care among Transgender Women in Oregon," *Transgender Health* 5, no. 4 (2020): 225–33, https://www.ncbi.nlm.nih.gov/pmc/articles/PMC7759275/.

forcefully called into question along with nature itself.[156] We should not be surprised, therefore, that what is sometimes experienced as discrimination might well be nothing more than resistance to the imposition of a new code of conduct, or rather, to the de-coding of the old code: the "queering" of natural norms, the unbinding of law, the rewriting of public policies, the overturning of social structures, the breaking down of traditions, and the reversing of cultural trends. In short, the new norm of queer theory is, as Mary Harrington observes, "anti-normie-ism," and the "heretic" or oppressor is one who "*resist[s]* the wholesale attack on rules, norms and traditions."[157] From this perspective, an act of "misgendering," or of refusing to address someone using their preferred pronouns, may, for example, be intended far less as an attack on another's person (nor even—as is sadly understood to mean the same—on that person's "gender") than as a refusal to collaborate with the new "gender" system, replete with its own rules, which contradict the "old" rules of timeless nature: of, that is to say, natural law.

Required by the new gender regime is, more specifically, the injunction that we use words that no longer reflect our knowledge of a visible, tangible, even audible reality or of a recent historical past—a time when, for example, my "daughter" was still my son or when my "father" was still my mother. Instead, we must employ words reflecting the invisible, inaccessible world of *another's consciousness*, not of things, but of inner states: of subjective convictions, inward desires, individual tastes, or personal feelings. Moreover, we are called to do so for the express purpose of complying with and even encouraging a new normative social pattern: one designed to bring "intelligibility" and even "materiality"—as Judith Butler would have it[158]—to otherwise "unruly" bodies: to bodies that do not "fit" a gendered choice, or one's personal project, to borrow from Sartre. In other words, by naming these bodies in accord with gender "consciousness"—which is not to be confused with consciousness *of the body*—we contribute to the establishment of a new normative code based on feelings rather than knowledge, on subjective consciousness rather than fact, on inner sentiment rather than objective truth, thereby contributing to the reversal of the order between signified (body) and signifier (word).[159]

---

[156] Brunskell-Evans, *Transgender Body Politics*, 122 (see also 83–90).

[157] Harrington, "The Tyranny of Queer Theory," UnHerd, October 15, 2020, https://unherd.com/2020/10/how-queer-theory-has-eaten-the-culture/.

[158] See my treatment of Butler's philosophy in chapter 2 of this volume.

[159] For a historical development of this turn to the feelings over reason, see Mary Ann Glendon, "Rousseau and the Revolt against Reason," *First Things*, October 1999, https://www.firstthings.com/article/1999/10/rousseau-the-revolt-against-reason.

When, in fact, it is possible for one to publicly affirm—as did Thomas Beatie—that "I used my female reproductive organs to become a father,"[160] or when a father is threatened by the courts with arrest without warrant into addressing his daughter using exclusively male pronouns;[161] when one must call a bearded man "madam";[162] when a journalist is fired for claiming that there are only two sexes;[163] when birth certificates are issued that present mother as "father" and father as "mother"[164] and likewise allow for a change of sex without so much as proof of surgery;[165] when grade-school children can change their gender status on school records in the absence of legal documentation;[166] when a husband is said to have saved his marriage by becoming "a woman;"[167] when those who claim "men are not women" are silenced on public media[168] or lose

---

[160] Cited by R. J. Wilson, "'First Pregnant Man,' Ten Years Later: Thomas Beatie Reflects on a Difficult Decade," Urbo, July 12, 2018, https://www.urbo.com/content/the-first-pregnant-man-10-years-later-thomas-beatie-reflectson-a-difficult-decade/.

[161] Jeremiah Keenan, "Authorities to Arrest Canadian Father if He Refers to Trans Child by Her Real Sex," The Federalist, April 29, 2019, https://thefederalist.com/2019/04/29/authorities-arrest-canadian-father-refers-trans-child-real-sex/; and Jeremiah Keenan, "Canadian Appeals Court Rules Father Can't Stop Teen Daughter from Taking Male Hormones," The Federalist, January 14, 2020, https://thefederalist.com/2020/01/14/canadian-appeals-court-rules-father-cant-stop-teen-daughter-from-taking-male-hormones/.

[162] See Rod Dreher, "Call the Bearded Man 'Madam'—Or Else," The American Conservative, October 2, 2019, https://www.theamericanconservative.com/dreher/transgender-doctor-britain-bearded-man/.

[163] Lindsey Ellefson, "Denver Post Columnist Says He Was Fired for His 'Insistence' That There Are Only 2 Sexes: Joe Caldara's Final Column Argued That to Be Inclusive, People Are Expected to 'Lose Our Right to Free Speech,'" The Wrap, January 20, 2020, https://www.thewrap.com/denver-post-columnist-says-he-was-fired-for-his-insistence-that-there-are-only-2-sexes/.

[164] See Jake Wittich, "Transgender Parents Welcome Baby Girl, Prompting Update to State's Birth Certificate System," *Chicago Sun Times*, January 6, 2020, https://chicago.suntimes.com/2020/1/6/21034801/transgender-parents-illinois-baby-update-birth-certificate-system; and Le Monde with AFP, "Une femme transgenre reconnue comme mère par la justice," *Le monde*, February 9, 2022, https://www.lemonde.fr/societe/article/2022/02/09/une-femme-transgenre-reconnue-comme-mere-par-la-justice_6112969_3224.html.

[165] See Laura Wilson, "New Colorado Law Allows Transgender People to Obtain New Birth Certificate without Proof of Surgery," *Fox Denver*, January 4, 2020, https://kdvr.com/2020/01/04/new-colorado-law-allows-transgender-people-to-obtain-new-birth-certificate-without-proof-of-surgery/.

[166] Selim Algar, "Changing Gender Is Easier Than Ever in NYC Schools," *New York Post*, June 28, 2019, https://nypost.com/2019/06/28/changing-gender-is-easier-than-ever-in-nyc-schools/.

[167] Asher Fogle, "My Husband Became a Woman—And It Saved Our Marriage," *Good Housekeeping*, June 17, 2015, https://www.goodhousekeeping.com/life/relationships/a32977/jonni-and-angela-pettit-transgender-marriage/.

[168] See Twitter's "Hateful Conduct Policy," https://help.twitter.com/en/rules-and-policies/hateful-conduct-policy; Hank Berrien, "Famed Feminist Furious after Twitter Says She Violated Rules by Saying Men Are Not Women," The Daily Wire, November 16, 2018, https://www.dailywire.com/news/38426/famed-feminist-furious-after-twitter-says-she-hank-berrien; and Jo Bartosch, "Twitter's War on Outspoken Women," Spiked, March 21, 2019, https://www.spiked-online.com/2019/03/21/twitters-war-on-outspoken-women/.

their jobs;[169] when international institutions are compelled to frame women's rights arguments as belonging to "people who menstruate"[170] and cultural icon J. K. Rowling is "canceled" for tweeting the same;[171] yes, when all of these and still innumerable other abuses are committed against our common language and the truth that it expresses, then clearly a parallel world of gender regime is well underway.

As each of these examples so effectively illustrates, in the name of "tolerance" we are required to forego our own knowledge of the sexed body, accessed by way of the senses, in favor of another's unqualified claims of "feelings" or inner "convictions." These claims, in contrast, have no point of objective reference beyond a subjective conscious state, which is to say that they are accessible to others on the sole basis of the claims themselves. Of course, this is not to deny that only the person whose gender is in question can know his or her own body *from within*. When, however, a so-called "trans" person claims to possess a gender other than the one assigned at birth—as in the common narrative, "I have always known that I was female" or "I have always been a male deep down"—it is not generally an experience *of the body* that is thereby invoked: the experiences of menstruating, developing breasts, growing a beard, or one's voice deepening, for example. In fact, it is readily admitted that such experiences of the body are causes of tremendous discomfort and even anxiety for these same persons, whence still another common narrative: that of a man "trapped" in a woman's body or a woman "locked" in a man's body. Indeed, the "feelings" of gender need not have any connection to the body at all.

In, however, the absence of a common object (a sexed body) serving as the point of reference for consciousness (whether one's own or another's), it is impossible—to return to the Pieperian analysis—to engage in authentic communication. That is why we are left with a clash between competing claims of authenticity or veracity, on the one hand, and those of justice or oppression, on the other. Such is a clash that is perhaps best expressed as a question: Why, in the new gender regime, do feelings and desires necessarily have precedence

[169] *BBC News*, "Maya Forstater: Woman Loses Tribunal over Transgender Tweets," December 19, 2019, https://www.bbc.com/news/uk-50858919.

[170] See, for example, Marni Sommer, Virginia Kamowa, and Therese Mahon, "Creating a More Equal Post-Covid-19 World for People Who Menstruate," USAID/DEVEX, May 28, 2020, https://www.devex.com/news/sponsored/opinion-creating-a-more-equal-post-covid-19-world-for-people-who-menstruate-97312#.XtwLnv0aEeR.twitter.

[171] "'People who menstruate.' I'm sure there used to be a word for those people. Someone help me out. Wumben? Wimpund? Woomud?" (J. K. Rowling, Tweet of June 6, 2020, @jk_rowling, https://twitter.com/jk_rowling/status/1269382518362509313).

over truth claims? Or, to put it still more straightforwardly, why do *your feelings* trump *my knowledge*?

The response to this question might be as simple as the fact that the substantial *person* of more metaphysically solid times has been replaced by the psychological "self" of the present era, whose fulfillment—as the testimonies of Chu and Chadra confirm—requires that inner "needs," desires, feelings, and convictions be socially acknowledged and affirmed. Moreover, for this same reason—that the self requires the social affirmation of his subjective state—the policing of language has become "central to society," as Carl Trueman observes.[172] After all, it is only through language that we can have access to the conscious states of others, wherein personal identity is somehow thought to be held captive.

Assuredly, we are not far from the typically Sartrian presentation of the conflictual mode of existence with others. Such, as we saw in chapters 4 and 5, is the constant struggle between the self (a pure freedom, or consciousness) and the Other (reduced to an object of my consciousness). Because the Other is also a self, however, he is acknowledged by Sartre as possibly possessing knowledge of me that is beyond my own realm of consciousness. Indeed, it is in virtue of this knowledge that he is said to exercise a certain power over me, just as I do over him. By his "look"—it bears repeating—he holds "the secret of my being, he knows what I *am*."[173] That is why, even in the game of love, as theorized by Sartre, what the lover "demands is a limiting, a gluing down of the Other's [in this case, the beloved's] freedom." Or, to put it more crudely, "I must be the inherent limit to his very transcendence."[174] It could hardly be otherwise if my own objective existence—my "facticity" beyond the *cogito*, who is unquestionably the starting and end point of Sartrian existentialism—is to be assured in the absence of God. For when the Creator is no more, it is uniquely within the Other's consciousness that my objective being is given to be. And that is why Sartre claims that "the world must be revealed [to the beloved] in terms of me. . . . I must be the one whose function is to make trees and water exist, to make cities and fields and other men exist, in order to give them later to the [beloved] Other who arranges them into a world."[175] In short, "if I am to be loved [or affirmed], I am the object by whose agency the world

[172] See Trueman, "Rise of 'Psychological Man,'" and Trueman, "Impact of Psychological Man."

[173] Sartre, *Being and Nothingness*, 473.

[174] Sartre, *Being and Nothingness*, 480.

[175] Sartre, *Being and Nothingness*, 481.

will exist for the Other; in another sense I am the world."[176] It is the "I," in other words, who necessarily takes the place of God.

At any rate, the fragile "self," or *cogito*, of the present era—whether in the Sartrian sense or in that spelled out by Trueman—is undoubtedly the origin of the attempt of the gender regime to force a way into the minds of others. Such, after all, is the unique manner of assuring the self's own survival. Desperate, therefore, is the attempt to gain access and even control over the way that others think of one's own self—including one's preferred gender—and likewise how they regard various basic realities of human existence that affect me. It follows, as a matter of course, that the traditional democratic values of freedom of speech and freedom of religion, along with the acknowledgement of objective truths, "are rapidly coming to be seen as vices," Trueman observes. For, "where the psychological self is normative, speech becomes violence and freedom of speech thus a license for violence." Indeed, even "silence is violence," Trueman adds, whence the impossibility of religious freedom assuming the form of silent disapproval without being judged as intolerant.[177]

Likewise "intolerant" are feminists known as TERFS (Trans-Exclusionary Radical Feminists) who stick to their guns, arguing that "the physical and social consequences of being female [like pregnancy and sexual assault] are so significant that women need specific protections in law and policy."[178] Anyone daring to make such claims that promote women *qua* women are shunned from the public square,[179] silenced,[180] and labeled as "bigots,"[181] as are all who refuse the "bait-and-switch" philosophy at the "heart of queer theory."[182] "Intolerant" too are those who question the fairness of competition between biological women and trans athletes[183] and even lesbians refusing to date "trans women with penises."[184] As for any scientific work that does not

[176] Sartre, *Being and Nothingness*, 482.

[177] Trueman, "Impact of the Psychological Man."

[178] Brunskell-Evans, *Transgender Body Politics*, 99. See also Shrier, *Irreversible Damage*, 150–52.

[179] See Brunskell-Evans, *Transgender Body Politics*, 132–43.

[180] See Brunskell-Evans, *Transgender Body Politics*, 104.

[181] See, for example, Chu, *Females*, 30–31.

[182] Harrington, "Tyranny of Queer Theory."

[183] See, for example, "LGBT Group Drops Martina Navratilova over Transgender Comments," *The Guardian*, February 20, 2019, https://www.theguardian.com/sport/2019/feb/20/lgbt-group-drops-martina-navratilova-over-transgender-comments.

[184] Rowling, "J. K. Rowling Writes about Her Reasons." See also the development by Brunskell-Evans, *Transgender Body Politics*, 32–34.

conform to the queer model, it is "taken hostage,"[185] and its authors are publicly humiliated and dismissed from their jobs, practices, or universities, as Lisa Littman, Kenneth Zucker, J. Michael Bailey, James Caspian, and Allan Josephson know only too well.[186]

There can be no policing of those, on the other hand, who are simply expressing their "inner selves" instead of making truth claims. After all, there are no means of entering into that sacred inner chamber where the self is constantly created and recreated by the power it has invested in itself. For, as Angela Franks wittily remarks, "If my identity is the residue of my performative action"—including the choices I make—"rather than the other way around, then I am never expressing myself, only creating it."[187] Hence, words do not so much acknowledge an objective reality as give birth to a subjective inner state, which in turn is charged—as Butler would have it—with giving meaning to otherwise "meaningless" matter. Or, to express this subjective phenomenon on a larger, sociocultural scale, the current preference for *selves* (who are created by feelings and desires) over *persons* (who are understood metaphysically in terms of substance) entails a corresponding reversal of the traditional metaphysical order between *knowledge*, by which truth claims are made, and *desire*, which is measured subjectively.[188] Hence, gender theorists have been granted license to confront their readers with "desire, not truth."[189] In so doing, they have begun undoing the essential "knots" of all that is tightly bound in virtue of our natures as sexed. In the profound insight of Margaret McCarthy:

> [The gender regime is] *diabolical* in the technical sense, because it *separates* (διάβολω) things that belong together—birth and sexual difference, sexual difference and sex, then sex and motherhood and fatherhood—and then reattaches them, on its own terms. To choose one's "gender" is to give birth to

[185] Mark Regnerus, "Queering Science," *First Things*, December 2018, https://www.firstthings.com/article/2018/12/queering-science.

[186] See Shrier, *Irreversible Damage*, 25–39, 123–29; Rachel del Guidice, "Academia Today 'Not for Faint-Hearted,' Says Professor Who Lost His Job for Talking about Gender," The Daily Signal, August 27, 2019, https://www.dailysignal.com/2019/08/27/academia-today-not-for-faint-hearted-says-professor-who-lost-his-job-for-talking-about-gender/; and BBC News, "Bath Spa University 'Blocks Transgender Research.'"

[187] Angela Franks, "The Plane Where Nietzsche and Jane Austen Meet," *Church Life Journal*, December 15, 2020, https://churchlifejournal.nd.edu/articles/the-plane-where-nietzsche-and-jane-austen-meet/.

[188] For more explanation, see Kenneth Schmitz, "Selves and Persons: A Difference in Loves?," *Communio* 18, no. 2 (1991): 181–206; and Gilles Emery, "The Dignity of Being a Substance: Person, Subsistence, and Nature," *Nova et Vetera* 9, no. 4 (2011): 991–1001.

[189] Chu, *Females*, 19.

> oneself (self-identification). It is then to avail oneself of an "unobstructed pansexuality" (self-determined orientation). Finally, it is to be the master of one's future by taking control of reproduction, "cut[ting] out all [our] posterity in what[ever] shape [we] please."[190]

Such, as Lewis puts it in another, albeit similar context, is the futile attempt "to take the living and seminal figures which God has painted on the canvas of our nature" and artistically "shift them about as if they were mere geometrical figures."[191]

[190] McCarthy, "Emperor's (New) New Clothes," 650. The internal reference is to C. S. Lewis, *Abolition of Man: Reflections on Education with Special Reference to the Teaching of English in the Upper Forms of Schools* (Oxford: Oxford University Press, 1943), 72.

[191] C. S. Lewis, "Priestesses in the Church?," in *Essay Collection: Faith, Christianity and the Church* (London: HarperCollins, 2000), 401.

CONCLUSION

A Plea for Respecting the Analogy between Divine Art and Human Art

In contrast to the transgender "body art" trend, which sets man up as his own creator, the ancient and medieval analogy of art, which we have drawn upon in these pages, is one that necessarily safeguards the *ever-greater difference* between the creature and the Creator. To be sure, man is like God in that he too "is the principle of his action, as having free-will and control of his actions."[1] Nonetheless, "no similitude can be expressed" between Creator and creature "without implying a greater dissimilitude."[2] Hence, unlike God, who "by one act understands all things in His essence" and "wills all things in His goodness," we know only in virtue of the fact that we are ourselves known and willed by God.[3] This accounts for the fact that the human word is, as we have seen, a "measured" word: it necessarily expresses (and thus corresponds to) the real world that God has created. In this way it radically differs from the Word of God in whom all things were created (cf. Col 1:16). Whereas—to put it more straightforwardly—human knowledge follows upon the existence of things, divine knowledge causes things to exist.[4] God therefore "does not gather knowledge from things [as we do]; rather, by His knowledge He produces things [including the human intellect] in being" and consequently renders human knowledge and creativity possible.[5]

---

1 Aquinas, *ST*, I–II, Prologue.

2 The Fourth Lateran Council (1215), in Heinrich Denzinger, ed., *Compendium of Creeds, Definitions, and Declarations on Matters of Faith and Morals*, 43rd ed., ed. Robert Fastiggi and Anne Englund Nash (San Francisco: Ignatius, 2012), 806.

3 Aquinas, *ST* I, q. 19, a. 5.

4 "Things are knowable" by us, Josef Pieper explains of Aquinas's teaching, "because they have been created" (Pieper, *The Silence of St. Thomas*, trans. John Murray and Daniel O'Connor [South Bend, IN: St. Augustine's Press, 1999], 56).

5 Aquinas, *SCG* IV, c. 13, 6.

As St. Thomas puts it in no uncertain terms:

> Now, just as an intellectual agent, because of the [imaginative] account [or model] he has in himself, produces things in being, so also a teacher, because of the account he has in himself, causes science in another, since the science of the learner is drawn from the science of the teacher, as a kind of image of the latter. God is not only the cause by His intellect of all things which naturally subsist, but even every intellectual cognition is derived from the divine intellect. . . . Necessarily, then, it is by the Word of God, which is the knowledge of the divine intellect, that every intellectual cognition is caused. Accordingly, we read in John (1:4): "The life was the light of men," to wit, because the Word Himself who is life and in whom all things are life [*sic*] does, as a kind of light, make the truth manifest to the minds of men.[6]

This important distinction between God's knowledge and ours is denied by Judith Butler's insistence that there is no prediscursive corporeality: no human body before human words bring it into being. To hold to such an assumption is, however, to forget, as Sylviane Agacinski points out, that those who speak are "living bodies." Hence, "when Aristotle defined man as 'a being endowed with *logos*,' the *logos* . . . appeared as a power of these particular living beings whom we are. Inversely, an *a priori* spiritualized or logo-centric position"—a position awarding ontological priority to language—"leads to the integral subordination of the living being to the speaking being."[7] In that case, the difference between a natural creature and an artisanal fabrication is simply obliterated, as is the difference between the Creator and the creature. When, on the other hand, we hold to this difference, we are reminded that the relation between matter and form is not the same for a body endowed with certain natural potentialities as it is for one that is organized from without by way of human intervention. Although, to be more specific, an animated being "acts and lives by actualizing . . . its natural and organic power"; it does not, Agacinski continues, "fashion or produce its own body."[8] Nor, we are to be reminded, does it fashion or produce the powers whereby it acts, whether in an artistic or ideological mode.

What we might retain from this important analogy between God's creation and our own is that common to both are the notions of purposefulness and ends—notions that are likewise present in the ancient and medieval sense of

[6] Aquinas, *SCG* IV, c.13.

[7] Sylviane Agacinski, *Femmes entre sexe et genre* (Paris: Editions du Seuil, 2012), 146.

[8] Agacinski, *Femmes entre sexe et genre*, 144.

the term "art" (*ars*), although they are denied by Sartre and Beauvoir. As for the art of acting and living well, which is the specific domain of ethics, it too is measured by a specific end, namely, the good of the human being as conceived by the Creator. The human person is not, in other words—as Sartre, Beauvoir, Butler, and other gender theorists would have us believe—his or her own creator. He or she is, rather, a responsible agent who creates within God's creation and who perfects his or her own natural powers and inclinations with respect for nature's own powers and inclinations, including those of his or her own bodily and spiritual nature.

It is thus "natural to man," as St. Thomas reasons in union with the Aristotelian tradition, "to take pleasure in contemplating truth and in doing works of virtue."[9] Indeed, virtue is fostered by the contemplation of truth: God's intentions, including his specific purpose and intention for human nature. Such, as we have seen, is the foundation of a classical understanding of morality. In fact, as Joseph Ratzinger has remarked, it was a common conviction of "almost the whole of mankind before the modern period . . . that man's Being contains an imperative." This, in turn, means "that he does not himself *invent* morality on the basis of calculations of expediency but rather *finds* it already present in the essence of things."[10] Such is the origin of the parallel conviction that "the *language of nature*" (in the present case, two distinct-yet-complementary sexes) "is *also the language of morality* (man and woman called to equally noble destinies, both eternal, but different)."[11] If, moreover, this is the case—that a classic understanding of morality entails a correlation between human nature and its end—this is not due to an arbitrary declaration on the part of God, as would befit the Nominalist vision of divine causality, whose influence continues to pervade contemporary thought. For there is "nothing so far" from the Aristotelian-Thomistic tradition as the conception of an arbitrary God, deciding what is good and what is bad in the absence of reason.[12]

Because, on the contrary, God is held by this tradition to create with purposefulness (or intent), all beings—including *human* beings—are recognized as created in view of certain ends and thus as endowed with the powers to

---

9 Aquinas, *ST* I–II, q. 31, a. 7.

10 Joseph Ratzinger, *Turning Point for Europe? The Church in the Modern World: Assessment and Forecast*, 2nd ed., trans. Brain McNeil (San Francisco: Ignatius, 1994), 34.

11 Joseph Ratzinger with Vittorio Messori, *The Ratzinger Report: An Exclusive Interview on the State of the Church*, trans. Salvator Attanasio and Graham Harrison (San Francisco: Ignatius, 1985), 97–98. Hence, "To respect biology is to respect God himself, hence to safeguard his creatures" (98).

12 Marie-Joseph Nicolas, "L'idée de nature dans la pensée de saint Thomas d'Aquin," *Revue thomiste* 74, no. 4 (1974): 564.

achieve those ends in accord with "his [God's] good purpose" (cf. Phil 2:13). In the reasoning of St. Thomas,

> If therefore we consider the order of things depending on the first cause, God cannot do anything against this order; for, if He did so, He would act against His foreknowledge, or His will, or His goodness. But if we consider the order of things depending on any secondary cause, thus God can do something outside such order; for He is not subject to the order of secondary causes; but on the contrary, this order is subject to Him, as proceeding from Him, not by a natural necessity, but by the choice of His own will; for He could have created another order of things.[13]

The Angelic Doctor thus explains how God allows the human person to create within the realm of his own (divine) causality without challenging his (God's) absolute sovereignty. God "operates immediately in every operation," St. Thomas holds, "without excluding the operation of the [human] will and [human] nature."[14] In other words, he works in creatures in such a way that they retain their own operations in virtue, namely, of the forms that he has given them. Again it is with recourse to the analogy of art that St. Thomas clarifies this distinction between first (divine) and second (human) causality: "For the craftsman is moved to action by the end, which is the thing wrought, for instance a chest or a bed; and applies to action the axe," which cuts in virtue of "its being sharp." Similarly, God "moves things to operate" by "applying their forms and powers to operation." God's intention in creating thus extends to the causal action of the beings whom he creates. Unlike the workman, however, who does not necessarily create the particular effect of the axe that he employs (he need not cause it to be sharp, even if he causes it to cut), God gives natural forms, or "principle[s] of action," to all the agents that he creates and likewise "preserves them in being." He might thus be said to work in all agents by bestowing "active powers" upon them in virtue of which they act for specific ends, which characterize them as such (as agents and as created).[15]

---

[13] Aquinas, *ST* I, q. 105, a. 6.

[14] Aquinas, *De Pot.* q. 3, a. 7. "God moves all things," St. Thomas argues, "but in diverse ways, inasmuch as each is moved in a manner befitting its nature. And so man is moved by God to will and to perform outwardly in a manner consistent with free will. Therefore, willing and performing depends on man as freely acting; but on God and not on man, as initial mover" (*Super Epistolam B. Pauli ad Romanus Lectura*, in Thomas Aquinas, *Commentary on the Letter of Saint Paul to the Romans*, trans. Fabien R. Larcher, ed. John Mortensen and Enrique Alarcón, *The Latin/English Edition of The Works of St. Thomas Aquinas* [Lander, WY: The Aquinas Institute for the Study of Sacred Doctrine, 2012], c. 9, lect. 3, no. 778 [p. 37]).

[15] Aquinas, *ST* I, q. 105, a. 5. Hence, as T. L. Short has argued: "Final causes are required to explain what mechanical causation by itself cannot explain, namely, the emergence of order from disorder or of

As for the specific power of the human will, it too "is natural, and [thus] necessarily follows upon the nature" that God has given it.[16] And this in turn means not only that "it is not free to not be free" but also that it is characterized by the fundamental (natural) inclinations of seeking the good—and thus also truth—and of acting accordingly. Hence, although the spiritual creature "does not give its nature to itself," it really does choose "this or that possibility of its nature."[17] It follows that the distinguishing characteristics of human persons, who share a common human nature, cannot be attributed uniquely to the Creator's intentions nor to the external causes of heredity or culture. Rather, it is in virtue of properly human, or free, acts that one assumes and appropriates or, on the contrary, refuses the given aspects of his given nature.[18]

Because, in other words, God profoundly respects human freedom, the latter implies "the power to assume or not [to assume] the end of one's own nature and consequently [to assume] this nature itself." Indeed, the spiritual nature of the human being implies the power to transform "general inclinations into precise and concrete desires (*vouloirs*)," whereby one realizes one's own self in the process of contributing to one's particular culture.[19] In virtue of the fact that the human will is defined by its nature, however, it necessarily follows that "its fundamental movement, anterior to every determination that it gives to itself and ever present within each of them" is "its necessary and constitutive object," namely, "*the good*."[20]

Hence, just as the natural inclinations that we share with other material beings are not limited to the preservation of our being and the avoidance of evil but more positively include the seeking of good and even—at the height of perfection—the passing on of the good (identical with being) by way of reproduction or generation, so also the natural inclinations of a spiritual nature are not limited to knowing the truth.[21] Instead, they include actively seeking it out and even sharing it; whence the natural inclination to live in society and

uniformity from variety. (Thus, Aristotle argued from uniformities in organic growth to there being final causes controlling these processes; and Newton argued that God created the solar system, on the grounds that the laws of motion and gravity could not themselves account for the emergence of so harmonious an order)" (Short, "Teleology in Nature," *American Philosophical Quarterly* 20, no. 4 [October 1983]: 311.) See also Charles Morerod, "A World of Natures and the Presence of God," *Nova et Vetera* 10, no. 1 (2012): 215–31.

16 Aquinas, *ST* III, q. 18, a. 1, ad 3.

17 Marie-Joseph Nicolas, "L'idée de nature," 553.

18 See Nicolas, "L'idée de nature," 560.

19 Nicolas, "L'idée de nature," 553.

20 Nicolas, "L'idée de nature," 554.

21 "The good is diffusive of itself and of being" (Aquinas, *SCG* I, c. 37).

to educate our offspring.[22] It is thus not surprising that Marie-Joseph Nicolas recognizes an analogy between the perfection of a material nature in physical generation and the perfection of a spiritual nature in intellection. In both cases we speak of a conception.[23] With due respect, however, to the difference between the Creator and the creature, the intellectual conception (or word) of the human being neither originates within the human intellect nor remains therein. Rather, it is an expression of the real beyond itself (or, in the case at hand, the real of its own spiritual-corporeal essence), and it is the knowledge of this created good that incites the will to seek it out.

In this way, human culture is achieved by the collaborative efforts of human persons, who transform general inclinations "into precise and concrete desires [*vouloirs*]" by the choices they make.[24] In the words of the Second Vatican Council, "it is one of the properties of the human person that he can achieve true and full humanity only by means of culture," by which is meant "all those things which go to the refining and developing of man's diverse mental and physical endowments," or "through the cultivation [and not the manipulation!] of the goods and values of nature. Whenever, therefore, there is a question of human life, nature and culture are intimately linked together."[25]

Hence, as Louis Dupré has put it, "culture performs its active function inadequately if it does not adopt a listening as well as a speaking role with regard to a given nature. Ideally it displays the creative give-and-take of a good conversation: we allow our ideas, values, and customs to be shaped by a given order, in the very process of transforming that order."[26] The alternative—the absolutizing of the human will in its function of self-determination, whether in the Butlerian mode of crafting one's own sex in an effort to avoid cultural determinism or in the Sartrian mode of inventing one's own nature and ethic in a conscious effort to usurp the Creator's prerogative—is to invite the destruction of the human person by the human self.

When, in fact, "belief in Genesis 1:27"—belief that "God created man in his own image, in the image of God he created him; male and female he created them"—is ruled "incompatible with human dignity," as it was in 2019 by an

---

22 "Even other animals have not at birth such a perfect use of their natural powers as they have later on. This is clear from the fact that birds teach their young to fly; and the like may be observed in other animals" (Aquinas, *ST* I, q. 101, a. 2).

23 See Nicolas, "L'idée de nature," 552.

24 Nicolas, "L'idée de nature," 553.

25 Second Vatican Council, Pastoral Constitution on the Church in the Modern World *Gaudium et spes*, §53.2–3.

26 Louis Dupré, *Passage to Modernity: An Essay in the Hermeneutics of Nature and Culture* (New Haven: Yale University Press, 1993), 11.

English Employment Tribunal, then it would seem that we are not far away from such self-destruction.[27] For as C. S. Lewis predicted, the "final victory" of "man's struggle with Nature" will be won when "the ultimate springs of human action are no longer . . . something given." Instead, conscience itself will be "*produce[d]*," as will human persons, who will henceforth resemble "artifacts" more than men. "They are . . . not men (in the old sense) at all," Lewis foretold.[28] After all, they do not regard themselves as engendered in virtue of forms particular to their species: forms that are handed down from one generation to the next through the procreative process. That is why they can no longer be understood as the "wise men" of our species (*homo sapiens*), who reach a perfected state of development when they are capable, in union with the other sex, of procreating in turn. Rather, to borrow again from Martine Rothblatt, they are of a new species, which no longer replicate by passing on their God-given forms and DNA.[29] Instead, they artistically "form" themselves at will. That is why, as Lewis saw it so well in advance, "'Good' and 'bad,' applied to them, are words without content": words no longer referring to a plentitude that is given with nature itself. Rather, "it is from them [this new species, which Rothblatt names *persona creatus*] that the content of these words is henceforward to be derived." That is why Lewis fittingly concludes in words that arguably summarize the ultimate goal of transgenderism: "Man's final conquest has proved to be the abolition of Man."[30]

---

27 "All three heads [*sic*], belief in Genesis 1:27, lack of belief in transgenderism and conscientious objection to transgenderism in our judgment are incompatible with human dignity and conflict with the fundamental rights of others, specifically here, transgender individuals" (Dr. David Mackereth v. the Department for Work and Pensions and Advanced Personnel Management, Final Merits Hearing, Employment Tribunals, case no. 1304602/2018. Hearing at Center City Towers, Birmingham, July 9–12; 18, 2019, judgment issued on September 26, 2019, §197, https://christianconcern.com/wp-content/uploads/2018/10/CC-Resource-Judgment-Mackereth-DWP-Others-ET-191002.pdf).

28 C. S. Lewis, *Abolition of Man: Reflections on Education with Special Reference to the Teaching of English in the Upper Forms of Schools* (Oxford: Oxford University Press, 1943), 74, 76–77.

29 See Rothblatt, "Are We Transbemans Yet?," *Journal of Evolution & Technology* 18, no. 1 (May 2008): 94–107, and Rothblatt, "Mind Is Deeper Than Matter: Transgenderism, Transhumanism, and the Freedom of Form" in *The Transhumanist Reader: Classical and Contemporary Essays on the Science, Technology, and Philosophy of the Human Future*, ed. Max More and Natasha Vita-More (West Sussex: Wiley & Sons, 2013), 318.

30 Lewis, *Abolition of Man*, 79, 77.

BIBLIOGRAPHY

Adolphe, Jane, and Robert L. Fastiggi. "Gender (in International Law)." In *New Catholic Encyclopedia Supplement 2012–13: Ethics and Philosophy*, II, 612–14. Detroit: GALE, 2013.

Aertsen, Jan. *Nature and Creature: Thomas Aquinas's Way of Thought*. New York: Brill, 1988.

Agacinski, Sylviane. *Femmes entre sexe et genre*. Paris: Editions du Seuil, 2012.

Allen, Prudence. "Can Feminism be a Humanism?" In *Women in Christ: Toward a New Feminism*, edited by Michele M. Schumacher, 251–84. Grand Rapids, MI: Eerdmans, 2004.

Althusser, Louis. "Ideology and Ideological State Apparatuses." In *Lenin and Philosophy and Other Essays*. Translated by Ben Brewster, 170–86. New York: Monthly Review Press, 1971.

Alvaré, Helen. "Religious Freedom versus Sexual Expression: A Guide." *Journal of Law and Religion* 30, no. 3 (2015): 475–95.

Anderson, Ryan T. *When Harry Became Sally: Responding to the Transgender Moment*. New York: Encounter Books, 2018.

Anscombe, Gertrude Elizabeth M. "Embryos and Final Causes." In *Human Life, Action and Ethics*, edited by Mary Geach and Luke Gormally, 45–58. Exeter, UK: Imprint Academic, 2005.

Aristotle. *De Anima* (On the Soul). Translated by J. A. Smith. In *The Complete Works of Aristotle: The Revised Oxford Translation*, edited by Jonathan Barnes, 641–92. Vol 1. Princeton, NJ: Princeton University Press, 1984.

———. *Ethica* Nicom*achea* (Nicomachean Ethics). Translated by W. D. Ross. Revised by J. O. Urmson. In *The Complete Works of Aristotle: The Revised Oxford Translation*, edited by Jonathan Barnes, 1729–1864. Vol. 2. Princeton, NJ: Princeton University Press, 1984.

———. *De generatione animalium* (On the Generation of Animals). In *The Complete Works of Aristotle: The Revised Oxford Translation*, edited by Jonathan Barnes, 1111–1218. Vol. 1. Princeton, NJ: Princeton University Press, 1984.

———. *Metaphysica* (Metaphysics). Translated by W. D. Ross. In *The Complete Works of Aristotle: The Revised Oxford Translation*, edited by Jonathan Barnes, 1552–1728. Vol. 2. Princeton, NJ: Princeton University Press, 1984.

———. *Physica* (Physics). Translated by R. P. Hardie and R. K. Gaye. In *The Complete Works of Aristotle: The Revised Oxford Translation*, edited by Jonathan Barnes, 315–446. Vol. 1. Princeton, NJ: Princeton University Press, 1984.

Augustine. *The Trinity* (*De Trinitate*). Translated by Stephen McKenna. The Fathers of the Church: A New Translation. Vol. 45. Washington, DC: The Catholic University of America Press, 1963.

Balthasar, Hans Urs von. *The Glory of the Lord: A Theological Aesthetics*. Vol. 1, *Seeing the Form*. Translated by Erasmo Leiva-Merikakis. Edited by Joseph Fessio and John Riches. San Francisco: Ignatius, 1989.

———. *Theo-Logic: Theological Logical Theory*. Vol. 1, *Truth of the World*, translated by Adrian J. Walker. San Francisco: Ignatius, 2000.

Bauman, Zygmunt. *Liquid Modernity*. Cambridge, UK: Polity, 2000.

de Beauvoir, Simone. *The Ethics of Ambiguity*. Translated by Bernard Frechtman. New York: Open Road Integrated Media, 2018. French: *Pour une morale de l'ambiguïté*. Folio essais. Paris: Gallimard, 1947.

———. *The Second Sex*. Translated by H. M. Parshley. New York: Vintage Books, 1989. French: *Le deuxième sexe*. Vol. 1, *Les faits et les mythes*. Paris: Gallimard, 1949. Vol. 2, *L'expérience vécue*. Paris: Gallimard, 1976.

———. "Sex, Society, and the Female Dilemma: A Dialogue between Betty Friedan and Simone de Beauvoir." *Saturday Review*, June 14, 1975.

de Beauvoir, Simone, Margaret A. Simons, and Jane Maine Todd. "Two Interviews with Simone de Beauvoir (1982)." *Hypatia* 3, no. 3 (Winter 1989): 11–27.

Bell v. Tavistock, [2020] EWHC 3274 (Admin). https://www.judiciary.uk/wp-content/uploads/2020/12/Bell-v-Tavistock-Judgment.pdf.

Benedict XVI, Pope. "Address of his Holiness Benedict XVI on the Occasion of Christmas Greetings to the Roman Curia." December 21, 2012. http://w2.vatican.va/content/benedict-xvi/en/speeches/2012/december/documents/hf_ben-xvi_spe_20121221_auguri-curia.html.

———. Encyclical Letter on Christian Love *Deus Caritas Est*. December 25, 2005. http://www.vatican.va/content/benedict-xvi/en/encyclicals/documents/hf_ben-xvi_enc_20051225_deus-caritas-est.html.

———. "The Listening Heart: Reflections on the Foundations of Law." Address to the Bundestag. Berlin, September 22, 2011. https://w2.vatican.va/content/benedict-xvi/en/speeches/2011/september/documents/hf_ben-xvi_spe_20110922_reichstag-berlin.html.

Berry, Wendell. "Feminism, the Body, and the Machine." In *What Are People For?*, 178–96. Berkeley: Counterpoint, 2010.

———. "Getting Along with Nature." In *The World Ending Fire*, 160–73. New York: Penguin Books, 2018.

Blanchette, Oliva. "The Logic of Perfection in Aquinas." In *Thomas Aquinas and His Legacy*, edited by David M. Gallaher, 107–30. Washington, DC: The Catholic University of America Press, 1994.

Blechschmidt, Erich. *The Beginnings of Human Life*. Translated by Transematics, Inc. New York: Springer-Verlag, 1977.

Bon, Sylvie le. "Le deuxième sexe, l'esprit et la lettre." *L'Arc* 61 (1975): 55–60.

Bonino, Serge-Thomas. "Aspects doctrinaux de la q. 2." In *Thomas d'Aquin, De la vérité Question 2 (La science de Dieu)*. Paris: Cerf, 1996.

Bostock v. Clayton County. 140 S. Ct. 1731. https://www.supremecourt.gov/opinions/19pdf/17-1618_hfci.pdf.

Bränström, Richard and John E. Pachankis. "Reduction in Mental Health Treatment Utilization among Transgender Individuals after Gender-Affirming Surgeries: A Total Population Study." *The American Journal of Psychiatry* 177, no. 8 (August 2020): 727–34.

Brugère, Fabienne. "'Faire et défaire le genre': La question de la solicitude." In *Trouble dans le sujet, trouble dans les norms*, edited by Fabienne Brugère and Guillaume le Blanc, 69–88. Paris: Presses universitaires de France, 2009.

Brunskell-Evans, Heather. "The Medico-Legal 'Making' of 'The Transgender Child.'" *Medical Law Review* 27, no. 4 (June 25, 2019): 640–57.

———. *Transgender Body Politics*. North Geelong, Australia: Spinifex, 2020.

Burggraf, Jutta. "Gender." In *Lexicon: Ambiguous and Debatable Terms Regarding Family Life and Ethical Questions*, edited by the Pontifical Council for the Family, 399–408. Front Royal, VA: Human Life International, 2006.

Butler, Judith. *Bodies That Matter: On the Discursive Limits of "Sex."* New York: Routledge, 1993.

———. *Ces corps qui comptent: De la matérialité et des limites discursives du 'sexe.'* Translated by Charlotte Nordmann. Paris: Editions Amsterdam, 2009.

———. *Excitable Speech: A Politics of the Performative*. New York: Routledge, 1997.

———. *Gender Trouble: Feminism and the Subversion of Identity*. New York: Routledge, 1990.

———. *Giving an Account of Oneself*. New York: Fordham University Press, 2005.

———. *Notes Toward a Performative Theory of Assembly*. Cambridge, MA: Harvard University Press, 2015.

———. "Performative Acts and Gender Constitution: An Essay in Phenomenology and Feminist Theory." *Theatre Journal* 40, no. 4 (December 1988): 519–31.

———. "Sex and Gender in Simone de Beauvoir's *Second Sex*." *Yale French Studies*. Special issue, *Simone de Beauvoir: Witness to a Century*, no. 72 (1986): 35–49.

———. *Subjects of Desire: Hegelian Reflections in Twentieth-Century France*. 1987. Reprint, New York: Columbia University, 2012.

———. *Undoing Gender*. New York: Routledge, 2004.

Byrne, Alex. "Are Women Adult Human Females?" *Philosophical Studies* 177 (2020): 3783–803.

Chu, Andrea Long. *Females*. New York: Verso: 2019.

Colapinto, John. *As Nature Made Him: The Boy Who Was Raised to be a Girl*. New York: HarperCollins, 2001.

Comité d'études sociales et doctrinales. *Connaître le* com*munisme*. Paris: Haumont, 1946.

Congregation for the Doctrine of the Faith. Instruction on the Respect for Human Life in Its Origin and On the Dignity of Procreation: Replies to Certain Questions of the Day *Donum vitae*. February 22, 1987. New York: St. Paul Books and Media, 1987.

Cottier, Georges. "Le concept de nature chez Saint Thomas." In *Le Désir de Dieu: Sur les traces de Saint Thomas*, 149–72. Paris: Editions Parole et Silence, 2002.

———. *Défis éthiques*. Saint-Maurice, Switzerland: Editions Saint-Augustin, 1996.

———. *Humaine raison. Contribution à une éthique du savoir*. Paris: Lethielleux, Groupe Parole et Silence, 2010.

———. "Nature et nature humaine," *Nova et Vetera* 4 (1991): 57–74.

———. "Questions sur l'embryon humain et l'âme spirituelle." In *Défis éthiques*, 179–97. Saint Maurice, Switzerland: Editions Saint-Augustin, 1996.

Crawford, David S. "Liberal Androgyny: 'Gay Marriage' and the Meaning of Sexuality in our Time." *Communio* 33 (2006): 237–65.

———. "Public Reason and the Anthropology of Orientation: How the Debate over 'Gay Marriage' Has Been Shaped by Some Ubiquitous but Unexamined Presuppositions." *Communio* 43, no. 2 (Summer 2016): 247–73.

Cucchiari, Salvatore. "The Gender Revolution and the Transition from Bisexual Horde to Patrilocal Band: The Origins of Gender Hierarchy." In *Sexual Meanings: The Cultural Construction of Gender and Sexuality*, edited by Sherry B. Ortner and Harriet Whitehead, 31–79. New York: Cambridge University Press, 1981.

Dawkins, Richard. "God's Utility Function." *Scientific American* (November 1995): 80–85.

Denzinger, Heinrich. *Compendium of Creeds, Definitions, and Declarations on Matters of Faith and Morals*. Edited by Robert Fastiggi and Anne Englund Nash. 43rd ed. San Francisco: Ignatius, 2012.

Descartes, René. *Discourse on Method*. Translated by Elizabeth S. Haldane. In *Discourse on the Method; and Mediations on First Philosophy*, edited by David Weissman, 3–48. New Haven: Yale University Press, 1996. French: *Discours sur la méthode*. Presented by Laurence Renault. Paris: GF Flammorion, 2009.

Diamond, Milton, and H. Keith Sigmundson. "Sex Reassignment at Birth: A Long-Term Review and Clinical Implications." *Archives of Pediatrics and Adolescent Medicine* 151 (March 1997): 298–304.

Drummond, Kelley, Susan J. Bradley, Michele Peterson-Badali, and Kenneth J. Zucker. "A Follow-up Study of Girls with Gender Identity Disorder." *Developmental Psychology* 44 (2008): 34–45.

Dupont, Charlotte, and Christophe Sifer. "A Review of Outcome Data Concerning Children Born Following Assisted Reproductive Technologies." *International Scholarly Research Network Obstetrics and Gynecology* (July 17, 2012): 1–5. https://www.ncbi.nlm.nih.gov/pmc/articles/PMC3385632/.

Dupré, Louis. *Metaphysics and Culture.* The Aquinas Lecture, 1994. Milwaukee, WI: Marquette University Press, 1994.

———. *Passage to Modernity: An Essay in the Hermeneutics of Nature and Culture.* New Haven: Yale University Press, 1999.

Editors of the English edition of *Nova et Vetera.* "Introducing the English Edition of *Nova et Vetera*: The Influence of Charles Cardinal Journet." *Nova et Vetera* (English) 1, no. 1 (2003): 1–9.

Emery, Gilles. "The Dignity of Being a Substance: Person, Subsistence, and Nature." *Nova et Vetera* 9, no. 4 (2011): 991–1001.

———. *The Trinitarian Theology of St. Thomas Aquinas.* Translated by Francesca Aran Murphy. Oxford: Oxford University Press, 2007.

———. "The Unity of Man, Body and Soul, in St. Thomas Aquinas." In *Trinity, Church, and the Human Person: Thomistic Essays*, 209–35. Naples, FL: Sapientia, 2007.

Emonet, Pierre-Marie. *The Dearest Freshness Deep Down Things: An Introduction to the Philosophy of Being.* Translated by Robert R. Barr. New York: Crossroad, 1999.

———. *The Greatest Marvel of Nature: An Introduction to the Philosophy of the Human Person.* Translated by Robert R. Barr. New York: Crossroad, 2000.

Fausto-Sterling, Anne. *Sexing the Body: Gender Politics and the Construction of Sexuality.* New York: Basic Books, 2000.

Finley, John. "The Metaphysics of Gender: A Metaphysical Analysis." *The Thomist* 79 (2015): 585–614.

Firestone, Shulamith. *The Dialectic of Sex: The Case for Feminist Revolution.* New York: William Morrow, 1970.

Fortin, Timothy. "Finding Form: Defining Human Sexual Difference." *Nova et Vetera* 15, no. 2 (2017): 397–431.

Franklin, Sarah. "The Cyborg Embryo: Our Path to Transbiology." *Theory, Culture & Society* 23, no. 7–8 (2006): 167–87.

Franks, Angela. "Deleuze, Balthasar, and John Paul II on the Aesthetics of the Body." *Theological Studies* 81, no. 3 (2020): 649–70.

Gallagher, David M. "Goodness and Moral Goodness." In *Thomas Aquinas and His Legacy*, edited by David M. Gallagher, 37–60. Washington, DC: The Catholic University of America Press, 1994.

Ganna, Andrea, Karin J. H. Verweij, Michel G. Nivard, Robert Maier, Robbee Wedow, Alexander S. Busch, and Abdel Abdellaoui. "Large-Scale GWAS Reveals Insights into the Genetic Architecture of Same-Sex Sexual Behavior." *Science* 356, no. 882 (August 30, 2019): 1–8.

Garcia, Jonathan, and Richard A. Crosby. "Social Determinants of Discrimination and Access to Health Care among Transgender Women in Oregon." *Transgender Health* (2020): 1–9.

Gillespie, Michael Allen. *The Theological Origins of Modernity*. Chicago: University of Chicago Press, 2008.

Gilson, Etienne. *Le Thomisme. Introduction à la philosophie de Saint Thomas d'Aquin*. 6th ed. Paris: Vrin, 1986.

Graham, Elaine. *Making the Difference: Gender, Personhood and Technology*. New York: Mowbray, 1995.

Greely, Henry T. *The End of Sex and the Future of Human Reproduction*. Cambridge, MA: Harvard University Press, 2016.

Goethe, Johann Wolfgang von. *Goethe, Collected Works*. Vol. 12, *Scientific Studies*. Edited and translated by Douglas Miller. Princeton: Princeton University Press, 1995.

Hanby, Michael. "When Art Replaces Nature." *Humanum: Issues in Family, Culture and Science* 2, no. 2 (2014): 22–25.

Haraway, Donna. "'Gender' for a Marxist Dictionary: The Sexual Politics of a Word." In *Simians, Cyborgs, and Women: The Reinvention of Nature*, edited by Donna Haraway, 127–48. New York: Routledge, 1992.

Heaney, Stephen J. "Fundamental Inclinations and Sexual Desires." *Nova et Vetera* 15, no. 1 (2017): 37–52.

Henri-Rousseau, Jean-Marie. "L'être et l'agir," *Revue Thomiste* 54, no. 2 (1954): 267–97.

Heyer, Walt. *Trans Life Survivors*. New Province, NJ: Bokwer Identifier Services, 2018.

Hipp, Stephen A. "Nature's Finality and the Stewardship of Creation according to Saint Thomas Aquinas." *Nova et Vetera* 10, no. 1 (2012): 143–91.

Hobbes, Thomas. *Leviathan*. Edited by William Molesworth. In *The English Works of Thomas Hobbes of Malmesbury*. Vol. 3. London: John Bohn, 1839–45.

Holdrege, Craig. "Delicate Empiricism: Practicing a Goethean Approach to Science." In *Beyond Biotechnology: The Barren Promise of* Genetic *Engineering*, by Craig Holdrege and Steve Talbott, 202–28. Lexington, Kentucky: The University Press of Kentucky, 2008.

Hruz, Paul W., Lawrence S. Mayer, and Paul R. McHugh. "Growing Pains: Problems with Puberty Suppression in Treating Gender Dysphoria." *The New Atlantis* (Spring 2017): 3–36.

Hvistendahl, Mara. *Unnatural Selection: Choosing Boys over Girls, and the Consequences of a World Full of Men*. New York: Public Affairs, 2011.

Irenaeus of Lyons. *Against Heresies*. In *The Ante-Nicene Fathers*, edited by Alexander Roberts and James Donaldson. Vol. 1, rev. ed. Sterling Heights, MI: Ex Fontibus, 2018.

John Paul II, Pope. "As Part of God's Original Plan, Sexuality Must Not Be Trivialized." *L'Osservatore Romano* (English) (June 29, 1994): 1–2.

———. Encyclical Letter on Human Work *Laborem Exercens*. September 14, 1981.

———. Encyclical Letter *Veritatis Splendor*. August 6, 1993.

Jonas, Hans. *The Phenomenon of Life: Toward a Philosophical Biology*. New York: Harper & Row, 1966.

Kass, Leon. "Teleology and Darwin's *The Origin of Species*: Beyond Chance and Necessity?" In *Organism, Medicine, and Metaphysics: Essays in Honor of Hans Jonas on His 75th Birthday, May 10, 1978*, edited by Stuart F. Spicker, 97–120. Boston: D. Reidel Publishing Company, 1978.

———. *Toward a More Natural Science: Biology and Human Affairs*. New York: The Free Press, 1985.

Kuby, Gabriele. *The Global Sexual Revolution: Destruction of Freedom in the Name of Freedom*. Translated by James Patrick Kirchner. Kettering, OH: LifeSite, 2015.

Kuhn, A., Christine Bodmer, Werner Stadlmayr, Peter Kuhn, Michael D. Mueller, and Martin Birkhäuser. "Quality of Life 15 Years After Sex Reassignment Surgery for Transsexualism." *Fertility and Sterility* 92, no. 5 (November 2009): 1685–89.

Kwasniewski, Peter A. *The Ecstasy of Love in the Thought of St. Thomas Aquinas*. Steubenville, OH: Emmaus Academic, 2021.

———. "St. Thomas, *Extasis*, and the Union with the Beloved." *The Thomist* 61, no. 4 (1997): 587–603.

Labourdette, Michel. *Cours de théologie morale I: Morale Fondamentale*. Paris: Editions Parole et Silence, 2010.

Laqueur, Thomas. *The Making of Sex: Body and Gender from the Greeks to Freud*. Cambridge, MA: Harvard University Press, 1990.

Larcher, Vic. "The Health of Children Conceived by Assisted Reproductive Technologies." *Archives of Disease in Childhood* 92, no. 8 (August 2007): 668–69.

Lawler, Michael G., and Todd A. Salzman. *The Sexual Person: Toward a Renewed Catholic Anthropology*. Washington, DC: Georgetown University Press, 2008.

Leak, Andrew N. *The Perverted Consciousness: Sexuality and Sartre*. London: Macmillan, 1989.

Letterie, Gerard, and Dov Fox. "Lawsuit Frequency and Claims Basis over Lost, Damaged, and Destroyed Embryos over a 10-Year Period." *Fertility & Sterility* 1, no. 2 (September 2020): 78–82.

Levet, Bérénice. *La théorie du genre ou le monde rêvé des anges*. Paris: Bernard Grasset, 2014.

Lewis, C. S. *The Abolition of Man: Reflections on Education with Special Reference to the Teaching of English in the Upper Forms of Schools*. Oxford: Oxford University Press, 1943.

———. "Good Work and Good Works." In *The World's Last Night and Other Essays*, 75–86. San Diego: Harcourt and Brace, 1987.

———. *Mere Christianity*. New York: Fount, 1977.

———. "Priestesses in the Church?" In *Essay Collection: Faith, Christianity and the Church*, 398–402. London: HarperCollins, 2000.

———. *Studies in Words*. New York: Cambridge University Press, 1967.

Lewis, Sophie. *Full Surrogacy Now: Feminism against Family*. New York: Verso, 2019.

Lilar, Suzanne. *A propos de Sartre et de l'amour*. Paris: Gaillimard, 1984.

Lubac, Henri de. *Catholicism: Christ and the Common Destiny of Man*. Translated by Lancelot C. Sheppard. London: Burns and Oates, 1950.

———. *The Drama of Atheist Humanism*. Translated by Edith M. Riley, Anne Englund Nash, and Mark Sebanc. San Francisco: Ignatius, 1995.

Luke, Barbara, Morton B. Brown, Ethan Wantman, David B. Seifer, Amy T. Sparks, Paul C. Lin, Kevin J. Doody, Bradley J. Van Voorhis, and Logan G. Spector. "Risk of Prematurity and Infant Morbidity and Mortality by Maternal Fertility Status and Plurality." *Journal of Assisted Reproduction and* Genetics 36, no. 1 (January 2019): 121–38.

Malet, André. *Personne et amour dans la théologie trinitaire de saint Thomas d'Aquin*. Paris: Vrin, 1956.

Malo, Antonio. *Transcending Gender Ideology: A Philosophy of Sexual Difference*. Translated by Alice Pavey. Washington, DC: The Catholic University of America Press, 2020.

Mamo, Laura. *Queering Reproduction: Achieving Pregnancy in the Age of Technoscience*. Durham, NC: Duke University Press, 2007.

McCarthy, Margaret Harper. "The Emperor's (New) New Clothes: The Logic of the New 'Gender Ideology.'" *Communio* 46 (Fall-Winter 2019): 620–59.

McHugh, Paul R. "Psychiatric Misadventures." *The American Scholar* 61, no. 4 (Autumn 1992): 497–510.

McHugh, Paul, and Lawrence S. Mayer. "Sexuality and Gender: Findings from the Biological, Psychological, and Social Sciences." *The New Atlantis* 50 Special Report (Fall 2016).

McHugh, Paul, Paul W. Hruz, and Lawrence S. Mayer. "Growing Pains: Problems with Puberty Suppression in Treating Gender Dysphoria." *The New Atlantis* (Spring 2017): 3–36.

Merrill, Jacqueline Pfeffer. "Embryos in Limbo." *The New Atlantis* (Spring 2009): 18–28.

Meyer, Jon, and Donna J. Reter. "Sex Reassignment Follow-up." *Archives of General Psychiatry* 36, no. 9 (1979): 1010–15.

Meyer, Walter J. III. "Gender Identity Disorder: An Emerging Problem for Pediatricians." *Pediatrics* 129, no. 3 (March 2012): 571–73.

Money, John. "Cytogenetic and Psychosexual Incongruities with a Note on Space Form Blindness." *American Journal of Psychiatry* 119, no. 9 (April 1963): 820–27.

Money, John, and Anke A. Ehrhardt. *Man & Woman, Boy & Girl: The Differentiation and Dimorphism of Gender Identity from Conception to Maturity*. New York: New American Library Mentor Book, 1972.

Montfort, Élizabeth. *Le genre démasqué. Homme ou femme? Le choix impossible . . .* Valence, France: Peuple Libre, 2011.

Moreau, Joseph. "L'homme est son âme, selon saint Thomas d'Aquin." *Revue Philosophique de Louvain* 74, no. 21 (1976): 5–29.

Morerod, Charles. "A World of Natures and the Presence of God." *Nova et Vetera* 10, no. 1 (2012): 215–31.

Newgent, Scott. "We Need Balance When It Comes to Gender Dysphoric Kids. I Would Know." *Newsweek*. February 9, 2021. https://www.newsweek.com/we-need-balance-when-it-comes-gender-dysphoric-kids-i-would-know-opinion-1567277.

Nicolas, Jean-Hervé. Footnotes to *ST* I, q. 5, a. 5; and *ST* I, q. 6, a. 1. In Thomas d'Aquin. *Somme théologique*. Vol. I. Paris: Cerf, 1984.

———. *Synthèse dogmatique. Complément. De l'Univers à la Trinité*. Paris: Editions Beauchesne, 1993.

Nicolas, Marie-Joseph. "Le corps humain." *Revue thomiste* 79, no. 3 (1979): 357–87.

———. "L'idée de nature dans la pensée de saint Thomas d'Aquin." *Revue thomiste* 74, no. 4 (1974): 533–90.

———. "Introduction à la Somme théologique." In Thomas d'Aquin, *Somme théologique*, translated by Albert Raulin, 13–66. Paris: Cerf, 1984.

———. “Vocabulaire de la Somme théologique.” In Thomas d’Aquin, *Somme théologique*, translated by Albert Raulin, 91–120. Paris: Cerf, 1984.

Nietzsche, Friedrich. *On the Genealogy of Morals*. Translated by Walter Kaufmann. New York: Vintage, 1969.

Nolan, Ian T., Christopher J. Kuhner, and Geolani W. Dy. “Demographic and Temporal Trends in Transgender Identities and Gender Confirming Surgery.” *Translational Andrology and Urology* 8, no. 3 (2019): 184–90.

Nutt, Amy Elles. Becom*ing Nicole: The Transformation of an American Family*. New York: Random House, 2015.

Oliva, Andriano. *Amours. L’Eglise, les divorcés remariés, les couples homosexuels*. Paris: Cerf, 2015.

Oliva, Blanchette. “The Logic of Perfection in Aquinas.” In *Thomas Aquinas and His Legacy*, edited by David M. Gallagher, 107–30. Washington, DC: The Catholic University of America Press, 1994.

Pasnau, Robert. *Thomas Aquinas on Human Nature: A Philosophical Study of* Summa theologiae *Ia 75-89*. Cambridge: Cambridge University Press, 2002.

Peeters, Marguerite A. “Gender: An Anthropological Deconstruction and a Challenge for Faith.” In *Woman and Man: The* Humanum *in Its Entirety: International Congress on the 20th anniversary of John Paul II’s Apostolic Letter* Mulieris Dignitatem*, 1988–2008*, edited by the Pontifical Council for the Laity, 289–99. Vatican City: Libreria Editrice Vaticana, 2010.

———. *Le Gender, une norme mondiale? Pour un discernement*. Paris: Mame, 2013.

Pesch, Otto Hermann. *Thomas von Aquin. Grenze und Grösse mittelalterlicher Theologie. Eine Einführung*. Mainz: Matthias-Grünewlad-Verlag, 1988.

Pieper, Josef. *Abuse of Language, Abuse of Power*. Translated by Lothar Krauth. San Francisco: Ignatius, 1992.

———. *The Concept of Sin*. Translated by Edward T. Oakes. South Bend, IN: St. Augustine’s Press, 2001.

———. “Future without a Past and Hope with No Foundation?” Translated by Jan van Heurck. In *An Anthology*, 207–21. San Francisco: Ignatius, 1989.

———. “Language and the Philosophizing Person: Aperçus of an Aquinas Reader.” In *For the Love of Wisdom: Essays on the Nature of Philosophy*, edited by Berthold Wald, translated by Roger Wasserman, 197–208. San Francisco: Ignatius, 2006.

———. *On Love*. In *Faith, Hope, Love*. Translated by Richard Winston, Clara Winston, and Mary Frances McCarthy. San Francisco: Ignatius, 1997.

———. *Problems of Modern Faith: Essays and Addresses*. Translated by Jan van Heurck. Chicago: Franciscan Herald Press, 1985.

———. *Reality and the Good*. Translated by Stella Lange. In *Living the Truth*, 107–79. San Francisco: Ignatius, 1989.

———. "Reality and the Knowing Mind." Translated by Lothar Kraus. In *An Anthology*, 91–93. San Francisco: Ignatius, 1989.

———. *The Silence of St. Thomas.* Translated by John Murray and Daniel O'Connor. South Bend, Indiana: St. Augustine's Press, 1999.

———. "Things Are Unfathomable Because They Are Created." Translated by Lothar Krauth. In *An Anthology*, 98–99. San Francisco: Ignatius, 1989.

———. *The Truth of All Things: An Inquiry into the Anthropology of the High Middle Ages.* Translated by Lothar Krauth. In *Living the Truth*, 9–105. San Francisco: Ignatius, 1989.

Pignat, Dominique. "Définition de l'âme chez Aristote." *Nova et Vetera* (French) 92, no. 1 (2017): 19–29.

Pinckaers, Servais. "Appendice I: Notes explicatives." In Thomas d'Aquin, *Somme théologique, I-II, qu. 6-17: Les actes humains.* Vol. 2. Translated by Servais Pinckaers. Editions de la revue des jeunes. Nouvelle édition. Paris: Cerf, 1997.

———. "Aquinas on Nature and the Supernatural." Translated by Sr. Mary Thomas Noble. In *The Pinckaers Reader: Renewing Thomistic Moral Theology*, edited by John Berkman and Craig Steven Titus, 359–68. Washington DC: The Catholic University of America Press, 2005.

———. *Morality: The Catholic View.* Translated by Michael Sherwin. South Bend, IN: St. Augustine's Press, 2001.

———. *The Sources of Christian Ethics.* Translated by Sr. Mary Thomas Noble. Washington, DC: The Catholic University of America Press, 1995.

Planned Parenthood v. Casey. 505 U.S. 833 (1992). Available at the Legal Information Institute of Cornell Law School. https://www.law.cornell.edu/supct/html/91-744.ZO.html.

Plotz, David. *The Genius Factory: The Curious History of the Nobel Prize Sperm Bank.* New York: Random House, 2006.

Pruss, Alexander R. "Not Out of Lust but in Accordance with Truth: Theological and Philosophical Reflections on Sexuality and Reality." *Logos* 6, no. 4 (Fall 2003): 51–80.

Putallaz, François-Xavier. "Pourquoi un corps si humain?" *Nova et Vetera* (French) 93, no. 1 (2018): 87–97.

Ratzinger, Joseph. *Introduction to Christianity.* Translated by J. R. Foster. San Francisco: Communio Books, 1990.

———. "The Renewal of Moral Theology: Perspectives of Vatican II and *Veritatis splendor*." *Communio* 32 (Summer 2005): 358–59.

———. *A Turning Point for Europe? The Church in the Modern World: Assessment and Forecast.* Translated by Brain McNeil. 2nd ed. San Francisco: Ignatius, 1994.

Ratzinger, Joseph, and Vittorio Messori. *The Ratzinger Report: An Exclusive Interview on the State of the Church.* Translated by Salvator Attanasio and Graham Harrison. San Francisco: Ignatius, 1985.

Reiner, William G., and John P. Gearhart. "Discordant Sexual Identity in Some Genetic Males with Cloacal Exstrophy Assigned to Female Sex at Birth." *New England Journal of Medicine* 350 (January 22, 2004): 331–41.

Rich, Adrienne. "Compulsory Heterosexuality and Lesbian Existence." *Signs* 5, no. 4 (Summer 1980): 631–60.

Richards, Janet Radcliffe. *Human Nature after Darwin.* New York: Routledge, 2000.

Rist, John. Foreword to *Transcending Gender Ideology: A Philosophy of Sexual Difference*, by Antonio Malo, ix–xv. Washington, DC: The Catholic University of America Press, 2020.

Ritter, William E. "Why Aristotle Invented the Word Entelecheia." *The Quarterly Review of Biology* 7, no. 4 (December 1932): 377–403.

Roberts, Timothy A., Joshua Smalley, and Dale Ahrendt. "Effect of Gender Affirming Hormones on Athletic Performance in Transwomen and Transmen: Implications for Sporting Organisations and Legislators." *British Journal of Sports Medicine* (December 7, 2020): 1–7.

Rothblatt, Martine. "Are We Transbemans Yet?" *Journal of Evolution & Technology* 18, no. 1 (May 2008): 94–107.

———. *From Transgender to Transhuman: A Manifesto on the Freedom of Form.* Edited by Nickolas Mayer. Self-published, 2011.

———. "Mind Is Deeper Than Matter: Transgenderism, Transhumanism, and the Freedom of Form." In *The Transhumanist Reader: Classical and Contemporary Essays on the Science, Technology, and Philosophy of the Human Future*, edited by Max More and Natasha Vita-More, 317–44. West Sussex: Wiley & Sons, 2013.

Sabot, Philippe. Foreword to *Subjects of Desire: Hegelian Reflections in Twentieth-Century France*, by Judith Butler, vii–xi. New York: Columbia University Press, 2012.

Salzman, Todd A., and Michael G. Lawler. *The Sexual Person: Toward a Renewed Catholic Anthropology.* Washington, DC: Georgetown University Press, 2008.

Sartre, Jean-Paul. *Being and Nothingness: A Phenomenological Essay on Ontology.* Translated by Hazel E. Barnes. New York: Washington Square Press, 1984.

———. *Existentialism and Human Emotions.* Translated by Bernard Frechtman and Hazel E. Barnes. New York: Philosophical Library, 1957.

———. *L'existentialisme est un humanisme.* Paris: Nagel, 1946.

———. *La nausée.* Paris: Gallimard, 1938.

Sax, Leonard. *Why Gender Matters: What Parents and Teachers Need to Know about the Emerging Science of Sex Differences.* New York: Harmony Books, 2007.

Schad, Wolfgang. "A Dynamic Morphology of the Cardiovascular System." In *The Dynamic Heart and Circulation*, edited by Craig Holdrege, translated by Katerine Creeger, 77–97. Fair Oakes, CA: AWSNA, 2002.

Schall, James V. "Nature and Finality in Aristotle." *Laval théologique et philosophique* 45, no. 1 (1989): 73–85.

Schiefsky, Mark J. "Art and Nature in Ancient Mechanics." In *The Artificial and the Natural: An Evolving Polarity*, edited by Bernadette Bensaude-Vincent and William R. Newman, 67–108. Cambridge, MA: Massachusetts Institute of Technology Press, 2007.

Schmitz, Kenneth. "Selves and Persons: A Difference in Loves?" *Communio* 18, no. 2 (1991): 181–206.

Schumacher, Michele M. "A Lamentation of *Eros*: Challenging the Sexual Revolution Fifty Years Later." In *Why* Humanae Vitae *Is Still Right*, edited by Janet Smith, 227–46. San Francisco: Ignatius, 2018.

———. "The Nature of Nature in Feminism, Old and New." In *Women in Christ: Toward a New Feminism*, edited by Michele M. Schumacher, 17–51. Grand Rapids, MI: Eerdmans, 2004.

———. "A Plea for the Traditional Family: Situating Marriage within John Paul II's Realist, or Personalist, Perspective of Human Freedom." *Linacre Quarterly* 81, no. 4 (2014): 314–42.

———. "The Reunification of Naturalism and Personalism in the Conjugal Act: A Contribution by Servais Pinckaers." *The Thomist* 84, no. 3 (2020): 435–66.

———. "A Woman in Stone or in the Heart of Man? Navigating between Naturalism and Idealism in the Spirit of *Veritatis Splendor*." *Nova et Vetera* 11, no. 4 (2013): 1249–86.

———. "Woman's Self-Interest or Sacrificial Motherhood: Personal Desires, Natural Inclinations and the Meaning of Love." *The Thomist* 77, no. 1 (January 2013): 71–101.

Second Vatican Council. Pastoral Constitution on the Church in the Modern World *Gaudium et spes*. December 7, 1965.

Sherwin, Michael S. *By Knowledge and by Love: Charity and Knowledge in the Moral Theology of St. Thomas Aquinas*. Washington DC: Catholic University Press, 2005.

Short, T. L. "Teleology in Nature." *American Philosophical Quarterly* 20, no. 4 (October 1983): 311–20.

Shrier, Abigail. *Irreversible Damage: The Transgender Craze Seducing Our Daughters*. Washington, DC: Regnery, 2020.

Simon, Yves R. *The Definition of Moral Virtue*. New York: Fordham University Press, 1986.

Simonsen, Rikke Kildevaeld, Gert Martin Hald, Ellids Kristensen, and Annamaria Giraldi. "Long-Term Follow-Up of Individuals Undergoing Sex-Reassignment Surgery: Somatic Morbidity and Cause of Death." *Sexual Medicine* 4 (2016): 60–68.

Singh, Devia. "A Follow-up Study of Boys with Gender Identity Disorder." PhD diss., University of Toronto, 2012. http://images.nymag.com/images/2/daily/2016/01/SINGH-DISSERTATION.pdf.

Sokolowski, Robert. *The God of Faith and Reason: Foundations of Christian Theology*. Notre Dame, IN: University of Notre Dame Press, 1982.

Spaemann, Robert. *Essays in Anthropology: Variations on a Theme*. Translated by Guido de Graaf and James Mumford. Eugen, OR: Cascade, 2010.

———. *Persons: The Difference Between 'Someone' and 'Something.'* Translated by Oliver O'Donovan. Oxford: Oxford University Press, 2012.

———. "A Philosophical Autobiography." In *A Spaemann Reader: Philosophical Essays on Nature, God, and The Human Person*, edited and translated by David C. Schindler and Jeanne Heffernan Schindler, 11–21. Oxford: Oxford University Press, 2015.

———. "*Vivere viventibus est esse*. Procréation, naissance, mort." In *Chasser le naturel?*, translated by Stéphane Robilliard, 129–61. Paris: Les Presses universitaires de l'IPC, 2015.

Stern, Karl. *The Flight from Woman*. St. Paul, MN: Paragon House Publishers, 1985. First published 1965 by Farrar, Strauss, and Giroux (New York).

Stewart, J. L., Leigh A. Spivey, Laura Widman, Sophia Choukas-Bradley, and Mitchell J. Prinstein. "Developmental Patterns of Sexual Identity, Romantic Attraction, and Sexual Behavior among Adolescents over Three Years." *Journal of Adolescence* 77 (December 2019): 90–97.

Sykes, J. B., ed. *The Concise Oxford Dictionary of Current English: Based on The Oxford English Dictionary and Its Supplements*. 6th ed. Oxford: Clarendon, 1976.

Taylor, Charles. *A Secular Age*. Cambridge, MA: The Belknap Press of Harvard University Press, 2007.

Thomas Aquinas. *Commentary on Aristotle's* De Anima. Translated by Kenelm Foster and Silvester Humphries. Notre Dame, Indiana: Dumb Ox Books, 1994.

———. *De Potentia*. In *Quaestiones disputate*, edited by Pio Bazzi. Vol. 2. Rome: Marietti, 1965. English translation by the English Dominican Fathers. Eugene, OR: Wipf & Stock, 2004.

———. *Opuscule* XIII: "De Differentia Divini Verbi, et Humani." In *Opuscules de Saint Thomas d'Aquin*. Vol. 3. Paris: Vrin, 1984.

———. *Opusculum* XIV: "De Natura Verbi Intellectus." In *Opuscules de Saint Thomas d'Aquin*. Vol. 3. Paris: Vrin, 1984.

———. *Quaestiones Disputatae de Anima*. Edited by B. C. Bazán. Rome: Leonine, 1996.

———. *Somme théologique*, I. Translated by Albert Raulin. Paris: Cerf, 1984.

———. *Summa contra Gentiles.* Leonine edition, vols. 13–15. Translated by Anton C. Pegis, James F. Anderson, Vernon J. Bourke, and Charles J. O'Neil. Notre Dame, IN: University of Notre Dame Press, 1997.

———. *Summa theologiae.* Translated by Laurence Shapcote. Edited by John Mortensen and Enrique Alarcón. Vols. 13–20 of The Works of St. Thomas Aquinas. Lander, WY: The Aquinas Institute for the Study of Sacred Doctrine, 2012.

———. *Super Epistolam B. Pauli ad Colossenses.* In *Commentary on the Letters of Saint Paul to the Philippians, Colossians, Thessalonians, Timothy, Titus, and Philemon.* Translated by Fabien R. Larcher. Edited by John Mortensen and Enrique Alarcón. Biblical Commentaries. Vol. 40 of The Works of St. Thomas Aquinas. Lander, WY: The Aquinas Institute for the Study of Sacred Doctrine, 2012.

———. *Super Epistolam B. Pauli ad Ephesios Lectura.* In *Commentary on the Letters of Saint Paul to the Galatians and Ephesians.* Translated by Fabien R. Larcher and Matthew L. Lamb. Edited by John Mortensen and Enrique Alarcón. Vol. 39 of The Works of St. Thomas Aquinas. Lander, WY: The Aquinas Institute for the Study of Sacred Doctrine, 2012.

———. *Super Epistolam B. Pauli ad Romanus Lectura.* In *Commentary on the Letter of Saint Paul to the Romans.* Translated by Fabien R. Larcher. Edited by John Mortensen and Enrique Alarcón. Volume 38 of The Works of St. Thomas Aquinas. Lander, WY: The Aquinas Institute for the Study of Sacred Doctrine, 2012.

———. *Super Evangelium S. Ioannis Lectura.* In *Commentary on the Gospel of John: Chapters 1–8.* Translated by Fabian R. Larcher. Edited by the Aquinas Institute. Biblical Commentaries. Vols. 35–36 of The Works of St. Thomas Aquinas. Lander, WY: The Aquinas Institute for the Study of Sacred Doctrine, 2013.

———. Truth. (*Quaestiones Disputatae de Veritate.*) Translated by Robert W. Mulligan, S.J. Chicago: Regnery, 1952.

Verlinde, Joseph-Marie. *L'idéologie du gende*r comm*e identité reçue ou choisie?* Mesnil Saint-Loup, France: Le Livre Ouvert, 2012.

Vollmer de Coles, Beatriz. "New Definition of Gender." In *Lexicon: Ambiguous and Debatable Terms Regarding Family Life and Ethical Questions*, edited by the Pontifical Council for the Family, 625–41. Front Royal, VA: Human Life International, 2006.

———. "New Feminism: A Sex-Gender Reunion." In *Women in Christ: Toward a New Feminism*, edited by Michele M. Schumacher, 52–66. Grand Rapids, MI: Eerdmans, 2004.

Wallien, Madeleine, and Peggy Cohen Kettenis. "Psychosexual Outcome of Gender-Dysphoric Children." *Journal of the American Academy of Child and Adolescent Psychiatry* 47, no. 12 (December 2008): 1413–23.

Zaliznyak, Micahel, Eric E. Jung, Catherine Bresee, and Maurice M. Garcia. "Which U.S. States' Medicaid Programs Provide Coverage for Gender-Affirming Hormone Therapy and Gender-Affirming Genital Surgery for Transgender Patients? A State-by-State Review and a Study Detailing the Patient Experience to Confirm Coverage of Services." *Journal of Sexual Medicine* 18, no. 2 (February 2021): 410–22.

Zucker, Kenneth J. "The Myth of Persistence: Response to 'A Critical Commentary on Follow-Up Studies and "Desistance" Theories about Transgender and Gender Non-Conforming Children' by Temple Newhook et al. (2018)." *International Journal of Transgenderism* 19, no. 2 (May 2018): 1–15.

WEBOGRAPHY

Adubato, Stephen G. "Andrea Long Chu's *Females* subverts subversiveness." *The Catholic World Report.* September 16, 2020. https://www.catholicworldreport.com/2020/09/16/andrea-long-chus-females-subverts-subversiveness/.

AFP. "Transgender Man Gives Birth in Finland First." *The Express Tribune.* April 4, 2018. https://tribune.com.pk/story/1677448/3-transgender-man-gives-birth-finland-first/.

Aldridge, Bailey. "One in Five Teens Reports a Change in Sexual Orientation in High School." *The State.* November 4, 2019. https://www.thestate.com/news/state/north-carolina/article236988434.html.

Algar, Selim. "Changing Gender Is Easier Than Ever in NYC Schools." *New York Post.* June 28, 2019. https://nypost.com/2019/06/28/changing-gender-is-easier-than-ever-in-nyc-schools/.

Allen, Mary Prudence. "Gender Reality vs. Gender Ideology: Ransoming the Concept of Gender." *Solidarity: The Journal of Catholic Social Thought and Secular Ethics* 4, no. 1 (2014). http://researchopruennline.nd.edu.au/solidarity/vol4/iss1/1/.

Anderson, Ryan T. "'Transitioning' Procedures Don't Help Mental Health, Largest Dataset Shows." The Heritage Foundation. August 3, 2020. https://www.heritage.org/gender/commentary/transitioning-procedures-dont-help-mental-health-largest-dataset-shows.

Anonymous Us. https://anonymousus.org/.

Armour, Stephanie. "Medicare Ban on Sex-Reassigment Surgery Lifted." *The Wallstreet Journal.* May 30, 2014. http://www.wsj.com/articles/medicare-ban-on-sex-reassignment-surgery-lifted-1401478303.

Associated Press. "Designer Baby Warning as Embryos Are Made Using TWO Women and One Man by Oregon Scientists." *Daily Mail.* October 22, 2012. https://www.dailymail.co.uk/news/article-2222622/Oregon-Health--Sciences-University-Scientists-swap-embryos-DNA-using-women-man.html.

Azad, Sonia. "Same-Sex Couple Carries Same 'Miracle' Baby in What May Be Fertility World First." *USA Today.* October 29, 2018. https://eu.usatoday.com/story/news/nation-now/2018/10/29/same-sex-couple-carries-same-baby-ivf-fertility-treatment-first/1804554002.

Bartosch, Jo. "Twitter's War on Outspoken Women." Spiked. March 21, 2019. https://www.spiked-online.com/2019/03/21/twitters-war-on-outspoken-women/.

Basic Rights Oregon. "Oregon Health Plan Coverage for Gender Dysphoria." November 2015. http://www.basicrights.org/wp-content/uploads/2015/09/OHP_FAQ_For_Individuals_Nov_2015.pdf.

Batty, David. "Sex Changes Are Not Effective, Say Researchers." *The Guardian.* July 30, 2004. http://www.theguardian.com/society/2004/jul/30/health.mentalhealth.

BBC News. "Bath Spa University 'Blocks Transgender Research.'" September 25, 2017. https://www.bbc.com/news/uk-41384473.

———. "Detransitioning: Reversing a Gender Transition." November 26, 2019. https://www.youtube.com/watch?v=fDi-jFVBLA8.

———. "Just a Girl." https://www.bbc.co.uk/programmes/b04v8czp.

———. "Maya Forstater: Woman Loses Tribunal Over Transgender Tweets." December 19, 2019. https://www.bbc.com/news/uk-50858919.

Berrien, Hank. "Famed Feminist Furious After Twitter Says She Violated Rules by Saying Men are Not Women." The Daily Wire. November 16, 2018. https://www.dailywire.com/news/38426/famed-feminist-furious-after-twitter-says-she-hank-berrien.

Berry, Susan. "Vermont to Allow Taxpayer-Funded Transgender Sex Reassignment Surgeries for Children." Breitbart. June 13, 2019. https://www.breitbart.com/politics/2019/06/13/vermont-taxpayer-funded-transgender-sex-reassignment-surgeries-children/.

Bhriaian, Niamh Ui. "Hey Women! We've Been Downgraded to 'Anyone with a Cervix' By the HSE." GRIPT. September 19, 2020. https://gript.ie/hey-women-weve-been-downgraded-to-anyone-with-a-cervix-by-the-hse/.

Bissinger, Buzz. "Caitlyn Jenner: The Full Story." Photography by Annie Leibovitz. Styled by Jessica Diehl. *Vanity Fair.* June 25, 2015. https://www.vanityfair.com/hollywood/2015/06/caitlyn-jenner-bruce-cover-annie-leibovitz.

Blanchard, Sessi Kuwabara. "Andrea Long Chu Is the Cult Writer Changing Gender Theory." Vice. September 11, 2018. https://www.vice.com/en/article/ev74m7/andrea-long-chu-interview-avital-ronell-gender.

Boston Children's Hospital Center for Gender Surgery (website). Accessed February 5, 2022. https://www.childrenshospital.org/centers-and-services/programs/a-_-e/center-for-gender-surgery-program#.

———. "Breast Augmentation Surgery." Accessed February 5, 2022. https://www.childrenshospital.org/conditions-and-treatments/treatments/breast-augmentation.

———. "Metoidioplasty." Accessed February 5, 2022. https://www.childrenshospital.org/conditions-and-treatments/treatments/metoidioplasty.

———. "Phalloplasty." Accessed February 5, 2022. https://www.childrenshospital.org/conditions-and-treatments/treatments/phalloplasty.

———. "Vaginoplasty." Accessed February 5, 2022. https://www.childrenshospital.org/conditions-and-treatments/treatments/vaginoplasty.

Business Today Desk. "Tinder's 'Let's Talk Gender' Online Glossary is the Guide We All Needed." *Business Today*, June 22, 2022. https://www.businesstoday.in/technology/news/story/tinders-lets-talk-gender-online-glossary-is-the-guide-we-all-needed-338709-2022-06-22.

Cantor, James. "Do Trans- Kids Stay Trans- When They Grow Up?" Sexology Today. January 11, 2016. http://www.sexologytoday.org/2016/01/do-trans-kids-stay-trans-when-they-grow_99.html.

Cave, Katherine. "The Medical Scandal That the Mainstream Media Ignores." Public Discourse. April 8, 2019. https://www.thepublicdiscourse.com/2019/04/50959/.

Cerretani, Jessica. "First-of-Its-Kind Study Links Puberty Blockers to Lower Odds of Suicidal Thoughts." Discoveries: Stories and News from Children's Hospital. January 24, 2020. https://discoveries.childrenshospital.org/puberty-blockers-suicidal-thoughts/.

Chadra, Daisy. "I'm Detransitioning." *YouTube*. October 27, 2020. https://www.youtube.com/watch?v=R_KD46_Ophg.

Chapman, Michael W. "Johns Hopkins Psychiatrist: Transgender Is 'Mental Disorder'; Sex Change 'Biologically Impossible.'" June 2, 2015. http://cnsnews.com/news/article/michael-w-chapman/johns-hopkins-psychiatrist-transgender-mental-disorder-sex-change.

Christensen, Jen. "Judge Gives Grandparents Custody of Ohio Transgender Teen." CNN. February 17, 2018. https://journals.plos.org/plosone/article?id=10.1371/journal.pone.0202330.

Chu, Andrea Long. "All Reproduction Is Assisted." *Boston Review*. August 14, 2018. https://bostonreview.net/forum/all-reproduction-assisted/andrea-long-chu-extreme-pregnancy.

———. "My New Vagina Won't Make Me Happy. And It Shouldn't Have To." *New York Times*. November 24, 2018. https://www.nytimes.com/2018/11/24/opinion/sunday/vaginoplasty-transgender-medicine.html.

———. "On Liking Women." *N+1 Magazine* 30, Winter 2018. https://nplusonemag.com/issue-30/essays/on-liking-women/.

Cleveland, Margot. "Supreme Court: Treat Men and Women as Interchangeable, Or Get Sued into Oblivion." The Federalist. June 18, 2020. https://thefederalist.com/2020/06/18/supreme-court-treat-men-and-women-as-interchangeable-or-get-sued-into-oblivion/.

Colapinto, John. "Gender Gap: What Were the Real Reasons behind David Reimer's Suicide?" Slate. June 3, 2004. http://www.slate.com/articles/health_and_science/medical_examiner/2004/06/gender_gap.html.

Congregation for Catholic Education. "'Man and Woman He Created Them': Towards a Path of Dialogue on the Question of Gender Theory in Education." Vatican City, February 2, 2019. https://www.vatican.va/roman_curia/congregations/ccatheduc/documents/rc_con_ccatheduc_doc_20190202_maschio-e-femmina_en.pdf.

"Correction to Bränström and Pachankis." *The American Journal of Psychiatry*. August 1, 2020. https://ajp.psychiatryonline.org/doi/10.1176/appi.ajp.2020.1778correction.

Council on Foreign Relations. "China's Baby Blues: When Better Policies for Women Backfire." July 5, 2018. https://www.cfr.org/blog/chinas-baby-blues-when-better-policies-women-backfire.

Crawford, David S. "The Metaphysics of Bostock." *First Things*. July 2, 2020. https://www.firstthings.com/web-exclusives/2020/07/the-metaphysics-of-bostock.

Crawford, David, and Michael Hanby. "The Abolition of Man and Woman." *The Wallstreet Journal*. June 24, 2020. https://www.wsj.com/articles/the-abolition-of-man-and-woman-11593017500.

Cretella, Michelle. "Gender Dysphoria in Children." American College of Pediatricians. November 2018. https://www.acpeds.org/the-college-speaks/position-statements/gender-dysphoria-in-children.

———. "I'm a Pediatrician. Here's What I Did When a Little Boy Patient Said He Was a Girl." The Daily Signal. December 11, 2017. http://dailysignal.com/2017/12/11/cretella-transcript/.

———. "I'm a Pediatrician. Here's What You Should Know About a New Study on Transgender Teen Suicide." The Daily Signal. September 18, 2017. https://www.dailysignal.com/2018/09/18/new-study-on-transgender-teen-suicide-doesnt-prove-kids-need-gender-transition-therapy/.

Cullinane, Susannah. "Second US Fertility Clinic Reports Egg Storage Tank Malfunction." CNN. April 5, 2018. https://edition.cnn.com/2018/03/12/health/frozen-eggs-second-clinic-malfunction/index.html.

Devlin, Amanda, and Richard Wheatstone. "UK's First Pregnant Man: Who Is Hayden Cross, How Can a Man Fall Pregnant, and How Did He Give Birth to Daughter Trinity Leigh?" *The Sun*. January 9, 2019. https://www.thesun.co.uk/news/2567386/hayden-cross-pregnant-man-first-uk-trinity-leigh/.

Devlin, Hannah. "Scientists a Step Closer to Mimicking Way Human Body Creates Sperm." *The Guardian*. January 1, 2018. https://www.theguardian.com/science/2018/jan/01/scientists-a-step-closer-to-mimicking-way-human-body-creates-sperm.

Dhejne, C., Paul Lichtenstein, Marcus Boman, Anna L. V. Johansson, Niklas Långström, and Mikael Landén. “Long-term Follow-up of Transsexual Persons Undergoing Sex Reassignment Surgery: Cohort Study in Sweden.” *PLoS ONE* (February 22, 2011). http://www.ncbi.nlm.nih.gov/pubmed/21364939.

Diamond, Milton. “Money’s Sex Claims.” Letter to the Editor. *The Listener*. September 5, 1998. http://hawaii.edu/PCSS/biblio/articles/1961to1999/1998-listener.html.

Doctor, Rina Marie. “Oregon Allows 15-Year-Olds to Have Sex Reassignment Surgery Even Without Parental Consent?” Tech Times. July 13, 2015. https://www.techtimes.com/articles/68319/20150713/oregon-allows-15-year-olds-to-have-sex-reassignment-surgery-even-without-parental-consent.htm.

Dr. David Mackereth v. the Department for Work and Pensions and Advanced Personnel Management. Employment Tribunals, Final Merits Hearing. Case no. 1304602/2018. Hearing at Center City Towers, Birmingham (July 9–12; 18, 2019). Judgment issued on September 26, 2019. https://christianconcern.com/wp-content/uploads/2018/10/CC-Resource-Judgment-Mackereth-DWP-Others-ET-191002.pdf.

Dreher, Rod. “Call the Bearded Man ‘Madam’—Or Else.” The American Conservative. October 2, 2019. https://www.theamericanconservative.com/dreher/transgender-doctor-britain-bearded-man.

———. “Gender Theory Outlaws Reality.” The American Conservative. October 9, 2019. https://www.theamericanconservative.com/dreher/gender-theory-outlaws-reality.

———. “Totalitarian Wars on Reality.” The American Conservative. December 19, 2019. https://www.theamericanconservative.com/dreher/maya-forstater-totalitarian-transgenderism/.

Deniz. “Existentialist Roots of Feminist Ethics: A Dissertation in Philosophy.” Ph.D. diss., The Pennsylvania State University, 2015. https://etda.libraries.psu.edu/files/final_submissions/11104.

Ellefson, Lindsey. “Denver Post Columnist Says He Was Fired for His ‘Insistence’ That There Are Only 2 Sexes: Joe Caldara’s Final Column Argued That to Be Inclusive, People Are Expected to ‘Lose Our Right to Free Speech.’” The Wrap. January 20, 2020. https://www.thewrap.com/denver-post-columnist-says-he-was-fired-for-his-insistence-that-there-are-only-2-sexes/.

English, Bella. “Led by the Child Who Simply Knew.” *The Boston Globe*. December 11, 2011. http://articles.boston.com/2011-12-11/lifestyle/30512365_1_twin-boys-transgender-jonas.

Equality Maps. “Conversion ‘Therapy’ Laws.” Accessed March 15, 2020. https://www.lgbtmap.org/equality-maps/conversion—therapy.

Favale, Abigail. "The Eclipse of Sex by the Rise of Gender." *Church Life Journal.* March 1, 2021. https://churchlifejournal.nd.edu/articles/the-eclipse-of-sex-by-the-rise-of-gender/.

Finlay, Janie, dir. *The Seahorse: The Dad Who Gave Birth.* 2019: Grain Media in association with Glimmer Films and *The Guardian.*

Fitzgibbons, Richard P., Philip M. Sutton, and Dale O'Leary. "The Psychopathology of 'Sex Reassignment' Surgery: Assessing Its Medical, Psychological and Ethical Appropriateness." The National Catholic Bioethics Center. 2009. http://ncbcenter.org/document.doc?id=581.

Fogle, Asher. "My Husband Became a Woman—And It Saved Our Marriage." *Good Housekeeping.* June 17, 2015. https://www.goodhousekeeping.com/life/relationships/a32977/jonni-and-angela-pettit-transgender-marriage/.

Franks, Angela. "Andrea Long Chu Says You Are a Female, and He's Only Partly Wrong." Public Discourse. December 10, 2019. https://www.thepublicdiscourse.com/2019/12/58719/.

———. "Deleuze on Desire." *First Things.* April 2020. Issue 302. https://www.firstthings.com/article/2020/04/deleuze-on-desire.

———. "The Plane Where Nietzsche and Jane Austen Meet." *Church Life Journal.* December 15, 2020. https://churchlifejournal.nd.edu/articles/the-plane-where-nietzsche-and-jane-austen-meet/.

Gagnon, Robert. "Supreme Court Ridiculously Demands Everyone Pretend Sex Differences Don't Exist." June 18, 2020. https://thefederalist.com/2020/06/18/supreme-court-ridiculously-demands-everyone-pretend-sex-differences-dont-exist/.

Gambino, Megan. "Ask An Expert: What Is the Difference Between Modern and Postmodern Art?" *Smithsonian Magazine.* September 22, 2011. http://www.smithsonianmag.com/arts-culture/ask-an-expert-what-is-the-difference-between-modern-and-postmodern-art-87883230/?no-ist.

Glendon, Mary Ann. "Rousseau and the Revolt against Reason." *First Things.* October 1999. https://www.firstthings.com/article/1999/10/rousseau-the-revolt-against-reason.

Goldberg, Alan B., and Katie N. Thomson. "Exclusive: 'Pregnant Man' Gives Birth to Second Child." ABC News. June 9, 2009. https://abcnews.go.com/2020/story?id=7795344&page.

Gordon, Lisa Kaplan. "Surgery Could Give Men Wombs of Their Own within Five Years." Yahoo Lifestyle. November 18, 2015. https://www.yahoo.com/lifestyle/surgery-could-give-men-wombs-1302360099545142.html.

The Guardian Staff. "LGBT Group Drops Martina Navratilova over Transgender Comments." *The Guardian.* February 20, 2019. https://www.theguardian.com/sport/2019/feb/20/lgbt-group-drops-martina-navratilova-over-transgender-comments.

GuessImAfab. "GenderFlux: How One Young Woman Fell Down the Rapid Onset Rabbit Hole." 4thWaveNow. May 15, 2019. https://4thwavenow.com/2019/05/16/genderflux-how-one-young-woman-fell-down-the-rapid-onset-rabbit-hole/.

del Guidice, Rachel. "Academia Today 'Not for Faint-Hearted,' Says Professor Who Lost His Job for Talking About Gender." The Daily Signal. August 27, 2019. https://www.dailysignal.com/2019/08/27/academia-today-not-for-faint-hearted-says-professor-who-lost-his-job-for-talking-about-gender/.

Hannon, Michael W. "Against Heterosexuality." *First Things*. March 2014. http://www.firstthings.com/article/2014/03/against-heterosexuality.

———. "Against Obsessive Sexuality: A Reply to My Critics." *First Things*. August 13, 2014. http://www.firstthings.com/web-exclusives/2014/08/against-obsessive-sexuality.

Harrington, Mary. "The Tyranny of Queer Theory." UnHerd. October 15, 2020. https://unherd.com/2020/10/how-queer-theory-has-eaten-the-culture/.

Hasson, Mary Rice. "'It Isn't Hate to Speak the Truth': J. K. Rowling Takes a Stand Against Gender Ideology, and We Should Stand With Her." *Our Sunday Visitor*. June 15, 2020. https://osvnews.com/2020/06/15/it-isnt-hate-to-speak-the-truth-j-k-rowling-takes-a-stand-against-gender-ideology-and-we-should-stand-with-her/.

Hatenstone, Simon. "The Dad Who Gave Birth: 'Being Pregnant Doesn't Change Me Being a Trans Man.'" *The Guardian*. April 20, 2019. https://www.theguardian.com/society/2019/apr/20/the-dad-who-gave-birth-pregnant-trans-freddy-mcconnell.

Health.am. "IVF Babies May Face Later Cardiac Risks." April 20, 2012. http://www.health.am/ab/more/ivf-babies-may-face-later-cardiac-risks/.

Health and Safety Executive of the United Kingdom (website). "What Cervical Screening Is." Accessed December 10, 2020. https://www2.hse.ie/screening-and-vaccinations/cervical-screening/what-cervical-screening-is.html.

Heller, Katia. "Widower of 9/11 Cop Returns Glamour Award over Caitlyn Jenner." November 17, 2015. http://edition.cnn.com/2015/11/16/living/widower-911-officer-glamour-award-caitlyn-jenner-feat/index.html.

Heyer, Walt. "'Sex Change' Isn't Surgically Possible, My Surgeon Testified in Court." The Stream. February 24, 2020. https://stream.org/sex-change-isnt-surgically-possible-my-surgeon-testified-in-court/.

———. Sex Change Regret. http://www.sexchangeregret.com/.

Hoffman, David I., Gail L. Zellman, C. Christine Fair, Jacob F. Mayer, Joyce G. Zeitz, William E. Gibbons, and Thomas G. Turner, Jr. "How Many Frozen Human Embryos Are Available For Research?" Rand Research Brief. RAND Corporation. 2003. https://www.rand.org/pubs/research_briefs/RB9038.html.

Human Rights Campaign Foundation. "Safer Sex for Trans Bodies." Whitman-Walker Health. 2020. Accessed January 29, 2021. https://assets2.hrc.org/files/assets/resources/Trans_Safer_Sex_Guide_FINAL.pdf.

International Theological Commission. "In Search of a Universal Ethic: A New Look at the Natural Law." 2009. http://www.vatican.va/roman_curia/congregations/cfaith/cti_documents/rc_con_cfaith_doc_20090520_legge-naturale_en.html.

Kearns, Madeleine. "A Thousand Parents of Trans-Identifying Children Beg Doctors to Listen." National Review. October 24, 2018. https://www.nationalreview.com/corner/american-academy-of-pediatrics-transgender-statement-parents-beg-doctors-to-listen/.

Keenan, Jeremiah. "Authorities to Arrest Canadian Father if He Refers to Trans Child by Her Real Sex." The Federalist. April 29, 2019. https://thefederalist.com/2019/04/29/authorities-arrest-canadian-father-refers-trans-child-real-sex/.

———. "Canadian Appeals Court Rules Father Can't Stop Teen Daughter from Taking Male Hormones." The Federalist. January 14, 2020. https://thefederalist.com/2020/01/14/canadian-appeals-court-rules-father-cant-stop-teen-daughter-from-taking-male-hormones/.

Khan, Shehab. "Within Thirty Years We Will No Longer Use Sex to Procreate, Says Stanford Professor." Independent. July 4, 2017. https://www.independent.co.uk/news/science/sex-procreation-hank-greely-stanford-professor-prediction-humans-no-longer-reproduce-a7821676.html.

Kidspot. "Meet Hayden, The First British Man Set to Give Birth." January 8, 2017. https://www.kidspot.com.au/parenting/real-life/in-the-news/meet-hayden-the-first-british-man-set-to-give-birth/news-story/a47bd06d1a189b1822c63efe13d82549.

Kuper, Laura E. "A Note on Research Methods and Gender Clinic Locations." In "Puberty Blocking Medication: Clinical Research Review IMPACT LGBT Health and Development Program." December 2014. http://www.impactprogram.org/wp-content/uploads/2014/12/Kuper-2014-Puberty-Blockers-Clinical-Research-Review.pdf.

Kuzma, Faith. "Are You Spiralling? Testosterone May Be the Reason." Psychreg. February 25, 2020, updated March 13, 2020. https://www.psychreg.org/testosterone-spiralling/.

Lahl, Jennifer. "Does IVF Cause More Cancer in Children or Not?" Center for Bioethics and Culture. October 7, 2013. http://www.cbc-network.org/2013/10/does-ivf-cause-more-cancer-in-children-or-not/.

———. "Modern Families and the Messes We Make," Public Discourse. November 1, 2013. https://www.thepublicdiscourse.com/2013/11/11111/.

Laidlaw, Michael K. "The Gender Identity Phantom." Mercatornet. November 12, 2018. https://www.mercatornet.com/mobile/view/the-gender-identity-phantom.

Le Monde with APF. "Une femme transgenre reconnue comme mère par la justice." *Le monde*. February 9, 2022. https://www.lemonde.fr/societe/

article/2022/02/09/une-femme-transgenre-reconnue-comme-mere-par-la-justice_6112969_3224.html.

Lee, Georgia. “Factcheck: How Many Trans People Are Murdered in the UK?” November 23, 2018. https://www.channel4.com/news/factcheck/factcheck-how-many-trans-people-murdered-uk.

Lewin, Tamar. “Babies from Skin Cells? Prospect Is Unsettling to Some Experts.” *The New York Times*. May 16, 2017. https://www.nytimes.com/2017/05/16/health/ivg-reproductive-technology.html.

Littman, Lisa. “Parent Reports of Adolescents and Young Adults Perceived to Show Signs of a Rapid Onset of Gender Dysphoria.” *PLoS ONE*. August 16, 2018. https://journals.plos.org/plosone/article?id=10.1371/journal.pone.0202330.

Lorusso, Marissa. “In ‘Females,’ the State Is Less a Biological Condition Than an Existential One.” NPR. October 30, 2019. https://text.npr.org/774365692.

Luke, Barbara, Morton B. Brown, Hazel B. Nichols, Maria J. Schymura, Marilyn L. Browne, Sarah C. Fisher, Nina E. Forestieri et al. “Assessment of Birth Defects and Cancer Risk in Children Conceived via In Vitro Fertilization in the United States.” *Jama Network Open* 3, no. 10 (October 29, 2020): 1–10. Corrected December 3, 2020. https://jamanetwork.com/journals/jamanetworkopen/fullarticle/2772342.

Mann, Denis. “Good Outcomes From First Five Years of Uterus Transplants But Concerns Remain.” *US News*, July 7, 2022. https://www.usnews.com/news/health-news/articles/2022-07-07/good-outcomes-from-first-5-years-of-uterus-transplants-but-concerns-remain.

Manning, Sanchez. “Does Your Child Really Need to Know How ‘Ben’ Became ‘Amy’? Furious Parents Slam ‘Damaging’ BBC Sex Change Show Aimed at Six-Year-Olds.” Mail Online. October 29, 2016. http://www.dailymail.co.uk/news/article-3885922/Parents-slam-damaging-BBC-sex-change-aimed-six-year-olds.html.

———. “‘A Live Experiment on Children’: Mail on Sunday Publishes the Shocking Physicians’ Testimony That Led a High Court Judge to Ban NHS’s Tavistock Clinic from Giving Puberty Blocking Drugs to Youngsters as Young as 10 Who Want to Change Sex.” *Daily Mail*. January 9, 2021. https://www.dailymail.co.uk/news/article-9130157/The-physicians-testimony-led-High-Court-judge-ban-child-puberty-blocker-drugs.html.

———. “NHS to Fund Sperm Bank for Lesbians: New Generation of Fatherless Families Paid for by YOU.” *Daily Mail*. August 2, 2014. https://www.dailymail.co.uk/news/article-2714321/NHS-fund-sperm-bank-lesbians-New-generation-fatherless-families-paid-YOU.html.

Manning, Sanchez, and Stephen Adams. “Wombs for Men: Astonishing Prospect as Fertility Doctors Back Operations on NHS So Transgender Women Born as Boys Can Have Babies.” *Daily Mail*. July 1, 2017. https://www.dailymail.co.uk/news/article-4657830/transgender-women-born-boys-babies-NHS-doctors.html.

Massachusetts General Hospital Journal. "Access to Pubertal Suppression Linked to Lower Suicidal Ideation Risks in Transgender Young Adults." July 1, 2020. https://advances.massgeneral.org/neuro/journal.aspx?id=1591.

Masters, James. "Martina Navratilova criticized for comments about trans women in sport." CNN. February 18, 2019. https://edition.cnn.com/2019/02/18/tennis/martina-navratilova-trans-women-comments-spt-scli-intl/index.html.

Matthews, Susan. "Does Tavistock GIDS Fast-Track 16+ Referrals of Adolescents with Gender Dysphoria?" Transgender Trend. August 4, 2019. https://www.transgendertrend.com/tavistock-gids-fast-track-referrals-adolescents-gender-dysphoria/.

Mattox, Mickey L. "Marquette's Gender Regime." *First Things*. April 2016. http://www.firstthings.com/article/2016/04/marquettes-gender-regime.

McCall, Becky. "Gender Identity Service at Crunch Point as Pressure Mounts." Medscape. January 3, 2020. https://www.medscape.com/viewarticle/923327.

McCarthy, Margaret Harper. "Overruling the Visible: The Emperor's New Gender." Public Discourse. October 6, 2019. https://www.thepublicdiscourse.com/2019/10/57542/.

———. "The Slavery of Radical Freedom." *First Things*. July 21, 2020. https://www.firstthings.com/web-exclusives/2020/08/the-slavery-of-radical-freedom.

McDonald, Leah. "'Looking to Transfer Before Christmas': Brooklyn Actress, 37, Posts Online Appeal Asking Women to Swap One of Their Male Embryos for Her Female One, Because She Wants Another Son." *Daily Mail*. November 3, 2018. https://www.dailymail.co.uk/news/article-6350193/Actress-37-New-York-appeals-offers-trade-female-embryo-male-one.html.

McHugh, Paul. "Surgical Sex: Why We Stopped Doing Sex Change Operations." *First Things*. November 2004. http://www.firstthings.com/article/2004/11/surgical-sex.

———. "Transgender Surgery Isn't the Solution: A Drastic Physical Change Doesn't Address Underlying Psycho-Social Troubles." *The Wall Street Journal*. June 12, 2014. http://www.wsj.com/articles/paul-mchugh-transgender-surgery-isnt-the-solution-1402615120.

McLelland, Euan. "Feminist Germaine Greer Accuses Caitlyn Jenner of 'Wanting to Steal the Limelight' from Female Kardashians." *Daily Mail*. October 24, 2015. http://www.dailymail.co.uk/news/article-3287810/Germaine-Greer-accuses-Caitlyn-Jenner-wanting-steal-limelight-female-Kardashians.html.

Midwives Alliance of North America. "Position Statement on Gender Inclusive Language." September 9, 2015. https://mana.org/healthcare-policy/position-statement-on-gender-inclusive-language.

Miller, Lisa. "The Trans-Everything CEO." *New York Magazine*. September 7, 2014. https://nymag.com/news/features/martine-rothblatt-transgender-ceo/.

Mitchell, Patrick. “60 Minutes Australia: Who Am I?” September 10, 2017. https://www.youtube.com/watch?v=vqSdcvIz4VI.

Morabito, Stella. “Trouble in Transtopia: Murmurs of Sex Change Regret.” The Federalist. November 11, 2014. https://thefederalist.com/2014/11/11/trouble-in-transtopia-murmurs-of-sex-change-regret/.

Moskowitz, Clara. “Transgender Americans Face High Suicide Risk.” NBC News. Updated November 19, 2010. http://www.nbcnews.com/id/40279043/ns/health-health_care/#.VsIZg_HVCt8.

“My Daddy’s Name Is Donor.” Institute For American Values. https://www.wearedonorconceived.com/uncategorized/my-daddys-name-is-donor/.

Newman, Alana S. “Children’s Rights, or Rights to Children?” Public Discourse. November 10, 2014. https://www.thepublicdiscourse.com/2014/11/13993/.

———.“Life as a Lab Specimen.” *Humanum: Issues in Family, Culture and Science* 2 (2014). https://humanumreview.com/articles/life-as-a-lab-specimen https://humanumreview.com/articles/life-as-a-lab-specimen.

Newman, Rickard. “Journey to Baby Gammy: How We Justify a Market in Children.” Public Discourse. August 18, 2014. https://www.thepublicdiscourse.com/2014/08/13701/.

O’Malley, Kate. “Two British Men Become First to Give Birth after Postponing Gender Reassignment Surgeries.” *Elle*. November 7, 2017. https://www.elle.com/uk/life-and-culture/culture/news/a36967/british-men-become-first-to-give-birth/.

Orange, Robert. “Teenage Transgender Row Splits Sweden as Dysphoria Diagnoses Soar By 1,500%.” *The Guardian*. February 22, 2020. https://www.theguardian.com/society/2020/feb/22/ssweden-teenage-transgender-row-dysphoria-diagnoses-soar.

“Parents Questioning the Transnarrative.” Transgender Trend. East Sussex, UK. 2019. https://www.transgendertrend.com/detransition/.

Payne, Daniel. “Causalities of a Social, Psychological, and Medical Fad: The Dangers of Transgender Ideology in Medicine.” Public Discourse. January 31, 2018. https://www.thepublicdiscourse.com/2018/01/20810/.

Pearson, Samantha. “Demand for American Sperm Is Skyrocketing in Brazil.” *The Wall Street Journal*. March 22, 2018. https://www.wsj.com/articles/in-mixed-race-brazil-sperm-imports-from-u-s-whites-are-booming-1521711000.

“Pediatric and Adolescent Center Clinic home page.” Stanford Lucile Packard Children’s Hospital. Accessed February 4, 2021. https://www.stanfordchildrens.org/en/service/gender.

Petherid, Sam. “Ex-Bath Spa Student James Caspian Fails in Court Fight Against University.” SomersetLive. February 20, 2019. https://www.somersetlive.co.uk/news/somerset-news/bath-spa-university-james-caspian-2557060.

Pflum, Mary. "Nation's Fertility Clinics Struggle with a Growing Number of Abandoned Embryos." NBC News. August 12, 2019. https://www.nbcnews.com/health/features/nation-s-fertility-clinics-struggle-growing-number-abandoned-embryos-n1040806.

Planned Parenthood. "What Are Puberty Blockers?" Accessed November 6, 2021. https://www.plannedparenthood.org/learn/teens/puberty/what-are-puberty-blockers.

Randell, Louise. "I'm A Celeb: Star Caitlyn Jenner's Brave Confession about Gender Reassignment Surgery." Mirror. November 14, 2019. https://www.mirror.co.uk/3am/celebrity-news/im-celeb-star-caitlyn-jenners-20879863.

Regnerus, Mark. "New Data Show 'Gender-Affirming' Surgery Doesn't Really Improve Mental Health. So Why Are the Study's Authors Saying It Does?" Public Discourse. November 13, 2019. https://www.thepublicdiscourse.com/2019/11/58371/.

———. "Queering Science." *First Things*. December 2018. https://www.firstthings.com/article/2018/12/queering-science.

Reid, Sue. "How Children as Young as 13 Are Asking Strangers Online to Crowdfund their Sex Change Drugs . . . and Even More Disturbingly—They Are Bypassing NHS Safeguards to Get Them." *Daily Mail*. January 28, 2022. https://www.dailymail.co.uk/news/article-10453837/How-children-young-13-asking-strangers-online-crowdfund-sex-change-drugs.html.

Reno, R. R. "A Striking Display of Sophistry." *First Things*. June 16, 2020. https://www.firstthings.com/web-exclusives/2020/06/a-striking-display-of-sophistry.

Respaut, Robin and Chad Terhune. "Putting Numbers on the Rise in Children Seeking Gender Care." Reuters, October 6, 2022. https://www.reuters.com/investigates/special-report/usa-transyouth-data/.

Ring, Avi. "Re: Pubertal Suppression for Transgender Youth and Risk of Suicidal Ideation." *Pediatrics*. February 12, 2020. https://pediatrics.aappublications.org/content/145/2/e20191725/tab-e-letters#re-pubertal-suppression-for-transgender-youth-and-risk-of-suicidal-ideation.

Riska, Roger. "US Supreme Court Stuns with Activist Ruling on Anti-Discrimination." June 22, 2020. https://christianconcern.com/comment/us-supreme-court-stuns-with-activist-ruling-on-anti-discrimination/.

Robbins, Jane, and Erin Tuttle. "What's Wrong with the New NIH Study on Transgender Kids?" Public Discourse. January 17, 2018. http://www.thepublicdiscourse.com/2018/01/20844/.

Ronchi, Federica Umani, and Gabriele Napoletano. "Uterus Transplantation and the Redefinition of Core Bioethics Precepts." *Acta Bio Medica* 92, no. 5 (November 3, 2021): 1–2. https://mattioli1885journals.com/index.php/actabiomedica/article/view/12257/10234.

Rosman, Katherine. "The Lost Embryos." *The New York Times*. April 16, 2021. https://www.nytimes.com/2021/04/16/style/freezing-eggs-and-embryos.html.

Rowling, J. K. "J. K. Rowling Writes about Her Reasons for Speaking Out on Sex and Gender Issues." June 10, 2020. https://www.jkrowling.com/opinions/j-k-rowling-writes-about-her-reasons-for-speaking-out-on-sex-and-gender-issues/.

———. Tweet @jk_rowling. June 6, 2020. https://twitter.com/jk_rowling/status/1269382518362509313?s=20.

———. Tweet @jk_rowling. June 7, 2020. https://twitter.com/jk_rowling/status/1269389298664701952?lang=fr.

Rueb, Emily S. "Second U.S. Baby to Be Born from a Dead Donor's Uterus Is Delivered." *New York Times*. January 9, 2020. https://www.nytimes.com/2020/01/09/health/uterus-transplant-baby.html.

Russell, Nicole. "What The First Nonbinary American Wants the Supreme Court to Know About Transgenderism." The Federalist. October 8, 2019. https://thefederalist.com/2019/10/08/what-the-first-nonbinary-american-wants-the-supreme-court-to-know-about-transgenderism/.

Sample, Ian. "UK Doctors Select First Women to Have 'Three-Person Babies.'" *The Guardian*. February 1, 2018. https://www.theguardian.com/science/2018/feb/01/permission-given-to-create-britains-first-three-person-babies.

Sax, Leonard. "Politicizing Pediatrics: How the AAP's Transgender Guidelines Undermine Trust in Medical Authority." Public Discourse. March 13, 2019. http://www.the publicdiscourse.com/2019/03/50118.

Scanlan, Rebekah. "Man Who Gave Birth Opens Up about Pregnancy Regrets." Kidspot. January 10, 2019. https://www.kidspot.com.au/parenting/real-life/in-the-news/man-who-gave-birth-opens-up-about-pregnancy-regrets/news-story/3b831b09b10e1eeb1996abd74b44ee43.

Senior, Jennifer. "Review: 'Becoming Nicole': A Young Boy's Journey to Girlhood." *New York Times*. October 21, 2015. https://www.nytimes.com/2015/10/22/books/review-becoming-nicole-a-young-boys-journey-into-girlhood.html.

Shrier, Abigail. "Inside Planned Parenthood's Gender Factory. An Ex-Reproductive Health Assistant Speaks Out." The Truth Fairy. February 8, 2021. https://abigailshrier.substack.com/p/inside-planned-parenthoods-gender.

Siddique, Haroon. "Appeal Court Overturns UK Puberty Blockers Ruling for Under 16s." *The Guardian*. September 17, 2021. https://www.theguardian.com/society/2021/sep/17/appeal-court-overturns-uk-puberty-blockers-ruling-for-under-16s-tavistock-keira-bell.

Sky News. "Special Report: NHS 'Over-Diagnosing' Transgender Children." December 11, 2019. https://www.youtube.com/watch?v=qXvdrSkBFqw&t=601s.

Smith, Wesley J. "Do Transgender Women Have a 'Right to Gestate'?" National Review. November 8, 2021. https://www.nationalreview.com/corner/do-transgender-women-have-a-right-to-gestate/.

Society for Evidence Based Gender Medicine. "Policy Change Regarding Hormonal Treatment of Minors with Gender Dysphoria at Tema Barn–Astrid Lindgren Children's Hospital." https://segm.org/sites/default/files/Karolinska%20_Policy_Statement_English.pdf.

———. "Sweden's Karolinska Ends All Use of Puberty Blockers and Cross-Sex Hormones for Minors Outside of Clinical Studies." May 5, 2021, updated May 8, 2021, and February 2022. https://segm.org/Sweden_ends_use_of_Dutch_protocol.

Solis, Marie. "We Can't Have a Feminist Future without Abolishing the Family: The Feminist Thinker Sophie Lewis Has a Radical Proposal for What Comes Next." Vice. February 21, 2020. https://www.vice.com/en_us/article/qjdzwb/sophie-lewis-feminist-abolishing-the-family-full-surrogacy-now.

Sommer, Marni, Virginia Kamova, and Therese Mahon. "Creating a More Equal Post-Covid-19 World for People Who Menstruate." USAID/DEVEX. May 28, 2020. https://www.devex.com/news/sponsored/opinion-creating-a-more-equal-post-covid-19-world-for-people-who-menstruate-97312#.XtwLnv0aEeR.twitter.

Spar, Debora L. "Opinion: The Poly-Parent Households Are Coming." *New York Times*. August 12, 2020. https://www.nytimes.com/2020/08/12/opinion/ivg-reproductive-technology.html.

Stark, Jill. "I Will Never Be Able to Have Sex Again. Ever." *The Sydney Morning Herald*. May 31, 2009. https://www.smh.com.au/national/i-will-never-be-able-to-have-sex-again-ever-20090530-br41.html.

———. "Sex-Change Clinic 'Got it Wrong.'" *The Sydney Morning Herald*. May 31, 2009. https://www.smh.com.au/national/sexchange-clinic-got-it-wrong-20090530-br3u.html.

Stewart, Jay. "Trans Youth Are Real." *Gendered Intelligence Blog*. January 20, 2017. https://genderedintelligence.wordpress.com/2017/01/20/trans-youth-are-real/. Accessed January 26, 2021.

———. "We are Living on the Cusp of a Gender Revolution." February 23, 2015. Accessed December 8, 2020. https://www.youtube.com/watch?v=UpQd-VrKgFI.

Sullins, Paul. "'Born That Way' No More: The New Science of Sexual Orientation." Public Discourse. September 30, 2019. https://www.thepublicdiscourse.com/2019/09/57342/.

Swimming World Editorial Staff. "Ivy League Parent Opens Up about Pain and Shock Met during Lia Thompson Controversy." Swimming World. March 1, 2020. https://www.swimmingworldmagazine.com/news/ivy-league-parent-i-want-people-to-wake-up-to-the-world-we-are-creating-for-women/.

Talbot, Margaret. "About a Boy: Transgender Surgery at Sixteen." *The New Yorker.* March 18, 2013. http://www.newyorker.com/magazine/2013/03/18/about-a-boy-2.

———. "Being Seen: Video Diaries of Transgender Youth." *The New Yorker.* March 11, 2013. http://www.newyorker.com/news/news-desk/being-seen-video-diaries-of-transgender-youth.

Talbott, Stephen L. "A Conversation with Nature." *The New Atlantis* 3 (Fall 2003). https://www.thenewatlantis.com/publications/a-conversation-with-nature.

———. "The Embryo's Eloquent Form." The Nature Institute: Biology Worthy of Life. May 22, 2008, updated March 18, 2013. https://bwo.life/mqual/embryo.htm.

———. "Evolution and the Purposes of Life. On Biology's Unasked Questions about the Goal-Directed Activities of Organisms." *The New Atlantis* 51 (Winter 2017). https://www.thenewatlantis.com/publications/evolution-and-the-purposes-of-life.

———. "The Unbearable Wholeness of Beings. Why the Organism Is Not a Machine." *The New Atlantis* 29 (Fall 2010). https://www.thenewatlantis.com/publications/the-unbearable-wholeness-of-beings.

———. "What Do Organisms Mean? How Life Speaks at Every Level." *The New Atlantis* 30 (Winter 2011). https://www.thenewatlantis.com/publications/what-do-organisms-mean.

Taylor, Rosie, and Katie Gibbons. "Breastfeeding Is Now Chestfeeding, Brighton's Trans-friendly Midwives Are Told." *The Times.* February 9, 2021. https://www.thetimes.co.uk/article/breastfeeding-is-now-chestfeeding-brightons-trans-friendly-midwives-are-told-pwlvmcnc7?utm_medium=Social&utm_source=Twitter#Echobox=1612890631.

Telegraph Reports. "Row over BBC Transgender Programme Aimed at Children." October 30, 2016. http://www.telegraph.co.uk/news/2016/10/30/row-over-transgender-programme-as-children-as-young-as-six-expos/.

Them before Us: Children's Rights before Adult Desires. https://thembeforeus.com/.

Trasancos, Stacy A. "The Death of Embryos and 'The Conception Problem.'" *The Catholic World Report.* May 2, 2018. https://www.catholicworldreport.com/2018/05/02/the-death-of-embryos-and-the-conception-problem/.

Tribune News Desk. "Stanford Professor Believes in the Future We Won't Have Sex to Procreate." *The Tribune.* July 2, 2017. https://tribune.com.pk/story/1448660/stanford-professor-believes-future-wont-sex-procreate/.

Trueman, Carl R. "The Impact of Psychological Man—and How to Respond." Public Discourse. November 10, 2020. https://www.thepublicdiscourse.com/2020/11/72190/.

———. "The Rise of 'Psychological Man.'" Public Discourse. November 9, 2020. https://www.thepublicdiscourse.com/2020/11/72156/.

Turban, Jack L., Dana King, Jeremi M. Carswell, and Alex S. Keuroghlian. "Pubertal Suppression for Transgender Youth and Risk of Suicidal Ideation." *Pediatrics* 145, no. 2 (February 2020). https://pediatrics.aappublications.org/content/145/2/e20191725.

Twitter. "Hateful Conduct Policy." https://help.twitter.com/en/rules-and-policies/hateful-conduct-policy.

United Nations Office on Drugs and Crime. "Global Study on Homicide: Gender Related Killings of Women and Girls." Vienna, 2018. https://www.unodc.org/documents/data-and-analysis/GSH2018/GSH18_Gender-related_killing_of_women_and_girls.pdf.

United States Department of Justice. "The Department of Justice Files Statement of Interest Defending the Constitutionality of Idaho's Fairness in Women's Sport Act." June 19, 2020. https://www.justice.gov/opa/pr/department-justice-files-statement-interest-defending-constitutionality-idaho-s-fairness.

Van Mol, Andre. "Transing California Foster Children and Why Doctors Like Us Opposed It." Public Discourse. October 28, 2018. https://www.thepublicdiscourse.com/2018/10/42612/.

Wiker, Benjamin D. "The New Gnosticism." *The Catholic World Report.* May 2, 2011. http://www.catholicworldreport.com/Item/514/the_new_gnosticism.aspx.

Wilson, Laura. "New Colorado Law Allows Transgender People to Obtain New Birth Certificate without Proof of Surgery." Fox Denver. January 4, 2020. https://kdvr.com/2020/01/04/new-colorado-law-allows-transgender-people-to-obtain-new-birth-certificate-without-proof-of-surgery/.

Wilson, R. J. "'The First Pregnant Man,' Ten Years Later: Thomas Beatie Reflects on a Difficult Decade." Urbo. July 12, 2018. https://www.urbo.com/content/the-first-pregnant-man-10-years-later-thomas-beatie-reflects-on-a-difficult-decade/.

Wittich, Jake. "Transgender Parents Welcome Baby Girl, Prompting Update To State's Birth Certificate System." *Chicago Sun Times.* January 6, 2020. https://chicago.suntimes.com/2020/1/6/21034801/transgender-parents-illinois-baby-update-birth-certificate-system.

Women's Liberation Front (WoLF). "Why the Harris Supreme Court Decision Is Not a Win for Women, Nor Is It Narrow." WoLF@WomensLibFront. Twitter. June 19, 2020. https://twitter.com/WomensLibFront/status/1274096937822834690.

World Professional Association for Transgender Health. *Standards of Care for the Health of Transsexual, Transgender, and Gender Nonconforming People*, 7th version. 2012. https://www.wpath.org/publications/soc.

Wright, Sydney. "I Spent a Year as a Trans Man. Doctors Failed Me at Every Turn." The Daily Signal. October 7, 2019. https://www.dailysignal.com/2019/10/07/i-spent-a-year-as-a-trans-man-doctors-failed-me-at-every-turn/.

Zeltner, Brie. "University Hospital Notifies 700 Fertility Patients of Freezer 'Fluctuation' and Potential Damage to Stored Eggs and Embryos." Cleveland.Com. March 8, 2018, updated January 30, 2019. https://www.cleveland.com/healthfit/2018/03/university_hospitals_notifies.html.

Zhang, Phoebe. "China's Gender Equality Falls and Falls." Inkstone. December 20, 2018. https://www.inkstonenews.com/society/china-falls-103-2018-global-gender-gap-report/article/2178898.